Leaders Who Dare

Pushing the Boundaries

Linda L. Lyman
Dianne E. Ashby
Jenny S. Tripses

Rowman & Littlefield Education
Lanham, Maryland • Toronto • Oxford
2005

Published in the United States of America
by Rowman & Littlefield Education
A Division of Rowman & Littlefield Publishers, Inc.
A wholly owned subsidiary of The Rowman & Littlefield Publishing Group, Inc.
4501 Forbes Boulevard, Suite 200, Lanham, Maryland 20706
www.rowmaneducation.com

PO Box 317
Oxford
OX2 9RU, UK

British Library Cataloguing in Publication Information Available

Library of Congress Cataloging-in-Publication Data
Lyman, Linda L.
  Leaders who dare : pushing the boundaries / Linda L. Lyman, Dianne E.
Ashby, Jenny S. Tripses.
       p. cm.
  Includes bibliographical references and index.
  ISBN 1-57886-264-7 (pbk. : alk. paper)
  1. Women school administrators–Illinois–Interviews. 2. Women
educators–Illinois–Interviews. 3. Educational leadership–Illinois. I. Ashby,
Dianne E., 1953- II. Tripses, Jenny S., 1948- III. Title.
  LB2831.624.I4L96 2005
  371.2'011'082–dc22   2005003609

*We dedicate this book to
Illinois Women Administrators
and to all women and men
who have found time, courage, and energy
to reach back and share leadership insights
to open doors for the next generation of leaders.*

Contents

Tables

Acknowledgments

The dedication and diligent work of a large number of persons impossible to name made this book a reality. First and foremost, we express deepest gratitude to the interviewers and participants, who are individually named in the preface. The book presents their collective wisdom. We gratefully acknowledge the financial and spiritual support for the book that came from Illinois Women Administrators as an organization, and also from individual members. We appreciate the several financial contributions from Illinois State University and Bradley University during the four years of this research and writing project. Each provided support to a particular aspect of the work. Madeline Hafner, University of Utah, not only wrote chapter 8 but also provided significant editorial assistance. Both Lilly Meiner and Nel Wallace from Illinois State University have made invaluable contributions. Thank you, Lilly, for the hours you devoted to transcribing the 18 lengthy interviews and for the professional quality of the transcripts. Thank you, Nel, for all the help with mailings and correspondence you have provided in your role as IWA administrative support. Finally, we acknowledge the support of our spouses, Dave Weiman, Jack Lockman, and John Tripses.

Linda, Dianne, and Jenny

Preface

THE CONTEXT

The book you are holding originated as a project of Illinois Women Administrators (IWA), a statewide organization with a rich history. At this time, the organization has its academic home in the Department of Educational Administration and Foundations, College of Education, Illinois State University, located in Normal, Illinois. The mission of IWA, as revised in 1999, is "to improve schools by networking and supporting women educational leaders into positions of influence in school administration." The original statement of mission was "Illinois Women Administrators is a professional organization that encourages the expansion of administrative opportunities for women. IWA provides women in administration the opportunity to share experiences and ideas, develop a viable support network, and promote self-growth." This original mission statement reflected urgency in Illinois at the end of the 1970s to increase the numbers of women school and district leaders.

The person credited with the founding of IWA was Joseph Cronin, Illinois' first appointed state superintendent. Coming to Illinois in the early 1970s, Cronin had a strong interest in affirmative action. He set in motion a self-study at the Illinois State Board of Education (ISBE) focused on equity in compliance with the requirements of Title IX. He appointed ISBE agency women in leadership positions to conduct the self-study. Their self-study data revealed substantial inequities at ISBE, particularly in the areas of salary and assignments reflecting qualifications. Over time these inequities were addressed.

In 1977 these same ISBE agency leaders were included on the task force Cronin appointed to conduct a follow-up study of the number of women administrators in Illinois schools. The task force charge was

> to study the status of women in educational administration and to make recommendations for improving that status. One of the findings of the task force was that the number of women in educational administration had declined in the preceding decade. The recommendation of the group was that management-training opportunities especially designed to enhance skills of practicing or aspiring women administrators be offered. The Illinois State Board of Education and the St. Charles School District #303 sponsored a statewide conference in November of 1978. The response was overwhelming and at the culmination of the conference, Illinois Women Administrators was formed. (Shores, 1989, p. 2)

Cronin appointed mostly ISBE agency personnel to the first IWA board of directors. During its first few years, IWA was open to women in business and higher education as well as K–12 education. Eventually the bylaws were changed and the focus narrowed to women in K–12 education. Early activities of the organization reflected an emphasis on professional development with a fall conference held every year.

Records are sparse from the founding event in 1978 until 1987 when the first executive director was selected and regular newsletters were produced. During some of the early years, the fall conference was the only IWA event. The Department of Leadership and Educational Policy Studies at Northern Illinois University formed a partnership with IWA in the fall of 1987, and appointed faculty member Patricia First as IWA's first executive director. During its sponsorship of IWA, Northern Illinois University provided funds for employment of an executive director, secretarial assistance, and office space. Carol Sager, also a faculty member at Northern Illinois University, was appointed the second executive director in the fall of 1988. The third executive director was Alice Ericksen, the IWA immediate past president and a principal in the River Forest School District. She held the position for two years. The IWA Fall 1991 newsletter announced the relocation of the IWA offices to Southern Illinois University–Edwardsville with Dr. Hazel Loucks, a full-time faculty member, taking on the job of executive director as part of her regular university assignment. This change made possible expanded services and increased visibility for the organization. Dr. Loucks kept the organization on the move by dramatically increasing membership during her three-year tenure. In the fall of 1994, IWA moved to its current academic home, Illinois State University, with Dr. Dianne Ashby as the new executive director. Dr. Linda Lyman was appointed executive director in April 2000. Dr. Dianne Gardner assumed the executive director position in January 2005.

In the course of its history the organization has sponsored and undertaken a variety of activities, including the now annual *Dare to Be Great* spring conference. A 1988 newsletter article reported planning for a regional mini-conference called *Dare to Be Great*. Then in 1989 the *Dare to Be Great* conference became a statewide spring event and has been held every year since. According to an IWA newsletter article,

> *Dare to Be Great* was born out of a concern noted by the Board of Directors at a strategic planning session several years ago. Because it is true that women often hesitate to be self-promoting, we very often don't get the chance to recognize or even know about the accomplishments of other women. *Dare to Be Great* does exactly that when it recognizes women who have dared to step out and lead others in all areas of administration. Previous nominees have been from the fields of education, politics, and business. Each has overcome personal and professional difficulties in order to make a positive contribution. (Ericksen, 1991, p. 1)

A strategic planning process in 1999–2000 under the leadership of then-president Dr. Jenny Tripses marked a critical point for the organization as it sought renewed purpose and meaning. Because larger numbers of women are serving in administrative positions throughout the state, the focus of IWA has shifted to *improving schools* by mentoring and supporting women leaders into positions of influence in school administration.

Although mentoring organizations such as IWA have contributed to the greater numbers of women in leadership positions, women throughout the country remain ambivalent about membership in such women's organizations. In the face of this ambivalence, IWA undertook an ambitious passionate project: the development of this book to tell the stories of Illinois' outstanding women educators, many who have been honored at *Dare to Be Great* conferences.

Year after year IWA members and friends come to the *Dare to Be Great* spring conference physically and emotionally weary. As the morning's storytelling unfolds, the atmosphere changes. Women sit up, lean forward, nod, whisper comments, take notes, often laugh uncontrollably, sometimes cry without embarrassment, and afterwards some hug presenters whose story lines mirror their own. For many participants, the *Dare to Be Great* experience means knowing they are not alone. They are not alone in their desires to serve and lead. They are not alone in feeling passion for their work. They are not alone in despair for unrealized potential in children and adults. They are not the only ones who are frustrated by bureaucracy and the frequent triumph of political survival over doing the right thing. Someone else found a way to raise difficult children of their own while helping the children of others. Someone else figured out how to find personal balance in an unbalanced world. And weariness turns to hope, optimism, energy, and even spiritual renewal. They leave with renewed energy, determined to become *leaders who dare*.

Book authors Linda Lyman, Dianne Ashby, and Jenny Tripses issued the invitation to help write what was initially called *Dare to Be Great: The Book* in the Spring 2000 issue of the IWA newsletter. We wanted to involve any interested members. Researching and writing the book served as a reflective and unifying act for the organization, with 23 persons joining the interviewing team. Having developed a qualitative methodology for the research, we conducted a one-day workshop for the book project volunteers on September 9, 2000. At the workshop we introduced the origin and purpose of the book project, presented a conceptual framework, reviewed interviewing techniques and protocols, and secured interviewer commitments.

During the 2000–2001 academic year, 18 IWA interviewers completed 19 of the projected 21 interviews. One of the leaders interviewed has withdrawn from participation. The interviewers included teachers, building and district administrators, and university professors representing three disciplines. Thirteen of the 18 interviewers had doctoral degrees, and many were experienced qualitative researchers. These credentials of the interviewers contributed significantly to the quality of the interviews and to this book. Without our interviewing team, the book could not have been written. Their reflections about how they have been influenced by their participation in the project are included in the book's final chapter. We list them alphabetically, along with their professional positions in 2000–2001 at the time of the interviews, and gratefully acknowledge their invaluable contributions to the research project:

Mary Ahillen, Administrative Intern, Chiddix Junior High, Normal CUSD #5

Jeanne Bodnar, Principal, Nathan Hale Intermediate School, District #130

Norma Borgmann, Superintendent, Patoka Community Unit #100

Dr. Pam Floit, Assistant Superintendent, Collinsville Unit #10

Dr. Nancy Gibson, Assistant Superintendent, Olympia CUSD #16

Dr. Madeline Hafner, Assistant Professor, Loyola University Chicago

Jana Hunzicker, Principal, Bolin School, District #86, East Peoria

Lynda Irvin, Coordinator, Gates Leadership and Technology Grant, Illinois State University

Dr. Frances Karanovich, Superintendent, Olympia CUSD #16

Dr. Gwendolyn Lee, Associate Superintendent, Thornton Township HSD #205

Dr. Ramona Lomeli, Assistant Professor, Illinois State University

Dr. Shari Marshall, Superintendent, Barry CUSD #1

Dr. Donna McCaw, Assistant Professor, Western Illinois University

Dr. Vita Meyer, Consultant/Retired Principal

Dr. Margaret Noe, Assistant Professor, University of Illinois–Springfield

Dr. Mary O'Brian, Assistant Professor, Illinois State University

Dr. Linda Searby, Principal, Mt. Pulaski Grade School

Dr. Jobie Skaggs, Assistant Professor, Bradley University

The particular themes and message of the book directly reflect the leadership practices of the distinguished educators we interviewed. In the following table we list these 18 individuals and their professional positions at the time of the interviews. Four women are African American: Gwendolyn Lee, Elizabeth Lewin, Aurthur Perkins, and Maxine Wortham. The others are Caucasian. Five of the subjects identified themselves as retired. Only one woman was a principal at the time of the interview, but many are former principals. Three were practicing superintendents, and several others are former superintendents. Two were district office administrators. One woman was a regional director of special education services. Two women were university deans of schools of education. Four women had statewide leadership roles: deputy superintendent at the Illinois State Board of Education, educational consultant/lobbyist for the Illinois Statewide School Management Alliance, president of a statewide academy for students gifted and talented in mathematics and science, and deputy governor for education and workforce appointed by the governor. All the participants agreed to ninety-minute interviews, to have their names used in any publications resulting from the research, and to be

Book Participants and Their Professional Positions in 2000–2001

Participants	Professional Positions in 2000–2001
Dr. Mary Jayne Broncato	Deputy Superintendent, Illinois State Board of Education
Ola Marie Bundy	Assistant Executive Director, Illinois High School Association (*Retired*)
Dr. Ann Duncan	Superintendent, Carlyle Community Unit District #1 (*Retired*)
Brenda J. Holmes	Educational Consultant/Lobbyist, Illinois Statewide School Management Alliance
Dr. Gwendolyn Lee	Associate Superintendent, Thornton Township High School District #205
Dr. Elizabeth I. Lewin	Superintendent, Carbondale Elementary School District #95
Dr. Hazel E. Loucks	Deputy Governor for Education and Workforce, Illinois Governor's Office
Dr. Vita P. Meyer	Principal, Bremen Community High School District #228 (*Retired*); Adjunct Instructor, Governor's State University
Diane Morrison	Director of Support Services, Northern Suburban Special Education District
Martha R. O'Malley	Regional Superintendent of Schools, St. Clair County (*Retired*)
Dr. Stephanie Pace Marshall	President, Illinois Mathematics and Science Academy
Dr. Sally Bulkley Pancrazio	Dean, College of Education, Illinois State University
Aurthur Mae Perkins	Principal, Harrison Primary School, Peoria School District #150
Dr. Mary M. Polite	Dean, School of Education, Southern Illinois University–Edwardsville
Dr. Carol L. Struck	Superintendent, Olympia CUSD #16 (*Retired*); Adjunct Instructor, Illinois State University; Co-Owner, About Books
Dr. Rebecca van der Bogert	Superintendent, Winnetka School District #36
Dr. Dorothy Weber	Superintendent, Glenview School District #34
Dr. Maxine A. Wortham	Executive Director, Early Childhood Education, Peoria School District #150

available for possible follow-up interviews. Without the collaboration of these outstanding individuals this book would not exist, and we proudly share their wisdom, experience, and insight. Toward the end of the book there are biographical sketches of each participant as well as information about each of the interviewers.

CONCLUSION

Every woman named in this book is authentic. No pseudonyms are used. Each subject has given permission for her story or selected parts of her story to be shared. Each has agreed that what is written about her in this book is accurate, including direct quotes. Some of the women named here may be taking extraordinary risks simply by being named. We appreciate the candor and generous spirit of each woman, all of whose lives have been made at least partially public so that all may learn to lead in ways that make a more powerful difference. A new scholarship of educational leadership is emerging. Whereas traditional leadership studies focused on *what* leadership is, *how* leadership is done, and *who* leaders are, according to Furman (2003) the new scholarship focuses on *what educational leadership is for*. The leadership stories included here focus on the larger purposes of leadership, exemplified by these women who have dared to lead themselves and others to new possibilities.

This coauthored book is the result of a unique collective qualitative inquiry. Because it began as a project of Illinois Women Administrators, we offer the organization's history as a partial context for your reading. Today, however, the book that began as a way to preserve the legacy of individual leaders who dared has moved into a larger context and become a book about what is needed from educational leaders who are facing 21st-century challenges. We offer common themes from the leadership practices of dynamic individuals to inform and influence practitioners, and to inspire and educate aspiring administrators. We encourage university professors to develop preparation program courses that address emerging new directions in leadership—in Furman's (2003) words, to address what leadership is *for*. May every reader take a larger view of her or his own possibilities and lead the dance of daring that will make a global difference to our interdependent world.

Chapter One

Introduction

This book is about leadership, especially leadership for schools. The book rests on three simple premises. First, leadership requires intellectual, moral, behavioral, and relational engagement. Second, a great deal can be learned about how to lead by studying those who do it well. Third, the leadership literature, especially literature that shares stories about the intellectual, moral, and behavioral engagement of leaders, draws heavily and almost completely on male models. Although several recent books have been published about the experiences of women as leaders (AhNee-Benham & Cooper, 1998; Blount, 1998; Brunner, 1999, 2000; Chase, 1995; Curry, 2000; Dunlap & Schmuck, 1995; Freeman, Bourque, & Shelton, 2001; Gardiner, Enomoto, & Grogan, 2000; Grogan, 1996; Harris, Ballenger, Hicks-Townes, Carr, & Alford, 2004; Jamieson, 1995; Reynolds, 2002; Rhode, 2003; Young & Skrla, 2003), leadership studies have generally not included women or failed to point to women leaders as role models who could, even should, be emulated by leaders of both genders. We argue that our analysis of the leadership practices of the 18 women interviewed for this book contributes to the discourse on contemporary issues of educational leadership. This book focuses on *leaders who dare* in multiple and significant ways, whose daring to lead their schools, districts, and organizations in new ways has made a difference to countless individuals and to the larger world.

These leaders' experiences provide counternarratives in terms of women in American culture generally, and the world of education and educational leadership specifically. We believe their examples will contribute to an emerging vision of constructive postmodern leadership. A central purpose of the research was to learn more about how these educational leaders have worked successfully within the boundaries of school bureaucracies. Of

1

particular interest to us was how they handled situations when their values clashed with the values of the bureaucratic systems in which they served. Due to powerful political, social, and economic shifts in society, as well as changes in understandings about ways schools should be led, the traditional bureaucratic models for school leadership must change. The traditional ways of thinking about school administration are inadequate for educational leadership in the 21st century (Murphy, 2002).

Leadership theory and practice are responding to societal changes by shifting focus from what leaders *do,* and *how* they do it, to what leadership is *for*. This shift provides leverage for change in bureaucratic systems that exist to serve the status quo. In this shift the new emphasis becomes leadership for valued ends, including social justice, democratic community, ethical schools, school improvement, and learning for all children (Furman, 2003). Increasingly, schools require leaders who "stand with their communities and against policies that divert education and resources away from the real needs of children and their families" (Larson & Murtadha, 2002, p. 157). School reform will not come about through uniform application of policy; rather, school reform requires moral leadership that interprets policy in light of local circumstances (Starratt, 1994). In this book we are dealing with major substantive issues for all educational leaders: (a) collaborative and discretionary decision-making processes; (b) getting things done in bureaucracies by pushing the boundaries; (c) claiming power through politics, including collaboration as a political choice; and (d) living and leading from values. The individuals we studied are leading by integrating *doing* and *being* to create new directions and possibilities for their organizations. This book illustrates through the work of impressive women leaders what counterbureaucratic moral leadership looks like. The book documents the transformative leadership images and practices needed in the *communities of difference* dominating schools in this postmodern world (Shields, 2003). The 21st century requires educational *leaders who dare*.

ORIGIN OF THE BOOK

Leaders Who Dare grew out of the storytelling tradition of the annual spring conference of Illinois Women Administrators (IWA). Since its founding in 1978, IWA has promoted inclusion of women in the leadership landscape of schools, particularly as principals and superintendents, but also as government, policy, and university administrators and teachers. *Dare to Be Great*, the IWA annual conference that began in 1988, features the honoring of a small group of three to five women leaders nominated by their peers for recognition. With the honor comes a special responsibility. Each honoree must tell her story. As the event has evolved, most honorees have abandoned unemotional recitations of their resumes to focus instead on life-changing events, mentors, families, insights, challenges, and the unintended consequences and surprises they encountered along the path. This storytelling has taken many forms and been accompanied by poetry, song, and metaphoric or visual representations of life themes. Participants in the conference leave inspired to live into new possibilities, to become *leaders who dare*.

PURPOSE OF THE BOOK

A few years ago some members of IWA became concerned that these rich stories and their lessons were lost beyond the moments of their sharing at the conferences. This book was born of a desire to capture the spirit and lessons of *Dare to Be Great* by collecting and analyzing stories of impressive women educational leaders. The book makes the *how* and *why* of the leadership practices of outstanding Illinois leaders available to all who are interested in improving the quality of educational leadership. Although those interviewed for the book are leaders in Illinois, characteristics of the state mirror many other parts of the country. Chicago is a major urban area that, together with the surrounding metropolitan area, reflects diverse dimensions of the United States. Downstate Illinois includes smaller urban cities and rural areas quite different from Chicago. In selecting leaders to interview, we sought to capitalize on the rich diversity of Illinois. We gave careful consideration to inclusion of distinguished educational leaders who represented the differences of community and geography, professional role and level, race, and institutional types.

The Participants

Eighteen IWA members who worked in Pre-K–12 schools and universities gathered on September 9, 2000, to learn more about the book project and how they could contribute. Those at the meeting committed to the project and worked with the coauthors to revise the demographic information form and refine the semi-structured interview guide. Components of productive interviewing were reviewed. Using purposeful reputational sampling (Patton, 1990), the group generated an initial list of 41 Illinois women educational leaders as potential participants. According to Patton (1990), "The logic and power of purposeful sampling lies in selecting *information-rich* cases for study in depth. Information-rich cases are those from which one can learn a great deal about issues of central importance to the purpose of the research, thus the term *purposeful* sampling" (p. 169).

Nomination criteria included professional distinction, political skill, a personality or story that would have an appeal beyond the boundaries of Illinois, and willingness to have their names used in publications resulting from the research. A desirable criterion was awareness of gender as having an impact on leadership. The group narrowed the list of 41 potential participants to create a pool of 21 individuals who represented a range of roles, a variety of institutions and levels, a geographic spread, and a racial/ethnic mix. Not surprisingly, the women interviewed for the book have all been honored at *Dare to Be Great* conferences. As the project evolved, 5 additional persons received training and joined the project interviewing team, but this team of 23 suffered some attrition due to illness, job pressures, and other conflicts.

The Interview Guide

We constructed the interview guide based on themes or patterns observed over the years in honorees' speeches at the *Dare to Be Great* conference. For example, one frequent pattern was the inclusion of values, such as care—care for others and care by others, including mentors and family. A recurring theme was tension in the interaction of personal and professional relationships, obligations, and ambitions. A theme less frequent but clearly present was how honorees dealt with conflicts of values and authority, their own and others. Many women talked about how they went around or beat the system to do what they believed to be necessary and right. Honorees also typically mentioned how their gender either had or had not affected their opportunities or leadership practices.

We created an interview guide to explore these and other issues associated with leadership.

We constructed a four-part interview guide. Some of the semi-structured interview guide questions were specific, while others were open-ended. Some questions asked for stories. In addition to asking the interview guide questions, interviewers were free to probe further into any interesting responses. In the introductory section of the interview guide, questions focused on career paths, values behind the participants' typical approaches to decision making, most difficult decisions, and experiences with the constraints of bureaucracy.

The second part of the interview guide focused on discretionary decision making. Questions asked how much discretion participants had in their present positions and about their comfort levels with discretionary decision making. For purposes of this study we defined discretionary decision making as decisions based on one's own judgment rather than on arbitrary bureaucratic rules and procedures. Questions asked participants for stories, for examples of discretionary decisions with positive results and also examples with problematic outcomes. Interviewers were asked to be alert to opportunities to open up the subject of politics.

The third part of the interview focused on creative insubordination. For purposes of this study, we defined creative insubordination as a counterbureaucratic approach to decision making that bends and/or ignores rules and otherwise subverts the authority of the chain of command when such subversion is justified by the greater authority of personal values, service to students, and common sense. Questions asked participants about their levels of comfort with creative insubordination and their stories. We asked whether they had practiced creative insubordination deliberately or unknowingly. Specific questions focused on the motivation for and the risks of creative insubordination. Interviewers were asked to be alert to opportunities to further explore a participant's level of political awareness.

The closing section of the interview included questions about gender issues and values. For example, we asked: "Has your gender affected your opportunities within the district/organization? To what are you unalterably committed? For what would you like to be remembered?" The closing question was open-ended, the "what else would you like for me to know" question.

Data Collection and Analysis

The 18 interviewers contacted their assigned participants using a prewritten introductory letter. They followed up by phone, scheduled, conducted, and taped the interviews. Transcripts of tapes from the interviews, as well as interviewers' reflections, were submitted to the book's coauthors, who analyzed the data inductively to find the recurring patterns using a combination of content analysis and constant comparative methodology (Glaser & Strauss, 1967; Merriam, 2001). An experienced transcriber produced all the transcripts. Whereas in a typical qualitative study the researcher would be the primary instrument for data collection and analysis (Merriam, 2001), the book's coauthors chose not to participate in the interviewing to allow greater objectivity during analysis of the transcripts. We note as a limitation that all the data is self-reported, and also note the confounding variable of different interviewers for each participant.

Member checking of the transcripts was completed by both the interviewers and participants to contribute to internal validity (Merriam, 2001). Both groups reviewed transcripts of the taped interviews and provided corrections and clarifications. A second level of member checking occurred when the participants had the opportunity to review and either delete, approve, or edit their direct quotations in the draft manuscript. The collaboration of the interviewers throughout the project also contributed to internal validity (Merriam, 2001). In addition to writing reflections on their interviews, in a focus group meeting in March 2001 the interviewers shared reflections on the project and their interviews, reacted to our preliminary analysis of the transcripts, and offered ideas about themes.

Although we have collected stories in response to certain of the interview guide questions, we have not pushed our analysis to the level required for narrative inquiry. We chose not to analyze the stories included in the transcripts structurally or linguistically (Polkinghorne, 1988). We are aware that "political conditions constrain particular events from being narrated, and have not attempted to interpret why individual stories have been told in particular ways" (Riessman, 1993, p. 3). We share our analysis of the interview data in thematic chapters (Seidman, 1991). The profiles included in the chapters present meaningful "descriptive, personal and concrete" stories about how life experiences shape who a leader is and what she does (AhNee-Benham & Cooper, 1998, p. 6). The personal stories suggest, as does Curry (2000), that self-knowledge and ego strength sustain *leaders who dare* in the daily work of leadership.

CATEGORIZING THE RESEARCH ON WOMEN IN LEADERSHIP

Several scholars (Rhode, 2003; Shakeshaft, 1987, 1999; Skrla & Young, 2003; Smulyan, 2000) have proposed conceptual and categorical schemes for organizing the existing research on women and leadership. Shakeshaft (1987) provided one of the first comprehensive scholarly overviews of issues confronting women who were seeking administrative positions in schools. She described what she called the "androcentric bias in educational administration theory and research," and detailed the historical underrepresentation of women in leadership roles, including analysis of the external and internal barriers to women's advancement. She called for researchers to document women's experiences or what she called the "female view of the school world" (p. 169). A decade later, summarizing advances in inclusion of women in the knowledge base, Shakeshaft (1999) categorized the research about women and gender in educational leadership into six stages (p. 113). Stage 1 research documenting the absence of women in administration took place mostly in the 1970s and 1980s, she reports. Shakeshaft characterizes Stage 2 research as identifying outstanding women administrators from the past and looking at "whether women have done the same things that men have done and if women's achievements meet male standards" (p. 114). Stage 3 research focuses on why there are so few women leaders in schools. Shakeshaft reports that these studies are ongoing, although much work on this topic was completed in the 1970s and 1980s. "Overall, Stage 3 research is plentiful, continuing the search for ways to overcome the barriers to women in administration first by describing the barriers and then by examining the effectiveness of responses" (pp. 114–115). In Stage 4 research, women are studied on their own terms. According to Shakeshaft these studies reporting how women experience leadership have become common in the last decade. Shakeshaft contends that Stage 5 research portrays women's experience as a challenge to traditional organizational and leadership theories. Finally, she projects that Stage 6 research eventually will document how theory has been transformed or reconceptualized to include experiences of women.

Blount's (1998) historical work on how women were moved out of leadership prominence to their current status is an example of research that bridges Shakeshaft's Stages 1–3. Blount documents in painstaking detail the historical changes in women's roles in education, illustrating how gender and interpretations of what was appropriate based on one's gender interacted with the historical context to eventually diminish women's opportunities (Stage 1). She identifies and profiles several important women superintendents from early in the 20th century (Stage 2). Her analysis clarifies in a new way why there are so few women in administration relative to their numbers in teaching, and the continuing gender barriers to leadership positions for women educators (Stage 3).

Other scholars are commenting about the scholarly research on women's leadership from a variety of angles. Taking a big-picture look, Skrla and Young (2003) write, "Especially within the past two decades, feminist epistemology and advocacy have played an important role in shaping the changes in the field" (p. 1). Smulyan (2000) identifies three shifts since 1980 in the study of women in administration. From her perspective, the first group of studies focused on discrimination, stereotyping, and socialization. The second group focused on the differences in male and female management styles, and contributed to what has become "the risk of essentializing women's characteristic approaches" (p. 17). In her view, a more recent third group of studies has a "focus on the organizational structures of schools and their reflection of larger social structures that perpetuate gender, racial, and class inequities" (p. 17).

Outside the field of education, Rhode (2003) addresses the underrepresentation of women in high-level formal leadership positions in law, politics, and business. Rhode clusters studies on women's leadership in two broad areas: issues related to gender differences in access or equal opportunity, and issues related to gender differences in the exercise of leadership. Research on leadership, gender differences, and the relationship between the two expanded rapidly in the last 25 years, according to Rhode, who reports that by the early 1990s, "surveys identified over 5000 scholarly works on leadership" (p. 4). She surmises that "gender inequalities in leadership opportunities are pervasive; perceptions of inequality are not. A widespread assumption is that barriers have been coming down, women have been moving up, and equal treatment is an accomplished fact" (p. 6). According to Rhode, analysis of existing studies demonstrates that access to leadership opportunities in the workplace is limited by traditional gender stereotypes, inadequate access to mentors and support networks, and inflexible workplace structures. Rhode calls commentary on gender differences in leadership a cottage industry, with "over two hundred empirical studies and a still greater volume of journalistic and pop psychological accounts" (p. 18) attempting to assess differences in leadership styles and priorities. She summarizes, "Perceptions of gender differences in style or effectiveness remain common, although the evidence for such differences is weaker than commonly supposed" (p. 19). In summary, her conclusion is that gender does make a difference to leadership opportunities, but not to style or priorities.

We considered our study in terms of these approaches to categorization. It does not fall neatly into any of Smulyan's (2000) three groups, although we touch on topics in each. Reflecting on Shakeshaft's (1999) six stages, we clearly began our work at Stage 4, inasmuch as part of our research purpose was simply to tell the stories of these outstanding women leaders in education. However, the themes and our conclusions certainly address Stage 5 in challenging traditional ways of leading. We consider our work a contribution to the eventual Stage 6 reconceptualization of leadership theory. Considering what Rhode (2003) labels the two major research categories, although not a major focus, we did ask participants in what ways their gender had affected their opportunities within their school district/ organization, including whether they perceived their status or power to have been affected by gender. We also addressed two issues in Rhode's second category, gender differences in leadership style or priorities. For example, one question we asked our participants was "What meaning does the phrase 'women's ways of leading' have for you?" Another question was "Do you perceive differences in your priorities/values and those of the establishment in your district/organization?"

Perceptions of Gender as a Factor in Access to Opportunities

Substantiating Rhode's (2003) observation that although "gender inequalities in leadership opportunities are pervasive, perceptions of inequality are not" (p. 6), our participants were divided when asked in what ways their gender had affected their opportunities for leadership. Some have experienced gender as a factor limiting opportunities, but others have not. Four reported *no effect*, while five others answered *yes and no*. An additional seven said *yes*, gender had affected their opportunities, and responses from two did not fit in any of these categories.

Responses from the four who perceived no gender constraints on their opportunities included a range of comments. For example, Superintendent Dorothy Weber was clear, "My gender has not impacted any opportunity for me to advance in the various districts I've worked. . . . I've always had the philosophy of being ready for opportunities that may arise so I was viewed as both qualified and capable when openings occurred." Rebecca van der Bogert answered, "I never felt like any doors were closed or anything like that." Stephanie Pace Marshall's response implied a *no*: "I've worked closely with men all my life. The boards I have chaired and been on have been mostly men, and the external world in which I work professionally is mostly men, although not necessarily here at IMSA [Illinois Mathematics and Science Academy]." Finally, one principal was included in this group of four who did not perceive gender to have limited their opportunities. Principal Aurthur Perkins was unequivocal in response to the question: "No. If there were a position tomorrow that I would apply for that I wanted in this district I think I could get it. I don't think they would see me as a woman or that I would hit that glass ceiling."

The five who answered *yes and no* had not forgotten earlier struggles and qualified their answers from a perspective of time, expressing how things had changed. For example, former superintendent Ann Duncan, now retired, said, "When I first got into administration I encountered some of the stuff [barriers] that came up. I decided early on that there were other things at play. There were times when I felt that being female made my job easier." Officially retired but still accepting interim superintendent positions, Carol Struck also commented on things having changed, at least for her personally. She said, "My gender has never caused me not to advance, but there have been problems along the way. I rarely see it anymore. It's just not the issue that it used to be." Dean Sally Pancrazio said, "Early in my career gender did definitely make a difference in my opportunities. But after a while you just keep working and doing your best and gender doesn't matter anymore." Two leaders in this *yes and no* category essentially said they had experienced limitations in previous situations, but not in their present positions. Superintendent Elizabeth Lewin explained, "Gender played a role in my climbing the ladder from assistant principal to principal within my high school. I think my gender caused a delay in my being offered the opportunity to move up. As a result, I was in my middle forties when I received the opportunity to move from principal to superintendent." Speaking of her present role her answer was, "I really don't believe that I have been impacted by my gender within the district in making decisions. And the reason for that is that the majority of my board has been female. So I really don't believe on a local level that my gender has impacted my opportunities." Illinois State Board of Education (ISBE) Deputy Superintendent Mary Jayne Broncato remembered applying for an assistant principal position and being told she was the best candidate, but they wanted a man for the job because it was a middle school. She expressed satisfaction with eventually becoming the superintendent in that district and the boss of the person who did not give her the job. Broncato did not believe her opportunities within ISBE had been affected by her gender, however. She viewed status and power as matters affected more by individual credibility than gender. These yes and no answers reflect that times have changed, but also that gaining a reputation, the particular role, and the type of organization all factor into whether gender is a limitation or not.

Seven women clearly addressed ways gender had limited their opportunities. Maxine Wortham, central office executive director of early childhood education, said, "I think my gender has caused things to be a little harder than they would have been had I been a male." Former regional superintendent Martha O'Malley also said, "I think it's harder. I had many battles along the way. It was very difficult when I started. . . . Gender did affect my opportunities with both obtaining and succeeding in my various career positions. The higher on the administrative ladder I went, the more problems presented themselves." On the other hand, O'Malley gave several examples of how men did offer her opportunities. Regional Special Education Coordinator Diane Morrison explained her *yes* answer in terms of differences in male and female career paths: "I got into my career later. Traditionally men have had to start their careers earlier, having fewer options than women have about careers versus families, kids, whatever. Had I been a man and spent more time in my career there probably would have been differences in where I would have gone in my career."

Ola Bundy spent her entire administrative career at the Illinois High School Association (IHSA), a position that came to her after eight-and-a-half years in teaching. Bundy shared several stories that illustrated how gender limited her. For example, for the first seven years when she was the only female administrator, she did all her own secretarial work. When the office was moved from Chicago to Springfield, discovering that she was still to be without secretarial help, she submitted her resignation, which was not accepted. That was what it took to achieve equal status with the men in terms of having a secretary. Additionally, Bundy, who remained at the assistant executive director level until her retirement, stated, "I believe I was passed over for a promotion to associate executive director because I was a woman."

Also from the *yes* category, Brenda Holmes explained, "In this position as a lobbyist sometimes I do feel somewhat stymied. Lobbying is still primarily a man's world, although it has changed significantly in the last 15 years. But I think the gender of being female has somewhat affected the opportunities." Hazel Loucks, as Deputy Governor for Education and Workforce Development, was also in the heart of the political world. Her perception about gender affecting her opportunities was, "I'm sure that it always has. I do think you have to work twice as hard and twice as long to show that you actually have the skills and knowledge to do the jobs. I saw some of my male counterparts sometimes get promoted faster, easier." Based on her own research, Loucks also believes that lack of mentoring is a factor in inequality of opportunities. Dean Mary Polite was adamant about gender as a factor in opportunities for women, taught about gender in her educational administration classes, and described herself as a person "extremely sensitive to gender issues." Taken as a group, these remarks suggest that things have been at least different, if not more difficult, for these seven leaders because they were women.

Responses from two women did not fit in the *no*, *yes and no*, or *yes* categories in terms of the issue of gender and opportunities. Associate Superintendent Gwen Lee did not answer the question directly, but observed, "All the boosts that I've had in my life have come from females." In response to whether gender affected her status and power, she was direct: "We now have two African American females who are leading the district. Both the superintendent and I, we've had some arrows come our way, you know, based on the fact that we're female and it certainly doesn't help if you're African American." Former high school principal Vita Meyer experienced a series of firsts for her district in her career. She was the first woman head swim coach, the first woman assistant principal, and the first woman high school principal. She said, "I look back and I always felt, and still do, that I was promoted and ended up a high school principal because I deserved it. I had proven that I could do the job." Meyer did express frustration at what had been the male domination of the Illinois High School Association and the Illinois Principals Association, two statewide organizations with which she had frequent dealings as a high school principal.

Looking at their perceptions by role, as a group the women who were superintendents perceived their experiences in terms of access to opportunities more positively than did the others. From the perspective of type of organization, women in highly political organizations (universities, state and regional agencies) generally experienced more limitations on opportunities than those in school districts. Looking at responses by race, three of the four African American women reported either constraints or mixed experiences, potentially reflecting the intersection of race and gender. Responses of the women in our study suggest that opportunity for a leadership position is closely interwoven with issues of status, power, race, and gender.

OVERVIEW OF BOOK STRUCTURE AND THEMES

The preface presented the context of our research. In chapter 1, "Introduction," we have elaborated on the purpose and procedures of the research. Chapter 2, "Studying Women's Leadership: Contemporary Issues," features an overview of four contemporary issues in the study of women's leadership: cultural tensions, essentializing, honoring diversity, and the role of feminism. In chapters 3–6, we broaden the focus from women's leadership to elaborate the four primary themes from our data in the context of the leadership literature. We share what we have learned through analysis of the stories of the individuals interviewed. Quotes and excerpts from their stories illustrate, validate, expand upon, and clarify the themes, subthemes, and our related conclusions. In addition, each chapter highlights a single leader who provides a clear example of powerful daring leadership relative to the theme and ideas explored in the chapter.

For example, chapter 3, "Developing Collaborative Decision-Making Processes," highlights a leader who is daring to make decisions her way: Dr. Rebecca van der Bogert, superintendent of Winnetka School District #36 and codirector of the International Network of Principals' Centers at Harvard University. Her commitment to collaborative leadership and shared decision making causes her to be a superintendent who "does not behave the way a lot of people expect me to behave." Her way is to diffuse power situations, break down authority, and stretch people's thinking. A published author, she frames problems that arise in her district as issues for research and learning. Becky said when interviewed, "My style is a little bit different than a lot of people, and things will take longer. I will involve people, and it's messy." Her leadership illustrates how a superintendent "challenges traditional notions of bureaucracy, creating power through relationships between equals rather than as an act of domination within a hierarchy—decentralizes and enlarges decision-making processes" (AhNee-Benham & Cooper, 1998, p. 146). Topics addressed in the chapter include the role of information in decision making, the complexity of collaborative decision-making processes, factors that can make discretionary decision making problematic, and exploration of why some decisions are more difficult than others.

Chapter 4, "Pushing the Bureaucratic Boundaries," features a person in the right place at the right time whose daring played out in a groundbreaking quest for equity for girls' athletics in Illinois. Ola Bundy was assistant executive director of the Illinois High School Association from 1967 until 1996. Her work on behalf of the girls and women of Illinois earned her a place in the National High School Sports Hall of Fame, as well as many other national honors. Ola Bundy pushed the boundaries. When interviewed, Ola said that the term *creative insubordination* was familiar to her, "maybe because I was being a little bit insubordinate all the time." She built networks of relationships and at the same time was never afraid to go "head to head" with the bureaucracy or the "good old boys" as the only woman on the leadership team to develop girls' interscholastic competition. In court over Title IX issues, she used the system to change the system. Her standards affected the entire educational arena in Illinois as women broadened their aspirations, sought new responsibilities, and assumed positions once reserved for men. Due to Ola Bundy's persuasiveness and commitment to equity, new possibilities exist for women who would coach and lead as well as for young women athletes. Ola Bundy is recognized nationally as one of the pioneers of girls' athletic competition. Topics addressed in the chapter include motivation for pushing the bureaucratic boundaries, types of creative insubordination, attributes and strategies for surviving the risks of creative insubordination, and approaches to transforming bureaucracies.

Chapter 5, "Claiming Power Through Politics," depicts an educational leader who dared to claim power in the political arena. Dr. Hazel Loucks was the first deputy governor for education and workforce in the country. Whatever her position has been, Hazel has centered her career on doing the right thing, making decisions based on core values, and daring to take risks. She has had to adjust to life in the political arena by forcing herself to also think of the political ramifications of her decisions. She has learned in this unique position to reckon with how politics works. By keeping an "I want to make a difference attitude," Hazel forges ahead in the political arena. Her power comes from her credibility and ability to bring together people of disparate views. She has been responsible for major changes in Illinois systems related to a wide range of educational issues and concerns. Working from her powerful political position, Hazel Loucks has created coalitions that have enhanced educational opportunities, created new possibilities, and made a difference to children, families, educators, and communities. Topics addressed in the chapter include collaboration as a political choice; positional versus personal influence and power; integrity, intent, and personal sacrifice; and outsider, insider, and gender politics.

Chapter 6, "Living and Leading From Values," highlights the leadership of Dr. Elizabeth Lewin, a dynamic superintendent of schools in Carbondale, a college town in southern Illinois where she was born. Skilled at community collaboration, Liz is always willing to make a risky decision to help children. "When I believe something is right, whatever risk may exist from a bureaucracy, board, or any tangible body is pretty low priority to me, because I answer to something much higher. When people say, you could have risked your job, I remind them that there are a lot of opportunities to make money. I am motivated by opportunities to get things accomplished and improving the quality of life for our children." She was called back to the community to be the superintendent in 1995 after extensive experience as an educator, having taught for 17 years and

served for 7 years as a principal and assistant principal at a large high
school in Edwardsville. Married for 30 years, with two grown children,
her experiences as a mother and her professional life are merged. Liz insists that educators in her district maintain a clear perspective that their
own families come first. When Liz talks about the importance of family,
she is clear to educators in her district not only about her values, but that
it is expected for them to express and live by what they hold most precious. She said, "I would not work for a board or in a situation where there
was not going to be sensitivity to the parent part of me." Elizabeth Lewin
also takes seriously her role as a role model: "I realize that I'm one of a
few African American females in a chief executive officer position to
serve as a role model for young ones out there. So I watch very carefully
what I do, and that's why I lean so heavily on my own personal values in
making decisions." Topics addressed in the chapter include values-based
leadership, benefiting children, maintaining integrity, honoring diversity,
and expressing spirituality.

In chapter 7, "Redefining Leadership: New Ways of Doing and Being,"
we examine our major themes in light of concepts of constructive postmodern leadership. We consider collaborative decision making, pushing
the bureaucratic boundaries, claiming power through politics, and living
and leading from values in the context of writings of contemporary leadership theorists. We also address international issues and perspectives about
educational leadership. We believe educators must dare to have a global
consciousness, must view their work as the creation of a compassionate
and sustainable world if we are to meet the needs of future generations.

Chapter 8, "Visionary, Provocative, Integrative," highlights a leader
with a global perspective. Dr. Stephanie Pace Marshall, president of the
Illinois Mathematics and Science Academy and former president
(1991–1993) of the Association for Supervision and Curriculum Development (ASCD) presents clearly the power of emerging leadership practices, of daring, and of commitment to generative learning and global consciousness. Stephanie is an inclusive decision maker who pays attention
to information, people, patterns, and language. An innovative leader with
an international influence, she continues to create new possibilities for
herself and to generate new possibilities for others. She believes that a
fundamental responsibility of a leader is "to offer people a chance to
choose a story of possibility that is worthy of their lives." She views lead-

ership and organizations as living systems of relationships. For Stephanie Pace Marshall, "leadership is not about *doing*; it is about *being*."

Finally, in chapter 9, "Concluding Reflections," we offer reflections on the dance of daring we have portrayed in the book. We share reflections of the interviewers on how this project has affected them as leaders. We offer reflections on how we have been strengthened by the collaborative processes through which we have developed the book and the conclusions we have reached. We circle back to issues in the study of women's leadership and consider contemporary educational leadership theory and practice in a global context. We consider the contemporary leadership and social justice challenges facing educational leaders across the globe, such as growing numbers of children living in poverty, increased accountability for the learning of all children, and ever-deepening funding concerns, to name only a few. We argue that the need for *leaders who dare* is greater than ever, and urge widespread attention to and adoption of the transformative leadership practices we have documented. Finally, we offer our hope that this book will contribute to closing the leadership gap and to the ongoing redefinition of leadership.

Chapter Two

Studying Women's Leadership: Contemporary Issues

A majority of the leaders interviewed for this book came of age professionally during a time when most administrators were white males and accepted leadership theory was based on white male perspectives. Six of the women are over sixty, and another ten are in their fifties. Many share ambivalence about identifying themselves as "women leaders." The story of each woman serves as a counternarrative in terms of American culture generally, and the world of education specifically. Chase (1995) defines counternarratives as "stories in which self images contrast with dominant cultural models for women" (p. 10). Speaking of the wider culture, she writes,

> Women educational leaders' narratives provide evidence that the counternarrative of the successful, accomplished professional woman has achieved at least a modicum of acceptance in contemporary American culture. Counternarrative is the appropriate term because the dominant script for women's lives continues to emphasize women's selflessness and orientation to domestic concerns. (p. 213)

In the world of education, women pursuing careers in administration still go against long-established cultural norms that teaching is for women and administration is for men. Women in leadership roles are perceived by many to be both role and status incongruent. Many leadership texts simply ignore the considerable influence of women educational leaders across the country. As Heilbrun (1989) argues, "because [power] has been declared unwomanly . . . women have been deprived of the narratives, or the texts, plots, or examples, by which they might assume power over—take control of—their own lives" (p. 17). The exclusion of women subjects from the research has deprived the field of educational leadership of a fully inclusive look at leadership patterns and practices. This exclusion has also limited our view of both leadership and the counternarratives that could lead others, women and men, to new possibilities.

Because we are living with a legacy of opportunity made possible by several iterations of the women's movement, we sometimes underestimate the power of historical and cultural realities to continue to constrain lives and opportunities of women. Cultural scripts for women and cultural stereotypes about women have deep roots. According to Blount (1998), women's 19th-century entry into teaching "allowed women to attain privileges previously available only to men" (p. 21). In spite of the competence of women as leaders in a variety of professional endeavors, women are still seen by many as less suited for leadership than men. The underlying tension still existing is that women in educational administration are taking public sphere roles when their natural place is the domestic sphere. This division of spheres persisted from the colonial period, became embedded in laws and policies, and was only dismantled legally in the 1970s. In the words of Blount, "The dismantling of separate spheres ideology prepared the way for legal activism on behalf of women seeking equity in educational employment" (p. 139). Although the separate spheres ideology has been legally dismantled, it still exists as a cultural script. "As recently as the 1980s," write Freeman and Bourque (2001), "conservative political and religious figures called for women's return to the home to heal the wounds of national life, suffered, presumably, because of women's exodus from the domestic sphere" (p. 3).

In writing the book we encountered both counternarratives of success and cultural barriers, as well as other issues associated with research into and generalizations about women's leadership (AhNee-Benham & Cooper, 1998; Blount, 1998; Brunner, 1999, 2000; Chase, 1995; Curry, 2000; Dunlap & Schmuck, 1995; Freeman, Bourque, & Shelton, 2001; Gardiner, Enomoto, & Grogan, 2000; Grogan, 1996; Jamieson, 1995; Reynolds, 2002; Rhode, 2003; Young & Skrla, 2003). At least four contemporary issues recurring in the scholarship about women and leadership are resolving cultural tensions, essentializing, the importance of honoring diversity, and questions about the role of feminism and feminist research.

RESOLVING CULTURAL TENSIONS

Gardiner, Enomoto, and Grogan (2000) write, "Women leaders say they often feel as though they 'don't quite fit' the accepted pattern, and are constantly attempting to either fit into the mold, or change the system" (p. 102). Calling it the balancing act, Smulyan (2000) writes, "One of the most striking balancing acts all three principals undertake is managing the tension inherent in being a woman in a position generally held by men in an institutional structure predicated on male definitions of power, authority, and leadership" (p. 2). Smulyan also contends, "A principal both constructs her role in context and is constructed by those contexts" (p. 5). Scholars have examined from a variety of perspectives how women leaders construct their roles and resolve cultural tensions associated with their leadership. Resolving cultural tensions inevitably involves either self-definition or redefinition of the leadership role.

An approach to resolving cultural tensions described by Blackmore (2002) is choosing to operate at work from one of several gender scripts of leadership. These include a "being strong" script, "superwoman" script, "choosing leadership over love" script, the "postmodernist" script, the "women's styles of leadership" script, the "power" script, the "professional success" script, and the "social male" script (pp. 56–62). Chase (1995) identifies four narrative strategies through which the 27 women superintendents she studied manage the coexistence of powerful positions and cultural subjection in their lives. Although the strategies differ slightly, a commonality is that these women construct "individual solutions to the collective problem of inequality" (p. 178). She distinguishes these individual solutions from what she calls the activist story, or "collective solutions to gender and race inequality" (p. 178). Chase refers to the co-optation story as another approach to resolving this cultural tension, and the one with which we are more familiar. This approach of fitting into a male-defined system by adopting masculine behaviors and values is what Blackmore labels the "social male" script. Writing about the same phenomenon, Curry (2000) identifies the costs of this approach, "Women who put on a masculine way of being in order to make up for their gendered socialization stand to lose the possibility of shifting from hierarchical leadership practice to a partnership of organizational members" (p. 102).

Curry (2000), an African American scholar, believes that women must deal with cultural norms and marginality by inventing or constructing a *leader persona*, often in the absence of female models. She studied eight women leaders in higher education or state offices of education. In the lives of these women, deliberate construction of a leader persona was an approach to living with cultural tensions associated with leadership. Each of the women constructed a leader persona differently as a result of differences in their backgrounds, their present contexts, and what Curry calls their defining experiences. She contends, "Leadership personas emerge from our individual psychology and are unique. They are part of our developmental experiences" (p. 21). Curry identifies a transcendent theme for each woman as "integral to the individual's adaptation to her way of being with regard to leadership" (p. 66). Examples of such themes are leadership as a lifestyle, service and obedience, and trust and advocacy (pp. 84–85). Each of these themes paradoxically embodies fundamental cultural tensions that must be resolved by women who would lead. This makes sense to Curry, who writes, "A transcendent theme is one that preoccupies the leader persona" (p. 66) until it is addressed or resolved. At that point a leader persona is achieved. A leader persona can be negative as well as positive. Maintaining a leader persona required some to compartmentalize certain features of themselves as a partner or parent. For others, arriving at a leader persona was an achievement of wholeness or identity congruence, and that congruence became a source of power.

Freeman and Bourque's (2001) words underline that any consideration of women and leadership must consider issues of power. They write,

> The exercise of leadership involves power, a concept where research has suggested gender variation. Power becomes an essential link in our study of women's changing leadership roles, for it is precisely in debates about the appropriateness of women's exercise of power, particularly over men, that gender is linked to leadership in society's most prestigious and highly compensated institutions. (p. 4)

Interestingly, Freeman and Bourque conclude that the amount of power a person has, rather than the gender, makes a difference in how a person uses power. Conway (2001) also addresses the need for discussions of women's leadership to explore the issue of power. She writes, "So we need to work steadily and deliberately to forge the images of female power that can inform notions of leadership. This is difficult to do in the face of the current 'relational' emphasis of feminist thought, but it is a task worthy of serious effort" (p. xix). Blackmore (2002) challenges us to consider power from a different angle when she writes, "Mainstream discourses continue to construct women as a problem for educational leadership rather than problematizing the concept of leadership itself, relative to dominant power and gender relations" (p. 55).

Blount's (1998) historical study of the superintendency encourages women to redefine the leadership role rather than themselves. She clarifies how men defined the superintendent's role during the second half of the 19th century using military and other strongly hierarchical male models in order to resolve the cultural tensions they experienced in what was by then a feminized profession. "Administrative work offered a gender-appropriate way for men to stay in education" (p. 47), Blount writes. As a consequence, she explains, "Women . . . have had little if any role in defining and shaping the structure of public schools and the superintendency in particular" (p. 162). If men created the masculine norms for the superintendent role, if men's numerical dominance in all administrative roles in education continues to perpetuate gendered approaches to leadership, then it seems not unreasonable to say that women, if given the opportunity, can redefine those roles and by extension the phenomenon of leadership itself. Blount, however, does not see greater numbers of women as the solution to gender inequity in schools. Instead, she would have us address the larger societal questions related to power: who has it and how it is constructed. It is a challenge we must tackle, because as Blount so powerfully expresses, "If we continue to support schools that systematically distribute power unequally by sex and gender, we send a forceful message to students about women's worth, their potential, and their place in society" (p. 169).

ESSENTIALIZING

A second issue in research about women as leaders is essentializing. Several scholars emphasize the importance of avoiding this error. For example, Smulyan (2000) writes: "Each of the women principals described in this book experiences her gender differently, as mediated by her own personal background and individual characteristics such as race, age, religion, and class" (p. 204). As a result, she concludes, "The cases illustrate that essentialized descriptions of women principals, while they have some validity, limit our ability to see women administrators negotiating leadership approaches in ways that meet their own needs and the demands of the communities and institutions within which they work" (pp. 213–214). Freeman and Bourque (2001) are also emphatic. "The evidence in these essays makes it clear that leadership qualities and requirements vary significantly from one context to another, among racial and ethnic groups and cross nationally" (p. 4). Essentializing typically shows up in generalizations about gender differences in leadership style.

Our participants' perceptions of gender differences in leadership style were in some cases directly stated and in other cases clearly implied in responses to the open-ended question, "What does the phrase 'women's ways of leadership' mean to you?" No clear categorical response differences emerged in terms of role, type of organization, or race. Almost every participant expressed belief that women lead differently, illustrating Rhode's (2003) observation that "perceptions of gender differences in style or effectiveness remain common, although the evidence for such differences is weaker than commonly supposed" (p. 19). Only one woman quite definitely disagreed, saying, "I don't think there's a woman's way of leading. I think there are a variety of management styles." She continued, "I think there are women who are very autocratic, who are very much in control. I think there are men who delegate, and who share decision making. I see those as the ends of the spectrum rather than a gender thing." From her perspective, a person's need for power, rather than gender, was a guiding factor in terms of leadership style.

Four women gave mixed responses to the question. The predominantly mixed responses included comments from two who viewed differences primarily in terms of individuals, while still making limited generalizations about women's leadership. Each expressed the impossibility, however, of making any sort of universal statement about men or women as leaders. For example, one said, "The longer I've been in administration the more I've come to see that it's really not about gender as much as it is about individuals." Another person stressed how the attributes of women and men as leaders overlap, that what used to be more true of women as a group—that women value nurturing more than men—is perhaps changing. On the other hand, she did find women to be more willing to talk through differences as opposed to what she described as the more task and outcome-oriented typically male approach. Generally, however, she believed there were more similarities than differences between men and women as leaders. Another woman in this group said that, in general, "you would find more women with collaborative styles. But," she continued, "I don't think it's just a female thing." Musing about greater acceptance of a collaborative style, she wondered about the parallel developments of more women coming into the superintendency and a collaborative style being more supported in the literature—"Which came first?" she asked.

The other 13 participants perceived women to lead differently than men. Four offered slight qualifiers, for example, "There are some men with similar qualities." One woman said, "I know some male superintendents who are very much committed to people and process. They are rare, especially in this time when we're being admonished to run schools like a business." Another said, "while there are individual differences among all people, if we looked at groups—male versus female—women differ from men in their leadership." The other nine women, exactly half of our subjects, stated unequivocally that in the field of education women's leadership is different from men's. Examples clustered in the categories of focus, interpersonal skills, and collaboration.

For the largest category, differences in focus, comments about women as leaders included: "They think more in terms of individual children." "They bring a human touch, a softness, a feeling for children that men do not." "They look at a larger picture." "They are more focused on children." "They are more visionary." "They take more risks." "They are better at accomplishing things. They pay more attention to details." For the category of interpersonal skills the differences noted included: "They are more compassionate and empathetic." "They are more nurturing and caring." "They express appreciation better." "Women listen more and differently." Several comments pointed to women as more collaborative, including: "They are more likely to share leadership, more collegial." "They are natural team builders." "They are more inclusive of those affected by a decision or issue." "They are more thoughtful and humane decision makers." "They mentor more consistently. They make better use of human resources." Four important responses belonged to no single category:

"Women have an ability to change persona to fit the needs of the situation." "Women are more creative." "Women are more able to trust intuition." "Women bring an unrecognized wisdom associated with women as the givers of life, a grace."

Although a majority of the participants in our study reflect an essentialist view of women's leadership, our intent in this book is to present a particularized look at how 18 different women lead. Their leadership patterns and practices display differences as well as commonalities. Freeman and Bourque (2001) clearly define essentialist descriptions of women as characterized by:

> [There is] the idea that there is an identifiable component found in every woman that marks her as female across cultures and over time. Although for many women the first catalyst to leadership may stem from their traditional domestic roles, women are no longer exclusively characterized by those roles. Similarly, few descriptions of women's leadership will hold across all cultures or throughout history or within American society across class, race, and ethnic lines. (p. 5)

We agree with their assessment that few generalizations will hold cross-culturally or within American society in spite of widespread perceptions that women lead differently. Such generalizations often overlook the realities of diversity, including diverse perspectives and contexts.

INCLUDING VIEWS OF DIVERSE WOMEN

A logical extension of the caution against essentializing is the admonition to include women of color and other minorities in studies of women's leadership. There is great value in hearing and learning from the "undersong of marginalization" (AhNee-Benham & Cooper, 1998, p. 141). Some scholars have focused studies exclusively on minority women (Ah-Nee-Benham, 2003; AhNee-Benham & Cooper, 1998; Alston, 1999; Atlas & Capper, 2003; Bloom & Erlandson, 2003; Brunner, 2003; Dillard, 1995, 2003; Jackson, 1999; Mendez-Morse, 1999, 2003; Murtadha-Watts, 1999; Ortiz, 1999). Our study included four African American women, 22% of the participants. In developing the thematic chapters, we note perspectives of these women, particularly when their perceptions differ from other participants.

One category considered in the scholarship on minority women is denial of access to leadership opportunities and positions. For example, Alston (1999) completed a study of "constraints and facilitators that black females encountered" (p. 79) in achieving superintendent positions. Her survey of the 45 black female superintendents in 1995–1996 identified five major constraints they had experienced:

1. Absence of "old boy network," support systems or sponsorship
2. Lack of awareness of the political maneuvers
3. Lack of role models
4. Societal attitudes that blacks lack competency in leadership positions
5. No formal or informal method for identifying black aspirants to administrative positions (p. 86)

Interestingly, Alston claims, they did not view racism or sexism as major obstacles. Ortiz (1999) reports that although they are few in number everywhere, Hispanic women superintendents are found most often in the Southwest where there is typically a contextual match. They are most likely to be selected for the positions in districts experiencing difficulties. Three Hispanic women superintendents profiled by Mendez-Morse (1999) each describe experiencing a redefinition of self on the way to a superintendent's position. In both the 1992 and 2000 American Association of School Administrators (AASA) studies of the superintendency, in sharp contrast to white respondents, much larger percentages of persons of color reported experiences with discriminatory hiring and promotional practices (Brunner, 2003). Brunner explores how dominant discourses used by researchers contribute to limiting the access of women and persons of color to the superintendency. Data collection and reporting categories can perpetuate norms that reinforce perceptions that the superintendency is a position for white males. She recommends that researchers involved in general studies such as those conducted by AASA give full reports of disaggregated data.

A second category in the scholarship on minority women concerns alternative values and visions for leadership. For example, as an extension of earlier work, Mendez-Morse (2003) describes three characteristics of

Chicana feminism: "a Pan-American perspective, an assertion of multiple oppressions, and an advocacy for social justice" (p. 163). She emphasizes the insights resulting from multiple interwoven experiences of oppression, and urges that future research always consider more than one category of difference. Other scholars who focused on leadership of women of color are coming up with new models of leadership that specifically challenge traditional conceptions. AhNee-Benham (2003) proposes a model of leadership grounded in both feminist thought and understandings from native/indigenous peoples. This model also offers values and visions for leadership that differ from the traditional. In developing the model, called *Go to the Source*, a conference of native educational leaders first identified what they wanted for their children:

> (a) to be fluent in their mother tongue (in most cases to be bilingual and/or multi-lingual; (b) to articulate a strong, positive native/indigenous cultural self-identity, to be centered in their unique ways of knowing, and to live as proud human beings; (c) to respect the land, the place of their ancestors; and (d) to be confident that they can make choices and define what they do, to be self-determined human beings. (p. 230)

The leadership model incorporates four dimensions: critical development of the intellect; health, body, and environment; preservation and revitalization of native languages, arts, and traditions; and native spiritual wisdom (p. 225). A fundamental principle of the model is balance—"an alternative worldview that focuses on the interconnectedness of family, community, culture, nature, and spirituality" (p. 226). Their belief is that if family is a first priority, then schools will be strong. AhNee-Benham recommends further study of educational leadership from the perspective of native women. She concludes, "It is through the dissemination of these ideas that we may learn more about the joy of living and the deeply held belief that embedded in one's heart, mind, and soul is the source of leadership" (p. 241).

Some scholars view a leader's deeply held beliefs from the context of religion or spirituality. Murtadha-Watts (1999) and Atlas and Capper (2003) emphasize the role of spirituality in the leadership of African American women. Murtadha-Watts writes, "African American women in leadership positions often draw upon profound historical traditions of inner spiritual strength" (p. 155). One such historical tradition is called *othermothering*. "Many Black women leaders act as Othermothers, a responsiveness to family in the larger community, thinking not only of themselves and the children they may have birthed, but offering care for children who have not experienced the loving and fussing nurturance of family," (p. 156) she explains. Murtadha-Watts posits a womanist model of leadership that includes spirituality and activism. Based on her own study of black women leaders from the past and interviews of 25 contemporary women in leadership positions, she offers this caveat: "Womanist spiritual leadership theory is neither static nor fixed in definition because there can be no unitary representation of African American women's lives" (p. 166). Murtadha-Watts does assert, however, "The women in this study clearly demonstrate that Black women's cultural, political, and economic status provides them with a distinguishing set of experiences, a particular set of spiritual beliefs and a different view of material reality than that available to other groups" (p. 166). Atlas and Capper (2003) examined through interviews how six African American women principals define spirituality and whether their spirituality influences their leadership. They also created a spiritual leadership theory for African American women based on analysis of their interview data. The theory is based on God or the Divine as an anchor in the lives of the women. The four facets of the theory are accountability to God, concrete experience of and relationship with God, receive and pass on God's care, and dialogue with God. In summary, the leadership patterns and practices of these six women, as well as those interviewed by Murtadha-Watts, clearly reflect the active presence of spirituality.

Dillard (1995) also reinterprets the meaning of leadership through an alternative vision. She writes about her case study of Gloria Natham, "Using the voice of this particular African American principal, the collective thought and action I seek to transform are our current conceptualizations of what leadership is and what leadership means" (p. 543). Natham talks back to established ideas of what principals do through her actions, like choosing to be a teaching principal in a large urban high school, for example. "In other words, Natham (re)interprets her actions within the role of the principal to take on the additional responsibilities of teaching instead of allowing the surplus teachers ('the sorry ones') to come into her building to teach her predominately African, Asian, and Latino students"

(p. 548). Her leadership authenticates through the nurturing and protecting of the children. Dillard describes Natham as leading with her life, from all of who she is as an African American female. "Nurturing and protecting children for African Americans hails from a history of communal responsibility for African children, for that matter all children, often extending beyond blood kinship ties" (p. 551). Dillard explains how "she [Natham] protects and nurtures both the parent's ability and the child's ability to succeed in school" (p. 553). Dillard understands Natham's work to be about values, a vision of what makes a school effective for African American students: "School principals always work on behalf of particular values, projects, and peoples, those choices arising from their personal subjective understandings of the world and the work" (p. 560). She describes Natham as acting deliberately on behalf of African American students to create a safe and nurturing inclusive environment.

Profiling nine minority women, AhNee-Benham and Cooper (1998) identify in their stories the importance of spirit as well as four other themes. They present these themes in the final chapter as a challenge to "traditional norms of school leadership, altering practice and adding, in significant new ways, to our current body of knowledge and understanding of educational leadership" (p. 141). The women they studied, seeing as they do from the margins, were aware of being different. Growing out of that sense of difference, the first theme is, "They carry in their hearts the desire to create communities for children that foster a sense of inclusion and value rather than oppression and alienation" (p. 142). A second theme is that "determination and courage lifts each woman's spirit" (p. 143). Having crossed boundaries in their own lives, they are determined to prevail against the odds. The third theme "focuses on the ways in which their difference has instilled in these women a sense of compassion toward all children and a determination to help children to learn, grow, and overcome whatever obstacles are placed in their way" (p. 144). The fourth theme is, "they have redefined power and authority in ways that equate power with connectedness" (pp. 145–146).

According to Bloom and Erlandson (2003), invisibility for women of color in leadership roles is as troubling as patterns, practices, and perceptions that limit their access to opportunities. Their stories illustrate how African American women administrators struggle for equitable recognition in the mostly urban schools they serve. Using black feminist standpoint theory from the work of Collins (1991), Bloom and Erlandson explain "diversities between and among Black women based on class, religion, age, and sexual orientation are real" (p. 342). This understanding is an important characteristic of feminist standpoint theory. Although their stories were different, the three women in their study were not defeated by discrimination or inequity, but demonstrated through their lives that "the force of marginalization . . . produced women who have pursued their dreams and lived up to visions of excellence for themselves" (p. 362). Researchers continue to be interested in the leadership of persons from marginalized groups. As their numbers increase, research of women and persons of color in university faculty positions is challenging traditional understandings of leadership. Feminist images of leadership, African American scholars and leadership for social justice, and spirituality, love, and leadership are examples of three strands of research developing new conceptions emerging in contemporary scholarship (Larson & Murtadha, 2002).

FEMINIST CONCERNS

Feminist concerns associated with the study of women's leadership must be included in a discussion of contemporary issues. Some feminist scholars focus on women's leadership; others view women leaders in the context of larger societal issues. Focusing on women's leadership, Gardiner, Enomoto, and Grogan (2000) identify three alternative approaches as characteristic of feminist leadership (p. 149). These are "instructional leadership, participatory or shared decision-making, and caregiving leadership" (pp. 149–150). Specifically, they describe an instructional leadership that is child centered and instruction oriented; they value the collaboration of shared decision making; and they understand caregiving to underlie all actions. They examine how mentoring of women by women may contribute to developing these approaches to leading, clearly alternatives to business-as-usual in schools. They write, "Collectively these three kinds of leadership contrast with the typically corporate managerial and bureaucratic functions of school administration" (p. 150). They link effective mentoring with the development of two of these approaches, participatory decision making and caregiving.

Blackmore (2002) takes us in a different direction. She speaks of the "need to move beyond the dualistic position that still remains embedded in feminist research in educational administration. This means focusing on the social relations of gender, and not just women in leadership" (p. 63). She believes that a masculine/feminine dualism traps both men and women and keeps the system stuck. Arnot (2002) perhaps has the social relations of gender in mind when she states, "Feminist post-structural research reminds us that more attention should be paid to the 'micropolitics' of power, which are as significant as macro-formulations" (p. 258). The popular view that women's leadership is superior because of women's sensitivity to relational concerns and skill in building relationships of care is challenged by Conway (2001). She writes: "Feminist psychologists have made an industry out of women's 'relational self,' presenting women as a nexus of relationships rather than an ego with boundaries and thus a potential to stand out from the group. We can't talk about women's leadership without exploring how we got to this highly gendered view and understanding its consequences" (p. xi). Conway argues against a strictly relational perspective of women leaders when sharing these observations of women leaders in a variety of institutions:

> They are super-efficient, visionary about the institution or business, and able to state their views and defend them strongly against contending opinions. Some are mothers, some are not. What they all have is the personal ability to call out the most performance from others and mobilize it around a common goal. They are no more lodged in a network of relationships than their male colleagues. (p. xix)

Young and Skrla (2003) urge reexamination of feminist research in educational leadership. Essays in their edited volume offer reconsiderations in three categories: feminist methodological dilemmas, feminist epistemologies, and possible applications of reexamined feminist research. Dillard (2003) is concerned with methodology and epistemology from the perspective of an African American scholar. She challenges our thinking about the meaning and validity of research. She explores the complexities of research about communities of color, suggesting that research requires alternative epistemological truths if we are to be open to the people we study. Rather than the researcher as detached and neutral, she argues for the metaphor "research as responsibility" (p. 134).

Smulyan (2000) also presents an example of a methodological dilemma when she ponders how to define her concern about feminist research on her nonfeminist subjects. To a large degree, her intended frameworks for analysis did not match how her subjects interpreted their experiences. She asks, "Could and should I challenge their strategies for defining themselves and succeeding within their given work contexts?" (p. 63). Speaking of the principals she studied, Smulyan writes, "To acknowledge the role of gender in their lives seemed to suggest an inability to function as a legitimate leader in the given structure of schools, an inability to control one's life and work" (p. 59). When they did see and acknowledge gender, she suggests they preferred not to give it much credit for influence—like subjects in Chase's (1995) study of superintendents—as if acknowledging gender placed interactions beyond their control and was negative and at some level paralyzing. Smulyan (2000) concludes,

If women approach leadership as feminists and want to develop different approaches, goals, and processes, they may be more frustrated and limited in what they are able to do. If their more "female" management styles are less conscious, they may be more unaware of the constraints, less able to draw on the support of others, and more likely to blame themselves for their lack of success in certain areas. (pp. 34–35)

Whether or not the women we interviewed would identify themselves as feminist is not important. In the words of Bunch (1991), "In this search for new leadership forms, it is useful to see cooperative, empowering models not as inherently female but as female-led" (p. xiii). Like the leaders profiled by Astin and Leland (1991) in an earlier work, one imagines that our subjects might agree with this definition of feminism: "a system of ideas and practices which assumes that men and women must share equally in the work, in the privileges, in the defining and the dreaming of the world (Lerner, 1984, p. 33)" (p. 19).

Strachan (2002) reminds us that feminist educational leadership is different from women's leadership. Although Illinois Women Administrators fits the definition of a feminist organization in its historical emphasis on collective action, the study we have conducted did not originate from feminism defined in terms of collective activism. We have not sought to impose a feminist interpretation on the stories told by our participants, nor to reinterpret their stories. Our objective in writing about what they have shared has been, insofar as possible, to let them speak for themselves. The result we seek is not collective action on behalf of women; rather, we are hopeful that this presentation of the *how* and *why* of women's leadership through stories will have an impact on the quality of leadership in schools. In this spirit, and using the definition presented by Gardiner, Enomoto, and Grogan (2000), our work is in the feminist tradition: "Feminist research validates multiple and diverse perspectives, in particular the value of examining these perspectives to clarify one's own beliefs and values, and for the pedagogical opportunities to help one to consider the viewpoints of other individuals. Women learn from other women's voices and experiences" (p. 29).

NEW QUESTIONS AND EMERGING THEMES

Through our focus on how women make decisions, how they get things done in bureaucracies, how they define and use power, and how they live their values, we address new questions and emerging themes pointed to in contemporary scholarship about women's leadership. We contend they are redefining leadership and agree with Smulyan (2000), "Efforts to examine gender differences in management style from a structural perspective have contributed to a gradual reshaping of the prevailing definition of leadership and power" (p. 24). For the women we interviewed, the important power was the power "'to get the job done' rather than power over people and resources" (Smulyan, 2000, p. 24). The chapter on how women get things done by pushing bureaucratic boundaries echoes the emphasis from Gardiner, Enomoto, and Grogan (2000) that "women also have to learn the rules and then bend them to their advantage—to be smart and have political savvy, able to change the face of educational leadership" (p. 125). We share stories of how the women interviewed got around systems and bureaucratic blocks as they accomplished things that were important to their constituents and to themselves. Some tell stories of how they have changed or recreated systems.

Blackmore (2002) advocates a shift in the research on women's leadership from focus on style to focus on substance. "We need to ask what we are leading for," (p. 64) she writes. Blackmore also directs us to attend to "the meaning-making processes of women leaders" (p. 55). Smulyan

(2000) points to our focus on values when she writes, "New questions emerge in the study of gender and schooling. For example: what are the preferred values and behaviors in the existing culture and what are the values and behaviors of those who tend to be marginalized within or excluded from school administration (e.g., women and minorities)?" (p. 26). We discuss perspectives of our participants about the degree to which their values conflicted with those of the prevailing culture. We share stories that illustrate how they lived their values in a myriad of ways. Although we do not generalize about minority women, we do point out when the perspectives of the four African American participants differ. Acknowledging these differences is a developing trend in the scholarship. Gardiner, Enomoto, and Grogan (2000) believe, "The different perspective of women, white and of color, in leadership may help bring about new forms of leadership, and necessary knowledge, understandings, and skills needed for teaching diverse school populations" (p. 99). We are similarly hopeful.

Speaking of their own book, Freeman and Bourque (2001) assert that "one of the most provocative hypotheses to emerge from these essays is that for many women leadership begins with an intensely experienced wrong" (p. 5). Many of the women we interviewed refer to awareness of injustice or intense wrongs in the lives of children as a source of their commitment to leadership. They are a group of risk-taking women who fit the definition of transformative leaders, leaders who take us on journeys to new places as they dare to live into new possibilities for themselves and others. They are redefining leadership by integrating *doing* with *being*.

Chapter Three

Developing Collaborative Decision-Making Processes

What constitutes good leadership is an evolving understanding in all institutions in this postmodern world. Making decisions might once have been a concept associated more with managing than leading; however, as we define leadership in new ways, the practices of lone decision making come under scrutiny. According to Goldring and Greenfield (2002), a

> recurring dilemma for school administrators is the need to balance participatory leadership with the simultaneous imperative to assume the responsibility to make and implement difficult decisions. . . . Participatory leadership, also referred to as shared, collaborative, distributed, or group leadership, focuses on decision processes that involve others. (p. 14)

From a participatory approach, it can be said, "The school leader becomes the keeper of the process" (Leithwood & Prestine, 2002, p. 46) through which decisions are made.

Murphy (2002) has posed that three metaphors provide a synthesis of leadership for a recultured profession of educational administration: "moral steward, educator, and community builder" (p. 75). The phrase *moral steward* suggests the primacy of values and a commitment to social justice. As an educator, a leader's primary concern is clearly learning. Community builder implies involvement in a process. Certainly a community builder must be comfortable with collaboration. To become builders of democratic community will require a change in practices for some educational leaders, particularly those who have not in the past practiced shared decision making. "Schools that build a democratic community would establish structures and procedures that allow all members of the school community to participate and have a respected voice in decisions and politics that affect them" (Furman & Starratt, 2002, p. 117). Whereas building a democratic community seems an ideal particularly well-suited for principals, other scholars propose that collaboration also become the norm at the district level. For example, Brunner, Grogan, and Björk (2002) view the 1990s and beyond as a new era for leadership by superintendents, offering the metaphor of *superintendent as collaborator*. They write, "above all, the most recent shift in the discourse [about leadership] encourages superintendents to be collaborators, working with others and sharing leadership. . . . Leadership in the superintendency, in particular, is now associated with words such as collaboration, community, cooperation, teams, and relationship-building" (p. 226).

We focused on decision making because of its centrality to the *doing* of leadership. We asked the leaders interviewed to characterize themselves as decision makers, to describe the processes they use in making decisions, the most difficult and important decisions they have made, and the values behind their decisions. We were particularly interested in discretionary decision making. In some cases, educational leaders are given the discretion or authority/freedom to make certain decisions by boards of education or superintendents. In other cases, educational leaders use their own discretion or authority/freedom when making decisions within a framework of rules, practices, and written and unwritten policies. Whether discretion is given or taken, skillful discretionary decision making distinguishes the politically astute leader. For purposes of the study, we defined discretionary decision making as making decisions based on one's own judgment rather than on arbitrary bureaucratic rules and procedures. Participants were asked to describe their level of comfort with discretionary decision making, give examples of discretionary decision making, and compare those decisions that had only positive outcomes with those where the outcomes were problematic. One major finding of our research is that, for 14 of the 18 leaders we interviewed, collaborative decision-making processes were the norm. In every case the commitment to collaboration grew out of the leader's values.

DR. REBECCA VAN DER BOGERT

The leadership beliefs and decision-making practices of Dr. Rebecca van der Bogert, superintendent of Winnetka School District #36, will be threaded throughout this presentation and discussion of our findings. Becky, as she prefers to be called, has a bachelor's in psychology (1967), and a master's in special education (1968), both from Syracuse University. She earned a doctorate in teaching, curriculum, and learning environments from Harvard University in 1991. She was a founding member and serves as codirector of the International Network of Principals' Centers at Harvard. She is the author, coauthor, or editor of numerous publications, including *Making Sense as a School Leader* (1996) with Richard Ackerman and Gordon Donaldson. Becky has been a teacher for 12 years and an administrator for 23. She has been a classroom teacher, guidance counselor, resource teacher, coordinator of a gifted and talented program, principal, assistant superintendent, director of curriculum, university instructor, and superintendent of schools in two communities. "In all these capacities she has engaged in the study and practice of shared decision-making and the nurturing of an environment in which all concerned" are respected and valued for their contributions and encouraged to grow" (Ackerman, Donaldson, & van der Bogert, 1996, p. xxiii). When asked how others would describe her as a leader, Becky responded, "reflective, collaborative or inclusive, I think they would say." Rebecca van der Bogert did not intend to become a superintendent, but in 1989 she was recruited for and took the position in the Lincoln Public Schools in Massachusetts because the board convinced her that they "really wanted somebody who was going to be an educator, a collaborative decision maker, and bring the board and staff together." She became the Winnetka District #36 superintendent in 1994. Her distinguished 35-year career and long-term commitment to collaborative decision making provides a singularly powerful exemplar of excellence in educational leadership.

DECISION-MAKING PROCESSES

Participants were asked how they would describe themselves as decision makers and to describe their decision-making processes. Answers to both questions intertwined. Rebecca van der Bogert described herself as a *researcher*. She elaborated, "I take time. I don't like to make a rushed decision. I like to be able to gather all the consummate data and play out many different options, including a lot of not-so-obvious options, all this involved with other people." Descriptors from others included: *collaborative, a delegator, thoughtful and decisive, a risk-taker, assertive*, and *reflective*. The variety of these descriptors seems to reflect the tensions surrounding leadership and decision making, especially for women. Does one follow the stereotypical male approach with its emphasis on being strong, assertive, and decisive, or does one take a more stereotypically female approach involving reflection and collaboration? Whatever the approach, decision making is risky business. Decisions have consequences. Often the consequences are as much a result of the process as of the decision itself.

The lengthy answers each person gave to describe her decision-making process reflect the tension between decisiveness and commitment to collaboration. The data contained themes of collaboration and information-based decision making. Fourteen of the 18 described involving others in decision making through a shared or collaborative process; 10 of those 14 described processes combining collaboration and information gathering. The remaining four leaders described a more individual approach to decision making, one that focused on analysis of information. Fourteen of the total group of 18 mentioned the importance of gathering and using information as part of the decision-making process.

Decision Making as a Collaborative Process Involving People

When she became a principal, Rebecca van der Bogert implemented democratic leadership practices in the school, and when she first became a superintendent she instituted shared leadership. Collaboration has been her trademark as an educator and why Winnetka sought her leadership. She said, "It's just my natural instinct to work with a group of people in a non-hierarchical way and not play a traditional leadership role. We're all in this together and we're all working on it. I actually went back to graduate school to try to be able to articulate what I'm doing and why I'm doing it!" Becky has an intuitive and philosophical commitment to collaborative decision making, and came to Winnetka when recruited because she saw the opportunity to fully actualize her beliefs in teacher autonomy. In Winnetka, she has pushed the envelope, focused on relationships, and lived with the messy ambiguity of shared decision making. She has been able to push the envelope because the district for decades has had a culture of collaboration and a board generally supportive of the complexity of collaborative decision making. Early in the 20th century the community of

Winnetka made a commitment to be a lighthouse district. Becky has written, "Much of what we do today in the Winnetka Public Schools is rooted in history and tradition—a history of excellence, a continual focus on research based teaching, an environment that enhances everyone's growth, and a community that works together on behalf of children"(van der Bogert, 2002, para. 4). Writing about her engagement with Winnetka, she acknowledged, "The commitment to growth and process that is such a strong part of the culture here has both complicated my quest and at the same time enabled its richness" (van der Bogert, 2002, para. 3). During a lengthy study in the 1990s, the district rewrote its philosophical document *Winnetka: A Community of Learners*. During that process a framework emerged "that still serves as a lens through which to examine the district and how it came to be. The phrase is: 'In Winnetka, we honor traditions, reflect on transition, and make choices about transformation'" (van der Bogert, 2002, para. 3).

"When a major decision needs to be made in Winnetka, everybody involved is going to be in on that final decision," Becky explained.

> Sometimes it will take longer than another way might, but it is important to really hear from other people. The process always stretches our thinking. Usually a decision doesn't come out the way I think it's going to when I start because other people add to it, and stretch my thinking. We try to get to a decision that everybody's comfortable with. By the time I make a decision everybody around me knows what it's going to be because they've been involved.

As an example, she described a process combining collaboration and data gathering that was underway in response to a concern that surfaced in a total community survey. The community survey process itself had been extensive, involving an outside researcher and focus groups, as well as a written survey. "Its purposes had been to determine if: 1) the community understands our philosophy, which is different from other communities; 2) do citizens agree or disagree with various parts of the philosophy; and 3) how well citizens think we're doing with the implementation." One concern that emerged was whether district programs challenged gifted and talented students. Although the easy response would have been to implement a pull-out gifted and talented program, the district is choosing to move slowly and take the time to research the need and explore all the program options. "The board has released two teachers full time for a year to research what we are doing to meet the needs of all students in hetero-geneous classrooms and what more we should be doing," Becky ex-plained. A steering committee of four administrators and seven teachers has been meeting regularly to share information. Information will be gath-ered from national conferences, observing other programs, questioning classroom teachers, and studying individual children. "The plan is for the steering committee to make a recommendation at the end of the year as to what the model will be, and it may even be different in each building," Becky said.

Around the time of Rebecca van der Bogert's interview, this teacher-led committee on which she also serves had just held a lengthy meeting to consider "what we want to do between now and the end of the year to make sure we have the data we need to determine the right model, and to have teachers feel that they're involved in that data gathering and conclu-sion." Reporting what happened at the meeting, she said,

> We decided that well before the end of the year we're going to bring in an outside researcher who works in our district and knows our district well. She is a person who taught a course on teacher research through funding we have for teacher research in the district. We are going to frame this data-gathering as a teacher research project. The outside consultant is going to help the committee come up with the right questions to ask when inter-viewing the teachers. She will help the committee articulate a lens to guide their classroom observations. This lens or framework will be shared with teachers who volunteer to become part of the data-gathering process so that they will know what the committee wants to observe and not feel threatened by the process. Then the committee will follow fifteen children and inter-view the children, interview their teachers, and go into their past education experiences to try to get a sense of what we can do for them.

Concluding the description of this process, Becky confided, "It wasn't un-til after about three hours of struggling about what would work, what wouldn't work, what we wanted to avoid, and where we wanted to go that we came up with this teacher research idea." She continued, "I'm totally convinced that by the time we're through, the two teachers leading this process are going to have an incredible amount of data and be able to present it in the context of a research study that supports their recommendations. The model will be something that all the teachers can feel they helped build, and then we're going to be able to present it to the board." Clearly this collaborative decision-making process involves serious data gathering, and any decision made will have grown out of information.

Of the 14 who describe themselves primarily as collaborative decision makers, a total of 10, including Rebecca van der Bogert, also addressed the importance of data gathering and information analysis to their decision-making processes. The 14 include other superintendents, whose perspectives are represented by the following selected quotations. One superintendent said quite directly, "I'm pretty much into shared decision making. I seek as much information as possible from people who might know about the problem. Then I weigh that information, put it together, and look at possible solutions, benefits, and side effects. Finally, I go with the one that has the greatest benefits and fewest disadvantages." Another explained, "I am very much collaborative. When I say collaborative, I mean I like to have a real good discussion. I don't hire yes people. I definitely use data but I also use people as a source of information as well. So I would spend time collecting history of any problem or situation requiring a decision."

Those outside the superintendent role spoke in the same language. For example, Ola Bundy (see chapter 4) said in describing how she approached decisions, "I would involve others in decision making, talk to a wide network of people, give people an opportunity to be part of the process." Additionally, Ola explained, "I would investigate and never support anything unless I had the reasons down and understood everything. I would do my homework." Asked to describe her decision-making processes, another person said,

> That depends upon what kind of decision that you're asked to make, but I would like to think that I do weigh all the evidence that I have. I try to get input from those other individuals who are specifically knowledgeable. It's been very important to have a wide variety of information. And once that occurs, I think the values behind my approach to decision making would be inclusive. I would not like to be characterized as someone who makes a decision completely and totally in a vacuum or without involving in most cases those individuals that the decision is going to affect.

Another representative quotation came from a former principal. She said, "I tried not to make quick decisions, because I wanted to involve other people in the decision making. I wanted information and shared all my information with my entire administrative team. I empowered teams to make decisions. When you withhold information you can't make a good decision."

The four African American women described their decision making primarily in terms of collaborative processes involving people. Elizabeth Lewin (see chapter 6) said, "I work as a team with two assistants and six principals. I think out loud and bring people along in my decision making. I lay things out like a puzzle and people pick up on my thought patterns and often draw the conclusion or verbalize it before I do." A second person said, "Before you make a decision you need to make sure that all parties are involved." Another person said, "I am a collaborative decision maker because I feel that whoever delivers the programs needs to be vested in the decision making of what happens in that program. . . . The collaborative process and doing what is best for persons being served — that's the process I use." Finally, the fourth person said in describing her decision-making processes, "I reflect myself and I bounce it off others. Before I make any decision that's going to change the school I always have a team of people with me."

Decision Making as an Individual Process Centered on Information

For the four who described a more individual decision-making process centered on information, people were still involved as part of the information-gathering process, but the emphasis was clearly on the individual as decision maker. All four worked in state agency or university settings that could be characterized as bureaucratic and male dominated, suggesting that a primary focus on data/information is perhaps situational, rooted in their large organizations. One woman said,

> I try to be very open-minded and objective and listen to all of the information and different aspects of what goes into the decision. I try to evaluate, depending upon the importance of the decision, what the right thing is to do, the integrity of what we're doing, the political ramifications, and then make

the decision. If my staff told me what they felt a decision should be and I was not comfortable with what they told me, I would make my own decision and take responsibility for it, because decision-making is a lonely experience, and you've got to live with it.

Another said, "I like to get the advice of all the affected parties and the knowledgeable people. I always let my people know that I want their honest opinion . . . and then I put that all together and in the long run it's my decision and I have to make it." Another called her approach that of a researcher. She said, "I'm an information gatherer. I want to know about the situation. I want to know what we've done in the past. I want quantitative information. Now I want to make a decision, though, because I can't stand people who study something to death. Once information is gathered and synthesized then I've no trouble being dictatorial about it, with a caveat: if it doesn't work then tell me and we'll change it." Hazel Loucks (see chapter 5) said,

I want the background information. I want to have the information to make an informed decision. I am not impeded by what others perceive to be reasons why not. I'm a very optimistic person. So I am always looking for: Why can't we do this? If we have the information, let's go for it. . . . If it's the right decision then I should move forward, and I'm willing to take the fallout or whatever it takes. I think an important process in decision making is the ability to move out front without always worrying about what's in it for me. How will most people benefit, that's how I make decisions. My decision-making style is to find the information, see who is going to benefit, and then go for it whatever the risks. It's not a very sequential process maybe, but there is a process.

For the women who described collaborative processes, as well as for those more focused on information, Helgesen's (1990) observation that "the women scheduled in time for sharing information" (p. 27) appears to be validated. Helgesen profiles a person she describes as a transmitter of information, "gathering information from everywhere, making sense of it, rearranging it in patterns, and then beaming it out to wherever it needs to go" (p. 179). This seems an apt description of many of the leaders in our study.

Complexity of Collaborative Decision-Making Processes

From the context of her work with developing teacher leaders, Lambert (1998) implies that collaboration is a choice and requires skill. She writes,

> Opportunities for collaboration are not enough in and of themselves. . . . The leadership skills for collaborative work involve the ability to develop a sense of shared purpose with colleagues, facilitate group processes, communicate well, understand transition and change and their effects on people, mediate conflict, and hold a keen understanding of adult learning from a constructivist perspective. (p. 18)

Even with highly developed leadership skills, several factors can be counted on to complicate collaboration. Two of these are politics and time pressures. Every leader has experienced the pressure of time surrounding a decision. As might be expected, two of the women who worked primarily at the state agency/government level mentioned the need to consider politics when making decisions. Others interviewed described their involvement in politics, and how political considerations could conflict with values as well as their preferred decision-making processes. Claiming power through politics will be explored in chapter 5, and living and leading from values will be the focus of chapter 6.

The four who specifically noted time as a factor in their decision-making processes explained that they refuse to make quick or rushed decisions, that investing the time required for collaboration and information gathering leads to a better decision. For example, Rebecca van der Bogert said, "I usually do take time. I don't like to make a rushed decision. I like to be able to gather all the data and play out many different options, all of this involving other people." In another representative comment, Stephanie Pace Marshall (see chapter 8) also discussed decision making and time: "On one level I am very decisive. If I have to make a decision quickly, I do. However, if I don't, I spend a fair amount of time gathering data from many sources. Sometimes staff may say I don't make decisions quickly enough for them. And that's tough. I could, of course, make them faster, but I don't think necessarily the quality of the decision would be enhanced. Faster does not mean wiser."

Complicating factors also arise from human issues involved in decision making. Frequently faculty and staff hold varying levels of commitment to collaborative decision making. Sometimes the motivation for collaborative decision making is misunderstood and a leader may be perceived as not doing his or her job. Lack of total commitment to collaboration on the part of a leader can result in perceptions of manipulation. On the other hand, some view shared decision making as a panacea, the answer to everything. In Rebecca van der Bogert's words, "Everybody thinks, oh, we'll collaborate and everybody'll get more. But it's like a marriage. In the long run everybody gets more, but people do have to give things up." Many persons support shared decision making when the outcomes are what they want, but commitment varies when the outcomes disappoint. Becky acknowledged this reality in these words, "With discretionary and shared decision making it always works if it comes out the right decision." It becomes problematic "if it was the wrong decision; [because] then everybody owns it." Experience with problematic outcomes can cause faculty and staff to back away from future involvement with shared decision making.

Bringing up another angle from which to view the complexity of collaborative decision making, Rebecca van der Bogert said, "There's a lot of psychological influence to collaboration. You have to really genuinely want to hear other people's opinions and you have to be able to tolerate the fact that possibly your opinion doesn't matter, and also believe it's going to be better because it's everybody's opinion." Another slant on psychological influence lies in temperament or personality. For example, Becky understands her intuitive preference for shared decision making to have something to do with the home she grew up in as a child. She said, "I'm good at avoiding power issues. I don't like them. I'm uncomfortable with them. I feel they take away something from someone else and I can't do that. As soon as you get into power issues, no one really wins. I think it's a part of my upbringing." Being more specific, she describes surviving childhood by developing resilience and "learning how to weave behind the scenes." In her family her mother served as a model who would buffer others from the tension of living with a father prone to unpredictable moods. She learned not to take things personally, and to stay calm. These interpersonal skills have served her well in the superintendency. Additionally, Becky describes herself as "a people person all the way. The reason I'm in education has a lot to do with having been actively involved in many extracurricular activities in high school," she said.

"There's no greater sense than working with a team of people and feeling like the whole team made it happen. You remember those people and moments the rest of your life." Paradoxically, her childhood experiences, which were not all positive, and her high school extracurricular experiences, which were positive, have both contributed to who she is as a superintendent and how she does things.

DISCRETIONARY DECISION MAKING

Participants had a wide range of responses to the interview question, "Can you tell me what the phrase 'discretionary decision making' means to you?" One woman answered simply, "I think it's one of the reasons I love my job." Rebecca van der Bogert said, "If discretionary means making decisions based on one's own judgment rather than bureaucratic rules, then I would say I can't think of too many instances where I just followed bureaucratic rules." Most seemed to understand it to mean making decisions based on your own judgments within certain parameters, but not necessarily bureaucratic rules or policy. Three answered essentially that all decisions are discretionary. Representative of their thinking is this quotation: "I think all decisions are discretionary. I think you have the discretion to follow policy or not, to see the bureaucratic monster or not, to share decision-making or not, to involve individuals or groups. And I think part of the discretion is to give people the knowledge and information to be involved." Other comments focused on values as self-chosen parameters that govern choices.

Level of Comfort with Discretionary Decision Making

As a group, 16 of the 18 participants, including Rebecca van der Bogert, expressed a high level of comfort with discretionary decision making. Becky is used to having a lot of discretion in the district educationally, in terms of hiring, curriculum, what goes on in the buildings, and what goes on in the administrative team. In fact, she has selected positions in her career partly based on whether she will have considerable discretion to "make happen what I believe should happen." Becky elaborated, "I've always been very careful that people up front know what they're getting.

My style is a little bit different from a lot of people, and things will take longer, I will involve people, and it's messy. I'm cautious getting in, and then I just sort of take the discretion." She is strongly opposed to bureaucratic procedures, saying,

> I feel it is part of my role to see that we don't have bureaucracy. When I see us getting in that mindset, hear comments like "Well, our policy says," then I try really hard to refocus thinking and get to the real issues. I'm usually the one to say "We're going to use our discretion, we're not just going to follow policy on this one. We're not just automatically going to do this, but I'll think about it." Then we will very often set up a committee to think things through. Or I will think it through with the administrative team at one of our Tuesday meetings. That's where many of the decisions are made in the district, and very often it'll take two or three meetings to make a decision.

Becky acknowledges that not every decision is shared, that "there are probably millions of decisions I make during the day," using my own judgment or discretion. "The only area in which I don't have total discretion is with the school board," she said. She gives the board information about financial decisions, for example, and makes a recommendation, "but it's not my final decision."

The two participants who did not feel comfortable with the term *discretionary decision making* posed interesting issues, both insisting that all decisions are in fact discretionary. For example, the first person elaborated in response to the comfort level question, "I am not comfortable. I think decisions that you make as a leader about people, programs, or with people about programs, are difficult. And there's a part of me that never wants to be comfortable making tough decisions because I feel like part of the very core of who I am would have to disappear for me to be absolutely comfortable with tough decision making." Stephanie Pace Marshall (see chapter 8), who also insisted that "at one level, every decision is discretionary," said simply that the term itself did not resonate with her. She would call her decision-making process identity or principle based or values driven. She elaborated,

> Discretion is not the operative discriminator to me. The question is what is the grounding or foundation for the decision. I always go back to the essence and the fundamentals. A decision is a judgment call; the issue is

what "rules," or principles, or parameters do you use to make the judgment. Do you use a procedural rule, such as, "It's in our policy; therefore, we have to." Or do you use a higher principle, such as what action can we take that will affirm our purpose and evoke us to embody who we are?

Discretionary Decision Making: Positive or Problematic?

A significant segment of each interview focused on having the participants describe a discretionary decision that only had positive outcomes, and then one that had problematic outcomes. They were then asked to analyze what made the difference between whether the outcomes were positive or problematic. Six persons either did not answer or were not asked the third question. Looking for meaningful categories, we analyzed answers of the 12 who did respond. The responses varied, with several clusters emerging.

Three proactive leaders explained how they simply would not let a decision become problematic, but would change directions if that became likely. One superintendent, for example, answered that she could think of no decisions where the outcomes were problematic because she routinely changed a decision before it got to such outcomes if things appeared to be heading in a problematic direction. "I try to learn from what doesn't work as the process is unfolding," she said. Her way is "to change directions and then tell people why you've changed, because it is very disconcerting to many when things aren't going as planned. You lose some credibility, but you'll lose credibility anyway if you carry something to the end that isn't going well." Another person gave a similar answer, emphasizing the importance of attitude. "I don't see things as problematic. Sometimes they're opportunities. I see challenges, but then all you have to do is go back, regroup, and ask 'how can I meet these challenges?' It has to do with your outlook." From a similar perspective, in discussing a complex reconfiguration of her district, Elizabeth Lewin (see chapter 6) explained, "Nothing became a long-term problem because we viewed each one as a challenge to be resolved jointly."

Two others qualified their responses in terms of time-frame considerations. Analyzing a problem involving a special education situation in which teachers were battling their own union for the freedom to serve the students as they wanted, one person interviewed commented directly on the passage of time,

The outcome really wasn't what I wanted it to be with the special education situation because they [the union] put it on hold. They didn't allow anything to happen for the semester. Finally the teachers fought themselves and they were able to do what they wanted for the good of the students and the union gave up the "it's not in the contract" fight. So it just became a situation where I don't want to say that any outcomes were negative. It just took a little longer for positive results to be realized.

Stephanie Pace Marshall (see chapter 8) had the same perspective, that one must consider short-term versus long-term outcomes in answering the question. She said,

Whether something is viewed as only positive or only problematic in many cases is a factor of time. In a short time horizon people are likely to judge immediate consequences—positive or negative. But in the longer term, the context emerges and the whole story becomes more complete. So even something you thought had a terrible consequence in the short term might be beneficial over time. Of course, some decisions might be positive for an institution but negative for an individual.

For another cluster of responses, the only possible generalization seems to be *it depends.* Three persons focused their analysis of the differences between positive and problematic in terms of whether the decision involved procedures and programs, or whether it primarily involved people. Analyzing the examples she presented, one person concluded, "It is easier to be successful with discretionary decisions involving procedures, but one can be too trusting in terms of people and work will remain undone." Another person had a slightly different angle. Looking at two situations, she described a decision that had positive outcomes for a program and people, and one that had a positive outcome for a program but problematic outcomes for the people. Problematic outcomes for the people involved developed when she caved into their pressure for her to decide and put a plan together for a program the group had been charged to create. "It's not been without its problems because of that. People didn't feel the ownership they needed to feel. They didn't have the level of understanding of how the pieces fit together. And it's taken almost a year to recover from some of the damage that was done." The third person spoke about lack of ownership as a reason for problematic outcomes for one of her decisions. She stepped in and wrote some of the assessment documents for a technology grant because she was uncomfortable with the quality of what was being produced. She acknowledged lack of ownership to be a consequence, "So it just becomes problematic in a way, because some of that stuff is mine instead of theirs." On the other hand, she justified her intervention, "But I think there comes a time when you know getting other people to do stuff for you is just not going to get it done, so you do it yourself." These responses indicate that discretionary decision-making outcomes can become problematic when people and collaborative processes are not honored.

Finally, four persons gave multifaceted answers, with factors that made the difference ranging from incomplete information and analysis to political pressures including timing to not trusting one's instincts. Comparing two decisions, one person described that rewriting job descriptions to create role expansion was a matter of making the title *intervention specialist* a better explanation of what people actually do than the previous titles *social worker* and *psychologist*. This decision has had only positive outcomes after some mild initial resistance, she said. However, for this same person, a push for inclusion, including getting students with BD disabilities back into neighborhood schools, has been problematic given the climate and context of increased school violence. Timing and politics were right for role expansion, but not for full inclusion of BD students. "There is a real sense that we're pushing against the political feelings of the time by having students back in their neighborhood schools when they could be potentially dangerous to themselves and others." Hazel Loucks (see chapter 5) compared two decisions she made as deputy governor for education and workforce. Decisions related to two education initiatives (Summer Bridges program and parent involvement) had only positive outcomes. However, without a strong workforce history and with only a limited knowledge base, she had to make a decision right away on implementation of the Workforce Investment Act (WIA), and in her words, "I didn't have a clue as to the extent of politics, didn't have the big picture like I do in education. I recommended the governor recertify the current 26 programs. The decision became problematic when one group complained loudly, with good reason." From her perspective, the difference between positive and problematic was clear. "It all has to do with the knowledge base, and knowing all the ramifications of a decision. With the situation I just described, I couldn't see what the ramifications might be. The better your knowledge base the broader your vision is for a discretionary decision and the more comfortable you can feel with your decision," she said.

Two final examples illustrate decisions that were problematic when the persons making them did not trust their instincts. Speaking from a state agency background, one leader described her decision to draft early childhood standards, even though they were not required, at the same time that standards were being developed in other areas. Having a draft of early childhood standards before they were required cast Illinois in a leadership role and the standards, which were well done, gained national prominence. In making this decision to draft the standards, she trusted her instincts. She had lots of data and had conducted a thorough analysis of it. The problematic decision happened when she was a superintendent and chose to put a teacher who was not performing well on probation, giving her an extra year. She explained that if she had spent more time going over with the teacher's supervisor the kinds of things the teacher was deficient in she probably would have made a different decision. Even without thorough analysis of the data, however, she was hesitant at an intuitive level about her decision, finally disregarding her own sixth sense and recommending probation on the advice of the supervisor. Because she did not trust her own instincts, letting the teacher go at the end of probation was more difficult. Better analysis, more data, and trusting her instincts contributed to positive outcomes in the first decision, whereas the reverse led to a problematic situation in the second.

Rebecca van der Bogert also described a situation that became problematic when she did not pay attention to her instincts and let a collaborative hiring process go too far, resulting in a hiring decision that wasn't right. "I've lots of questions that I keep asking myself about that process, like what parts could I have hung onto more, because, bottom line, I'm the one that made the recommendation to the school board. Should I have taken more of the responsibility and not listened so much to others? Because I think my gut would have gone elsewhere. There was a piece of me that wasn't sure this was the right person for the job." Becky shared the story as an example of how involving people can have a down side. "I thought long and hard, because I believe in shared decision making, but maybe on this one I let it go too far. I am still thinking about it. I don't know whether I did or I didn't let it go too far, but I do know right now that I don't feel good that lots of other people are feeling responsible when, bottom line, it was my decision."

MOST IMPORTANT AND MOST DIFFICULT DECISIONS

Although the questions about most important and most difficult decisions were asked separately, responses are presented together because of the considerable overlap. A few of these decisions involved career moves and personal risk. These included getting a doctorate, becoming a superintendent, taking a university position, and accepting an interim university administrative position without right of return to a previous role. The largest category was personnel. Two decisions involved dismissals of persons who had been relating inappropriately with students. In one case this involved preparing to dismiss someone at all costs. "It was difficult," the person said, "because it impacted kids who didn't have any defense for themselves." The other situation involved a series of decisions with regard to a man who was accused of being a pedophile, ending with the decision about how to tell staff and students about his suicide. More routine terminations of administrators and teachers, each difficult, were mentioned by several persons. One person mentioned the hiring of an administrator as a most important decision. One difficult decision was whether to authorize extensive psychiatric evaluation of a teacher prior to making a decision about termination. Assisting a staff member in crisis was mentioned. Finally, a decision that resulted in a court battle, not giving the head football coach job to an African American male, was a difficult decision for an African American woman to make. She calls it "one of the best decisions she ever made," however, because she made it on what was best for kids.

The second-largest number of responses to these questions included decisions involving value conflicts. A principal who prided herself on being able to establish good relationships with parents had to ask authorities "to keep certain parents off of the school premises, because I would not allow them to come over and intimidate teachers. It was tough," she said, "because of calling the authorities to come and do something that I feel like

I should be able to handle." Several persons described instances where they have had to make a decision that did not match their value systems because someone else had more power. One superintendent experienced a conflict between a board that "wanted a 'take-charge' person and instead got me. I resisted the pressure, deciding to be myself." Risky and difficult decisions involving values and politics included staying the course on inclusion, speaking up at the Illinois State Board of Education, challenging the legislature over funding and honoring an excess number of admissions at the Illinois Mathematics and Science Academy (Stephanie Pace Marshall, see chapter 8), and confronting the Illinois High School Association (Ola Bundy, see chapter 4). A small cluster of responses described decisions that affected programs or students. A university dean closed the counselor education program because it was no longer a quality program. A principal had no choice but to expel twelve good students for drinking because of a zero tolerance policy, a difficult decision because she cared about them. Postponing the state final for girls' volleyball when the IHSA executive director could not be found was a difficult and risky decision for Ola Bundy (see chapter 4)—one that almost cost her job. Another person faced a decision about whether to place a student whose parent was a board member in an advanced or traditional course, a decision made difficult because of the political environment. Finally, two important decisions involved politics and money. Hazel Loucks (see chapter 5) made the decision to focus significant state resources on developing teachers' skills, and a regional superintendent reorganized the regional office to become the fiscal agent for her region of the state.

The hardest decision she ever made, said Rebecca van der Bogert, was around a referendum question that the district had studied for two years. With all the pieces in place, a referendum recommendation that was modest and had been cut to what was essential went to the board, a group that had seemed to be engaged in the process. When the proposal was formally presented, however, one board member said "I can't support that." Becky struggled over time, given what was at stake and the shock of this sudden opposition, with what to do—to let the democratic process work, and not become uncharacteristically authoritarian or try to manage the outcomes proactively. "Our mode was research, discuss, everyone has their voice, we get consensus, and even though everybody doesn't agree that's okay.

We get as close as we can to consensus and then we move on." In this situation, as the weeks passed, the amount for the referendum continued to be cut and Becky was really torn. "Do I tell people how strongly I believe that this is too low? It was the first time I've ever publicly not been forthright because I really was torn within myself." When the vote was taken, the final amount authorized was below what the district needed, low enough possibly to result in financial trouble in a couple of years. Becky is still pondering this experience, concluding her discussion of this example, "I know I made a mistake. I don't know how I'd replay it again. I felt, for the first time ever in my life, boxed, and I couldn't figure my way out." In what was an incredibly complex situation, Becky remained true to her principles and her belief in the democratic process, although others might have made a different choice. For example, as Kellerman (2003) has noted, "Although virtues such as cooperation and collaboration do now permeate the leadership literature, we also know that when the going gets tough, the tough tend to revert to command and control" (p. 56). For Rebecca van der Bogert that was not an option, because she has never been about command and control.

CONCLUSIONS

"Do women make decisions differently?" is a question raised by this chapter and embedded in considerations of whether women lead differently. As one of our participants said, although she did not agree, "Women's ways of leading, I think, are often perceived as soft, indecisive, way too collaborative." Helgesen's (1990) discussion of whether women lead differently begins with the observation that "nuance is so often the key to style" (p. 17). However, she also wrote, "Females learn to value cooperation and relationships; to disdain complex rules and authoritarian structures; and to disregard abstract notions like the quest for victory if they threaten harmony in the group as a whole" (p. 38). Generally, Helgesen contended that women's ways of leadership differed from men's. Representative of the same view, Gardiner, Enomoto, and Grogan (2000) say participatory or shared decision making is characteristic of feminist leadership (pp. 149–150). Those scholars who disagree regard such a generalization as an example of essentializing. As presented in the context of our discussion of essentializing in chapter 2, almost all the women in our study expressed the belief that women lead differently in response to the question, "What meaning does the phrase 'women's ways of leading' have for you?" Included in their responses were the following comments that relate to decision making: "They are more likely to share leadership, more collegial." "They are natural team builders." "They are more inclusive of those affected by a decision or issue." "They are more thoughtful and humane decision makers." "They mentor more consistently. They make better use of human resources." These statements correspond with the conclusion of Björk (2000) that "common attributes of women leaders identified in studies conducted over the past 30 years confirm the notion that women approach school leadership differently than men do and that their characteristics tend to correspond to emerging demands for school reform" (p. 10). He continues, "Women are also perceived as being more likely to be facilitative and collaborative in their working relationships, and they tend to use democratic leadership styles and power" (p. 10).

Gender and Decision Making

Examining the *doing* of leadership leads one to decision making. The relationship between gender and decision making can be viewed from many angles. It seems clear that Rebecca van der Bogert, who understands the nuances of leadership, does not think collaborative decision making is gender specific. When asked what meaning does the phrase "women's ways of leading" have for you, Becky responded, "I have mixed feelings about the phrase, because I have stereotypes myself—that a woman's way of leading is collaborative, being a good listener, good problem solver, usually a workaholic. But I don't think it's just a female thing. I'm part of a network of principals around the country [International Network of Principals' Centers] and most of the men on the advisory council with me are very collaborative." Reflecting on whether more women use a collaborative style than men, she wondered if that perception could be associated with the arrival of more women in the superintendency along with the collaborative style becoming more in vogue. She said, "Now who knows which is first? Is it because women with that style are in positions, or is it that the style is much more supported in the literature? I'm not sure which came first."

Reflecting on herself as a leader, Rebecca van der Bogert made what she said could be considered an outrageous statement: "I don't think of myself as a woman." She repeated, "I don't think of myself as a woman or a man. I just know how to make happen what I believe in." With regard to the question of whether women are more collaborative, Becky expressed that, if they are, a reason could be society's expectations. "I don't behave the way a lot of people expect me to behave." She has wrestled with expectations of how she should behave as a superintendent. When Becky first came to Winnetka, one principal (who is now a good friend) called her after she had been there for about a month and said, "Van der Bogert, you're not going to make it here if you don't come out stronger and let people know what you stand for and who you are." Becky replied, "If you don't know what I stand for in about six months, I'll leave." Her response to such pressure to put herself out front has simply been, "It's not who I am and how I work with people." Referring to being decisive, she said, however, "I think I have less pressure maybe than some men who have to appear as a strong [decisive] leader—if you define 'strong leader' as someone who sits up tall and has a booming voice, and says 'this is the way it's going to be.' I think it might be harder for some men to do what I do. Most of the men I know experience tremendous pressure to feel like they're the authority, they're the voice, they're the right one, they're the last stand." But Rebecca van der Bogert at an intuitive level, perhaps influenced by her childhood, refuses to engage around issues of power. She is one of the superintendents, some female and some male, who are redefining the role through commitment to collaborative decision making. Her leadership brings life to the emerging metaphor of *superintendent as collaborator* (Brunner, Grogan, & Björk, 2002).

Collaborative Decision Making in a Historical Context

Mary Parker Follett, who died in 1933, is known for ideas about human resource management that were popular for a time and that reemerged toward the end of the 20th century. "She looked to approach organizations as group networks rather than as hierarchical structures, and attended to the influence of human relations within the group" (Smith, 2002). "One of the key aspects of Mary Parker Follett's approach was the 'circular' theory of power she initially developed in *Creative Experience* (1924). . . .

She distinguishes between power-over and power-with" (Smith, 2002). Follett's circular theory suggests Helgesen's (1990) leadership from within a web, or what others have called *heterarchic* leadership (Shields, 2003). Power with, rather than power over, is another idea that has reemerged in the literature on women's leadership (Brunner, 1999; Rosener, 1990). Tracing the history of women in the superintendency, Blount (1998) documents women teachers' preferences for superintendents to practice collaborative decision making. As hierarchical industrial models of administration were implemented, with men in positions of power, teachers complained, including Gail Hamilton, who in 1880 wrote "a scathing critique of these changes that were overtaking schools and diminishing the autonomy of teachers" (Blount, 1998, p. 49).

> Teachers were often better educated and more sophisticated than administrators, whom many regarded as incompetent. As teachers grew more qualified, they also become more critical of strictly hierarchical administrative practices that placed them at the bottom. . . . Rather than accept these administrative practices, some women teachers suggested alternative structures based less on hierarchy and more on shared power, equality, and consensual decision-making. (Blount, 1998, p. 50)

Blount writes that "ambitious women seeking school leadership positions briefly enjoyed broad-based and enthusiastic support from a powerful emerging political constituency of women" (p. 61) in the early 20th century. But numbers of women in leadership roles gradually diminished, and bureaucratically run schools became the norm. In the next chapter, we explore how leaders today get things done in bureaucracies by pushing the boundaries.

Chapter Four

Pushing the Bureaucratic Boundaries

Getting things done in educational bureaucracies requires tenacity, communicating with skill, making wise discretionary decisions, and pushing the boundaries. Leaders may experience conflicts between personal values and rules designed to perpetuate bureaucratic organizational structures. The leaders we studied made decisions and acted from their values even when that required going outside the rules. Although quite real, this pushing the boundaries aspect of effective educational leadership is not often talked about or studied. Although more often unnamed, it goes by many names, including *creative insubordination*. We believed that women leaders, in part because of their marginalized status, might have something to share about pushing boundaries. In the words of Blackmore, "Once women have gained leadership roles, they can be construed as creating trouble. Strong women often are seen as difficult, dangerous, and even deviant, because they 'trouble' dominant masculinities and modes of management by being different" (2002, p. 53). Whatever the terminology, the topic explored in this chapter is how women and men might *trouble* bureaucracies to get things done.

As an entry to understanding how they pushed the boundaries to get things done, we explored the concept and practice of creative insubordination with the leaders we interviewed. Of the 18 interviewed, six said they were familiar with the term creative insubordination. Six more were familiar with the practice, giving us data from a total of 14, including the two interviewers who were also participants in the study. Three others said the concept was not familiar. One woman was inadvertently not asked. Probing their understanding, we also asked participants to consider whether they practiced creative insubordination deliberately, to share stories as examples, to explain their motivation, and how they perceived the risks. Responses to a question about their comfort level with creative insubordination fell on a continuum from positive to negative, with 12 unequivocally at the high comfort end, two toward the middle, and three not comfortable with the concept.

Among the 12 whose comfort level was high were the four African American women, in every case because of strong motivation to serve the needs of the students and to make a difference. One of the four, now a central office administrator, spoke eloquently of her creative insubordination as a principal, "I guess I have the reputation in the district of being always very creatively insubordinate. As long as I did not go against board policy, I pretty much did whatever I wanted to. I always found a way. We were considered the renegades. We were off doing wonderful things for kids and we enjoyed every minute of it." When asked about her comfort level specifically, she said, "I'm very comfortable if it's doing the right things for kids." Elizabeth Lewin (see chapter 6) said, "Have I used creative insubordination? Absolutely. Probably me and every other visionary leader, or anyone who is determined to get something accomplished. I am comfortable with it because what I ultimately answer to is what is right." A principal said, "I'm very comfortable with it [creative insubordination]. If I feel that I'm right or it is going to make a difference in the lives of my students, my staff, and my families then I am willing to be forceful." Finally, the fourth African American, a central office administrator, said, "I'm very comfortable. It goes back to what's best for kids. I know what I'm doing."

Three leaders interviewed were not comfortable at all with the term or concept of creative insubordination for a variety of interesting reasons. For example, Rebecca van der Bogert spoke of her more direct approach as a superintendent to breaking down authority. She said, "I work with people directly so they know what I am doing. I just tell them the hierarchy and bureaucracy has got to change. I am good at avoiding power issues. People might think of me as creative but not insubordinate." Another person interviewed said that if she were faced with the repeated necessity for creative insubordination she would seek a new work environment. Illinois Mathematics and Science Academy President Stephanie Pace Marshall (see chapter 8) called the concept "part of an old language system. It constrains me, suggests classic hierarchy. In some sense any insubordination is creative because it perturbs the system and that causes the system to reexamine itself." A total of five of the participants were more inclined to transcend and transform the systems in which they worked than to even think about creative insubordination as a way to get things accomplished. This chapter uses data from our interviews with these leaders serving in various roles—principals, superintendents, state agencies, state associations, and office of the governor—to explore how they have accomplished things, in part by refining the concept and practices of creative insubordination, in part by working to transcend and transform bureaucratic structures.

THE CONCEPT AND PRACTICE OF CREATIVE INSUBORDINATION

For purposes of the study, we defined *creative insubordination* as a counterbureaucratic approach to decision making that bends and/or ignores rules and otherwise subverts the authority of the chain of command when such subversion is justified by the greater authority of personal values, service to students, and common sense. Morris, Crowson, Porter-Gehrie, and Hurwitz (1984) identified the practice of creative insubordination in a major study of Chicago principals conducted in the late 1970s and early 1980s. Their work was motivated by a desire to know what actually goes on during a principal's workday. The researchers were also curious about what they called discretionary decision making, which they defined as something principals exercise in "the spheres of activity which are not routine or merely clerical, not dictated by strict rules, mandatory procedures, or the severe, even if unstated, expectations of immediate superiors" (p. 29). Their reasons for focusing on discretionary decision making included the following: to investigate the idea that the school principal has no power; to understand a relatively unstudied phenomenon; to see and reflect on the dynamic of human interaction; and to learn more about principal effect (pp. 29–30). The target sample for their ethnographic research included 26 men and women principals of elementary and secondary schools in the Chicago Public School System (p. 26). The number of principals of each gender is not included in the report. The researchers spent more than 300 logged hours of observation, with someone spending up to twelve days with each principal.

Terminology and Context

Analysis of how the 26 principals they studied handled discretionary decision making led the authors to coin the term *creative insubordination*, which they also called civilized disobedience (Morris et al., 1984, p. 149). Acknowledging the conventional wisdom that managers are bound by a chain of command, Morris et al. (1984) observed that "Precisely because decision making in large organizations relies on impersonal expectations, the need to disobey orders to counter their dehumanizing effects becomes more compatible with principles of good management. Knowing where and how to disobey is central to discretionary decision making among school principals" (p. 150). The point is to be unobtrusive and subtle in taking an action with a maximum positive effect for one's school and a minimum impact on one's superiors. "Among sophisticated administrators, particularly those who are sensitive to the human needs of their surroundings, such disobedience to the chain of command has developed into an art form" (p. 150). The authors comment on the ability of skillful principals to thrive in chaos. "Our inquiries revealed a new form of entrepreneurialism: the ability to turn confusion to one's own advantage. Indeed some principals find bureaucratic chaos the most exciting and productive state in which to practice their art" (p. 163). This comment brings to mind Wheatley's (1992, 1999) ideas about the power of chaos to produce meaningful change.

Traditional command and control leadership styles thrive in the bureaucratic organizational structures pervasive in our society. Communication in hierarchical organizations typically follows strict rules about the degree to which one can be candid and with whom one can talk. Isolation is perpetuated by structures of rank and status (Bolman & Deal, 2003). As a consequence, leaders tend to become isolated from the information needed to adapt their organizations to changing environments. Wheatley (1999) argues that leaders must embrace new ways of organizing, communicating, and relating with others in order for their organizations to thrive in today's rapidly changing environments. Wheatley (1999) argues that Newtonian (traditional bureaucratic) organizational structures are not adequate in today's quantum age. Bureaucratic models fail to explain how to use chaos to allow new forms of order to emerge, how to simultaneously maintain organizational standards and individual freedoms, and how to create participative, inclusive, and open organizations. Wheatley uses insights from the new science to critique bureaucracy and bureaucratic leadership. She proposes that relationships, information, and vision can be understood differently using the new science lens. The new science explored by Wheatley also offers a radically different understanding of chaos and its power to set change in motion as a natural and continuous process that creates organizations responsive to their environments. The destruction of old forms brought about through chaos is seen as positive, as necessary for the creation of anything new (Wheatley, 1999). Creative insubordination can provide such a disruption of order by breaking through bureaucracy's old forms and prescribed ways of doing things. Increasingly, the populations served by our educational institutions are diverse. Diversity is reality; pluralism, however, is a creation. The growing achievement gap suggests that schools continue to fall behind in their effort to meet the educational needs of a pluralistic society. When something needs to change, troubling bureaucracy can be a good thing.

Does Creative Insubordination Still Exist?

We were interested in whether the originally identified (Morris et al., 1984) practices of creative insubordination would be found in the stories told by the leaders in our study. The five types of creative insubordination identified in the original study are the ploy that failed, the numbers game, the gentlemen's agreement, planned delinquency on deadlines, and the literal response (Morris et al., 1984, pp. 150–155). Only one practice, playing the numbers game, was found both in the original study and in our study. In both cases the purpose of playing or manipulating the numbers was to keep a teacher. In the Chicago study, principals manipulated enrollment numbers to protect a school's head count for purposes of keeping the allocation of teachers the same. One example was manipulating the suspension policy to keep student numbers up. In our study a central office administrator told of working with student enrollment numbers creatively for the purpose of keeping a teacher.

Morris et al. (1984) documented other strategies related to creative insubordination. They found common practices of skillful principals to include seven examples of short-circuiting what they called the *labyrinth* of standard operating procedures. These strategies included wielding the community as an ad hoc weapon, management by loophole, employing the old-crony network, short-circuiting standard operating procedures from necessity, shortcuts to image building, putting new wine in old bottles, and creating spontaneous policy statements (pp. 156–161). Our interviews did not uncover examples of three—shortcuts to image building, putting new wine in old bottles, or creating spontaneous policy statements—but the other four practices were clearly described by persons in our study. Five persons gave clear examples of mobilizing the community to get something done. Four told stories of taking advantage of loopholes in policies and procedures to accomplish something important. One person told a story of short-circuiting a standard operating procedure capping at 25 the number of teachers allowed to be gone on any given day for professional development. Creatively, she made possible the simultaneous attendance of 122 early childhood educators at a state conference. Finally, there were examples too numerous to count of how relationships helped people get things done that were not technically possible, what Morris et al. (1984) labeled "calling on the old crony network." Table 4.1 offers brief descriptions of examples of these four strategies related to creative insubordination that were found in both the original study and in our study.

Several examples of the practice of creative insubordination described by participants in our study did not match any from the original study, so they are not included in the table. Some of these examples represent the practices of experienced confident administrators who are willing to be direct and aggressive in confronting bureaucratic rules, procedures, and expectations. For example, a regional superintendent told a remarkable story of *negotiating* with county bureaucrats to give up her courthouse office space, space highly valued by the county official, but not meaningful in itself to her. Understanding the politics, she offered to give up the space if other space could be found, and was ultimately successful in negotiating a $100 per month lease on another building containing 40 offices. In other examples, at least two participants reported *just going ahead and doing something*. Hazel Loucks (see chapter 5) was told a program could not be implemented because there was no money, so she went out and raised it. Without asking permission, a principal simply replaced the district read-

Table 4.1. Four Practices Related to Creative Insubordination Found in Both Studies

Four Practices Related to Creative Insubordination	Examples from 1984 Chicago Study	Examples from 2000 Illinois Study
1. Using the community as an ad hoc weapon	Mobilizing community support to force a decision from central office bureaucracy to transfer an uncooperative custodian	Appealing to the larger community through board members; talking with fellow lobbyists to mobilize opinion; involving parents and teachers to keep a drug prevention program that the superintendent opposed; going through the union for support against unreasonable edicts designed to intimidate teachers; going directly to parents to get money needed for new chairs when told there was no money
2. Management by loophole	Working through a loophole involving pay authorization forms to go around the established procedure for getting substitutes by just calling them directly	Working around legal residency requirement by declaring students homeless; ordering computer for self and delivering it to high school offices when their request for computers had been denied; taking advantage of a law permitting third-party lease agreements that made possible the building of a new school without seeking the community's approval; taking a student home without following due process to suspend
3. Short circuiting standard operating procedures from necessity	Handling problems with supplies by working with other principals rather than depending upon central office to remedy distribution errors	Going around a district "cap" and arranging for 122 early childhood educators to attend a professional development conference when district policy only allowed 25 teachers to be gone on any given day for professional development
4. Calling on the old crony network	Calling upon a network of friends within the system to get things done for your school	Numerous examples were given of how relationships helped participants accomplish things not technically possible

ing curriculum because it was not getting results with her students. She also departmentalized her third- and fourth-grade classrooms, a practice at the time not found in other buildings. Creative insubordination as a counterbureaucratic leadership practice seems to be alive and well.

MOTIVATION FOR CREATIVE INSUBORDINATION IN EDUCATIONAL BUREAUCRACIES

Morris et al. (1984) are not the only scholars who have been interested in creative insubordination. Haynes and Licata (1995) viewed creative insubordination as "one component of discretionary decision-making" (p. 21). They identified principals with a reputation for creative insubordination. They found that these principals were "said to be veterans and more aggressive. They liked to run their own schools as they saw fit and were willing to take the initiative. . . . Some of these principals were described as 'strongly student-oriented.' They were ready to do what was necessary to help their students" (p. 30). These descriptors match motives for creative insubordination given by the leaders we studied, several of whom also acknowledged that veteran status created greater independence of action. A primary motivation was serving the needs of students, also found in a later study of principals by McPherson, Crowson, and Brieschke (1986). Referencing the work of Morris et al. (1984), McPherson, Crowson, and Brieschke offer this definition of creative insubordination: "It is a workable form of disobedience carried out in the least obtrusive manner using the organizational apparatus so that the ultimate client, the student, is served" (p. 72). They explain it as a counterbureaucratic behavior that is both a balancing tool and a survival mechanism for administrators. They analyze four factors that contribute to the need for creative insubordination, including the reality of a dual set of expectations or goals, that is, both long-term educational goals and short-term operational goals. In accounting for why two administrators can look at the same situation and see differing response possibilities, McPherson, Crowson, and Brieschke (1986) cite three factors: "the combination of personality with training and professional experience" (p. 75). They characterize the average or typical principal as having greater allegiance to the district, and the less typical, more skillful principal as having allegiance first to the school (p. 75). They describe the less typical principals as initiators, experienced, entrepreneurial, and concerned with service delivery. They interviewed one of the elementary women principals who participated in the original Morris et al. (1984) Chicago study. When interviewed, Marjorie Stallings explained that her success with bending the rules resulted from making key contacts, and cultivating relationships face-to-face to create a network of persons who function as "a miniature system for doing things the wrong way" (p. 83). McPherson, Crowson, and Brieschke conclude that for skillful administrators like Marjorie Stallings, "civilized disobedience is a learned behavior for these men and women, a benchmark of the maturing career" (p. 83).

Defining Creative Insubordination

We asked the leaders in our study what the term *creative insubordination* meant to them. The answers revealed a range of motivation for pushing the boundaries and a rich level of understanding about how to get things done in bureaucracies. Generally, their answers displayed a commitment to the *why* of leadership (Furman, 2003), or what Fullan (2003) calls leadership's moral imperative. Responses were as varied as the individuals. For example, one woman said, "I think we are all creative in getting things done that we want to get done. I would never do anything to put the organization in jeopardy, but being told 'no' doesn't necessarily stop me from figuring out a better way of presenting something to get it done." Another replied, "I guess creative insubordination means to me that you take an alternative approach to achieve the expected, or the desired, or the required outcome of the typical boss-driven stated approach." Superintendent Elizabeth Lewin (see chapter 6) elaborated on the complexity of leading:

> There are times that I must do things that I know people may not want done, or that they'll think best be done by someone else. We know there are rules and regulations in our business, and people will say no, the law says you can't do this, or the board says well, we prefer to do this, or we have this policy that says we can and cannot do this. But if I feel that something is

going to be best for children, or it will help the district reach a goal, I will find or create flexibility to get the task accomplished. There is always a way to get good things done.

Someone else spoke from a similar framework, "Within a set of values, to me that means what is really good for children over the long run. It's a method of getting something done that you really believe in and that you feel would be good for the kids when your superior has said better not try that. You can't do that. We don't have the money. Or whatever." One person was blunt, "I would have defined it [creative insubordination] as up-front, straightforward, candid. . . . My style would be, if the rule is stupid change the rule." Speaking of flexibility, another person said, "It's getting the job done. I think there are lots of ways to go under, around, and through things. And sometimes we just need to get our minds thinking out of the box." A superintendent also spoke in terms of creativity, "You close the door and you do what needs to be done, assuming it's all ethical and all those other values important when you work with people; creative insubordination is more against the system of bureaucracy rather than person related—which would have contract ramifications. It is more about being creative." The definitions they articulated revealed their values.

Stories of Creative Insubordination

The leaders in our study also told stories to illustrate when they had practiced creative insubordination, whether deliberately or not. The examples they chose give insights into their motives. Several spoke of creative insubordination as having been common for them at the level of the principalship, but not so common at this point in their careers. Generally the revealed motivations fell into the following three categories: congruency with personal values such as integrity, to serve the needs of the students, and to accomplish goals or get things done. In giving examples of creative insubordination from her career, one person described these actions as springing from her sense of integrity. She explained, "In everybody's career there comes a time of intensity. It may be something small. It may be something big, when you say 'you're not buying my soul.' In my career I can point to three or four times when I said 'you will not make me do this.' It's that thing in your soul. It's just too much. If you give in then you aren't a good person any more. You have to listen to that voice of conscience that wakes you up in the night or you're not a moral person." As an example, she told of a time when the state agency was putting out a publication on sex equity. One of the writers wanted to include a certain manager who had written an article on Title IX.

> Because he was a sexist pig, I said "I'll be damned if I'm going to put his article in this [publication]." He had had affairs with his colleagues and supervisors. We didn't have a sexual harassment policy then, but he would have been guilty of it tenfold. I said, "I don't care if you fire me or not, I'm not going to do it." And I didn't do it. That was liberating. I didn't get fired, and the article didn't get put in with our stuff. I felt like either you accept my explanation or fire me, but I'm not going to let you do this to me.

Reflecting on her actions to get services for students from a migrant family by classifying them as homeless, Elizabeth Lewin (see chapter 6) explained that the risk to her as a superintendent was clear, that the family and the district could have been embarrassed. But she said, "To me the bottom line is that children come first. And if we were the only ones willing to provide the services, it was worth the risk to me personally to do that." She has the satisfaction of knowing that the family flourished— they even opened a business in the area—because she was willing to be creative and take a risk. She said, "Throughout educational history, many children have been let down by adults. It is my desire not to be among that count of the adults who failed our children. Frankly, I refuse to be among the count." Her motivation to serve the needs of children is consistently clear.

Describing similar administrative decisions, another central office administrator said, "You kind of work on the fringes of the road in bureaucracy." She explained her proactive approach,

> I don't see things as problematic. Sometimes they're opportunities. I see challenges, but then all you have to do is go back and regroup and say, "How can I meet these challenges?" Sometimes you have to just re-look, get some feedback, and learn how to move forward. Maybe you can't turn left, but you can turn right, go up the street, then come back around. Rules and procedures are there to make sure that people don't get in trouble, but that doesn't stop you from doing what's best for your program.

Secure in the values of integrity, honesty, and love behind her decisions, she elaborated further, "I do a lot of creative insubordination. I must tell the truth. Would anybody ever say I was ever insubordinate? No, I'm never insubordinate. But sometimes you have to express yourself in a manner that will enable people to understand where you're coming from and what your purpose is and what your goals are." Asked for examples, she replied, "These are some tough questions. You want all of my secrets!" She gave two examples, one that served the needs of students indirectly through making possible widespread professional development; the other addressed a need with a particular misbehaving student.

> I'm not supposed to suspend children without going through due process. But I took a child home without suspending the child. I knew I was doing it; I knew I wasn't supposed to do it. At that moment the child and that parent needed to be together. We needed to talk out some things in order for that child to get a better experience in the classroom. The child was back in school the next day, and the parent came in with the student. In fact, I knew that parent. Because I have relationships with people in the community I could do that. I knew the risk was minimum on my part. Could anybody else have done that? No. I think it was because of the relationships.

She explained, "I've been doing this a lot of years. You know exactly what you're doing. I guess, honestly, I've not had anybody to call me on a lot of things. A lot of time they say, 'You know her, that's the way she is.'" She understands her freedom to be partly about her reputation, and partly because her supervisors approve of what she is doing. As she explained, "The school code really doesn't say that you *have to* suspend. It says you may. It doesn't say you have to. We're not told to give up on the kids. That's why it says 'you may.' There are instances where that should be used, but they're very infrequent." This woman's success illustrates this advice: "If we follow all of the rules, our schools won't work. If we break too many, we won't, either. But still, we have to take chances" (Machievelli, 1992, p. 35).

Machievelli's [pseudonym] article includes the story of two administrators who "both believed the ends they sought were more important than the rules they were expected to follow" (p. 36). One was successful; the other was soon out of a job. The difference was the perception of constituents of their purposes. The author observes that it takes people who are willing to look the other way for creative insubordination to work. "But if you have, along the way, created the impression that you are being selfish, or if you have created enemies, there will always be someone who's only too happy to trip you up in the middle of your fancy dance" (p. 36). Creative insubordination by definition is risky.

Living With the Risks of Creative Insubordination

For those who practice it, the risks of creative insubordination are potentially serious. For principals they include, at a minimum, loss of influence with the superintendent and others, loss of reputation within the community, or loss of one's position. The leaders we interviewed were aware of these risks. For example, one person said, "You have to live with yourself, but you have to weigh the risks. Is winning the battle more important than winning the war? You have to ask yourself, is this my fight? What are the consequences of what I do? The risks are very great. You risk being derided and labeled as someone who is not loyal and de-professionalized." Another woman said, "You always run the risk of someone smacking you on the hands. And that's okay because you can always say, well, I'm sorry. I really didn't mean for that to happen." She believed in the wisdom of asking forgiveness rather than begging permission. Elizabeth Lewin (see chapter 6) said, "I take risks to do what I need to do to help children. But when I take a risk I have already told myself that I am prepared for a worst-case scenario, even if it means my job." Speaking of a different kind of risk, a former superintendent said, "A few times I put myself in physical jeopardy." She was also clear about political risks but viewed them to be at a different level. Stephanie Pace Marshall (see chapter 8) described a complex situation where her decision based on integrity meant "that I might lose my job, and others might lose their jobs." She was the only person to describe the risks from yet another angle:

> You run the risk over time of not having your voice heard if, as a creative insubordinate, you are not very clear about the issues that really matter. Not everything matters. Therefore, over time, someone who is "always insubordinate" even for the best reasons can become marginalized; if this happens, then no one's going to pay attention to them and the potential for their voice to be a perturbation that can move the institution to a higher level is lost.

Many of the leaders in our study were willing to take the risks of creative insubordination when the alternative was compromise of their values. They seemed to rely on previously built relationships as well as political skill and competence to manage the risks. They also relied on what Haynes and Licata (1995) call the *legitimacy of the justifiable* to protect them from consequences. In other words, they could defend their actions because the creative insubordination could be justified in terms of values larger than obedience to authority. Calling creative insubordination "one component of discretionary decision making" (p. 21), Haynes and Licata (1995) found that principals tend to use creative insubordination when district policies and rules do not make sense in terms of the reality of a local situation. They were interested in "how principals who use creative insubordination acquire social protection or avoid negative sanctions from superiors" (p. 21). Haynes and Licata offer two propositions: 1) "Creative insubordination is most likely among veteran elementary principals who value demonstrated on-the-job competence over completion of degrees or certificates and who are thought to be instructional leaders by their central office supervisors" (p. 32); and 2) "The more school principals are able to access the legitimacy of the justifiable in responding to superiors' questions about creative insubordination, the more likely they are to enjoy social protection or avoid negative sanctions for such conduct" (p. 33). We perceive a link between the concept of competence grounded in larger principles than obedience and the willingness of the leaders in our study to risk creative insubordination.

A former superintendent spoke of being totally comfortable with creative insubordination as a principal, but more political in using it as a superintendent. In fact, she used her competence to protect herself from political risk. She explained,

> I would certainly try to maneuver my forces in such a way that I would protect what I felt the outcome needed to be, and any good superintendent does that. I would always do a lot of background work. If we had a crucial vote coming up on something that I needed for teachers and principals, I'd do a lot of legwork, a lot of background work with board members, educating them, making sure they understood, and answering questions over and over again.

From her perspective, her competence and the relationships she had built protected her and protected the outcome. She never approached a job worrying about making a living. Describing getting things done, she said, "Frequently there are programs or money that a school might need to initiate a program. I'd say, in the face of resistance, okay, let's back off this a couple of months. Let's rework it and come back at it again. Let's look at it a little differently and see how we can approach it. I did that a lot." Sometimes her approaches were more direct. Once when she had a central office position, and an administrative peer continually denied the requests from the high school for new computers for their offices, her way of helping was every year to order a new computer for herself. Her request would be approved. When the computer came she would put it on a cart, wheel it past the man's office, and take it to the high school.

Gender as a Factor in Creative Insubordination

Because the patterns of bureaucracy are considered the norm, other ways of organizing and leading, particularly if preferred by many women, may appear deficient and not worth studying. The original Morris et al. (1984) study gave no attention to the factor of gender, not even indicating how many of their sample of 26 principals were men and how many were women. Neither of two more recent studies of creative insubordination (Haynes & Licata, 1995; McPherson & Crowson, 1994) addressed gender. However, women may be inclined toward creative insubordination by virtue of an affinity for relational leadership (Drath, 1996; Gilligan, 1982), discomfort with bureaucratic structures (Helgesen, 1990), marginalized status (Dunlap & Schmuck, 1995), and general student centeredness (AhNee-Benham & Cooper, 1998; Dunlap & Schmuck, 1995; Shakeshaft, 1987). One might expect that successful women school administrators, in part because of their marginalized status, have practiced a variety of forms of creative insubordination in their exercise of discretionary decision making as they tend to have valued a more personal and student-focused school.

Within the context of creative insubordination, significance was found for gender in a study (Piazza, 1996) focused on principals' level of confidence in surviving risky decisions as it related to their tenure status. Female principals were found to be more confident about surviving risky decisions, although confidence in surviving risky decisions was not significantly related to creative insubordination. Similar confidence is revealed in comments made by several of the participants in our study. As one woman said, she did not worry about losing a job because she knew she could always get another one. Interestingly, two women in our study described either *not getting* or *losing* a job because of creative insubordination. When she was a high school counselor, for example, Hazel Loucks (see chapter 5) organized the teachers and counselors to change an unfair system of student scheduling. They voted to implement a new system even though it meant going against the principal. When she wanted a principalship in that same district, the principal blocked her advancement several times. She would be interviewed, but never given the job. Later in a position in another high school in that district, she worked aggressively to address a drug problem that the superintendent preferred to deny. After a successful program was in place as a result of buy-in from the faculty, she chose to leave the system and was immediately hired as a principal by another district.

One of our participants had pursued a career in government working with the legislative process, eventually becoming director of governmental relations and chief lobbyist for a large state agency. In that position she continued "to speak up internally relative to public positions and policies that the agency had taken. I felt very much compelled to make sure that my colleagues and my boss had information that perhaps they didn't want to hear, but that I felt was important as it impacted the agency's image and how they were perceived not only in the legislative but in the public arena." She elaborated further, commenting again on how important it had been to her "to talk with fellow colleagues or even fellow lobbyists or legislators about issues that were occurring within the agency." She concluded her explanation by sharing, "I truly do believe that the outcome of this type of creative insubordination is that I was ultimately fired."

TRANSFORMING BUREAUCRACIES

Some of the leaders we interviewed were not content to get things accomplished through occasional acts of creative insubordination. Five of our leaders were changing bureaucracies deliberately through a variety of transformative leadership practices. They gave examples of practices and actions undertaken directly with the intent of *transforming or transcending the system*, thereby eliminating the need for creative insubordination. Believing their reasoning to be important, we will give attention to the ideas of each of the five. For example, the term *creative insubordination* was not familiar to one administrator although she was quite comfortable with discretionary decision making. In responding to the question of how she would define creative insubordination, she said,

> It would be like if a situation came up in my job, and my boss said, you know, maybe you shouldn't go down that road, or why don't you think twice about that. And I thought for some reason it was a good idea, and would continue to gather data and continue to push for that when maybe I felt somebody, either a colleague or somebody over me, was giving me a subtle message that maybe it wasn't a right way to go, either for the timing or political things, or whatever.

In fact, she had recently experienced such a disagreement with her boss with regard to issues of accountability in the monitoring of progress of students with disabilities, an issue about which she has strong beliefs. As she stated, "I think we just have been satisfied with not pushing kids with disabilities and not being accountable and dumbing down the curriculum and all these terrible things. And if it takes this kind of accountability to get people to be accountable, then I think that's what's driving me on this." After the meeting where she and her boss disagreed, she continued to share the reasons she felt like she did. He also continued to talk. Eventually they came to a point of agreement.

Thinking again about her continued articulation of her ideas as a form of creative insubordination, she said that because she works in a culture that supports risk taking based on your values, one that values creativity and thinking outside the box, creative insubordination seemed an anachronism. Speaking of her level of comfort with the concept of creative insubordination, she explained,

> If I had a daily diet of insubordination I wouldn't like that on a daily basis because it would make me question where I was working. One of the good things I've done is find an environment that suited me and pushed me and where I could accomplish things with the support of other people. So if I

started finding myself in a lot of these creative insubordination situations, I'd probably have to start questioning the leadership and the direction of the agency or that school or whatever.

In other words, she would transcend a system requiring the practice of creative insubordination by leaving it.

The second person who spoke of transforming the system was a superintendent. She explained a practice that had been a constant throughout her career, *using information* in ways untypical of bureaucratic organizations. It began when she was a principal in a very hierarchical, controlling, left-brain, traditional system that typified the mid 1970s. Decisions were made at the level of central office and meetings did not last long because you were told what to do and you left. She reported changing the format in meetings in her own building, using these words.

> In addition to saying that we are going to use these reading materials or whatever, *I also said why.* And then I would also say let's discuss what this means to us with the children we're teaching. In this way I demonstrated my strong belief in the staff as competent, intelligent, and articulate participants in this thing called school. I also let the staff know that I was aware that what I was doing was different from their past experience. They knew it was a risk for me. I was very up front. I put it right out there and they kept my trust. The risk, of course, is that if it gets back to the superintendent the fact that I'm sharing background information and I now have a building staff that knew more than other building staffs, that reality could be a real concern in terms of dissention across the system. But I can think of only two times there were issues in the seven years I was principal there. And it was typically a teacher who traveled between schools and just got used to operating the way we did at our school and started to act that way in another building. Then I'd get a call from a principal saying how did they even know this, leaving me to explain how I worked with my staff. This way of operating made meetings longer because of the questions, dialogue, and suggestions. But the atmosphere of professionalism and cooperation that this generated was unique to my school at the time.

Now as a superintendent who intentionally attempts to transcend rigid systems, she found the term *creative insubordination* familiar, defined it as "against the system," and more about being creative than being insubordinate to people. She stated, "If there is a lot of that going on then there's something inherent [to the system] that you need to look at." She elaborated,

> In my role as a superintendent I always felt I answered to a higher standard and that I needed to "walk my talk." It would mean that if there was a rule or practice or policy with which I disagreed, then I set up a process to have it reviewed and/or changed. Because I could create action to make a change, I didn't need to be "creatively insubordinate." I also wanted to gain and uphold the trust of the school board. I don't believe that can be obtained if the superintendent bends or ignores or is creative about the rules.

When asked to describe her level of comfort with creative insubordination, she responded:

> That's an interesting question because I am a left-brain, rules-and-regulations individual. Yet I know my sense of structure, which provides support and order for me, can be stifling or limiting to others. What I have tried to create is a system that truly does flow and move with the people and the tides of ideas and environment, and that says we look at what we do, we think about it, and we aren't so wedded to what we've always done that we can't do what we need to do on behalf of kids. I'm all for ideas, but I'd rather that we have a place where we bring them out. You don't close your door and do them. So, I guess in a way, I'm all for creative insubordination as long as it's done publicly and we all grow from it.

Neither Rebecca van der Bogert nor Stephanie Pace Marshall (see chapter 8) were familiar with the term *creative insubordination* nor were they comfortable with the concept. Their understandings of organizational realities and possibilities clearly have transcended bureaucratic structures that call forth such practices. They are transformative leaders. Rebecca van der Bogert knew instinctively what the term meant, even though she had never heard of it, saying "It probably means ways of getting around bureaucracy. I think probably it's being creative and bending those rules." She understands that her approach to leading pushes the envelope. As a superintendent she is about dividing authority and influence, working in a positive, problem-solving mode. Becky views herself as *direct* in her approach to breaking down authority so that genuine collaboration can happen. She concluded, after thinking it over, "To be perfectly honest with you, I don't think I'd be creatively insubordinate. I think I'd just say this has got to change. And that's why I don't put myself in that kind of situation. I get too outraged." Speaking of her past experience, Becky said, "I thought of myself in the past as antiauthority, but it was a real awakening to me in the sixties when I realized those who stayed outside the system didn't have as big an impact. Maybe they play a function, but it was those who got in and actually changed the system who have made a difference." She is a leader who believes, "When you get into power issues, no one really wins. And it becomes an issue over adults and the kids are forgotten." The preceding chapter featuring Rebecca van der Bogert's collaborative approach to decision making illustrated how her leadership creates a new kind of system.

Stephanie Pace Marshall's (see chapter 8) first reaction when asked about creative insubordination was, "Who is coming up with these words anyway?" Elaborating, she said,

Insubordination is just a funny word, because subordination means you need an ordinate in order to have a subordinate. We have translated the natural hierarchies in nature, which are organic and fluid, to a rigid structural and positional hierarchy that is equated to power and this does not serve. There are hierarchies in nature but they're not about who is controlling or has authority over. So when you use the word *insubordination* what I hear is the classic "I'm above you, I'm more important, I have more power. I have more authority." But I also hear something else. Subordination suggests less access to information directly. Subordination means information access is through someone else. This is not reality. The lifeblood of any system is its information. When you use these unnatural structures of ordination and subordination, you're saying that the only way you can access certain kinds of information about the organism in which you are living is through certain pathways. So I guess I would say in some sense, any insubordination is creative because it perturbs the system, and any system perturbation causes the system to reexamine itself, giving it the potential for growth, new life, new opportunity.

Stephanie's final statement about creative insubordination was that the words caused her to feel constrained: "They put me in a box." She concluded, "When someone is using these phrases, I put my psychological hat on and say, why is creative insubordination necessary? Ideally, creativity is welcomed." These statements were made in the context of her belief that we need a new language of leadership that comes from nature, and that is not mechanistic, linear, and objective. A fifth person who transformed a system was Ola Bundy.

OLA MARIE BUNDY

We close the chapter by focusing on one woman whose singularly impressive career brought about equity for girls and women, something she accomplished by getting things done in a statewide bureaucracy. Ola Bundy was assistant executive director at the Illinois High School Association (IHSA) from 1967 until 1996. Her fight to bring equity to girls and women in athletics is a classic story of working within a bureaucracy to accomplish something of moral importance. Working from inside, she transformed an entrenched system to bring about an equal role for girls' athletics in Illinois high schools and expanded opportunities for women at the same time. When she retired, she was regarded not only as the "first lady" of Illinois girls' athletics, but of America's girls' interscholastic athletics, having been the first woman state association administrator to earn a place in the National High School Sports Hall of Fame. When asked, she said the term *creative insubordination* was familiar to her, "maybe because I was being a little bit insubordinate all the time." Her voice was many times the only one heard in support of the rights and opportunities for girls within the structure of the Illinois High School Association. She is recognized as one of the pioneers of girls' athletic competitions and she never gave up the fight to provide equal opportunities for girls and women.

Ola Bundy was born in 1935 on a farm just north of Allerton, Illinois, one of five children. When she was born, her "papa" was a farmer, and her "mama" was a farm wife who was recognized for good cooking. When she was nine years old, the family moved to Champaign, where her parents, neither of whom had a high school education, bought a student rooming house near the University of Illinois campus. Her father worked on the University of Illinois farm. A number of years later her mother became a cook at a neighboring boys' rooming house. Ola graduated from the University of Illinois in 1958 with a bachelor's in physical education, and taught at the high school level for eight-and-a-half years before accepting a position at the Illinois High School Association in 1967. At the time, the association had in place a statewide Girls Athletic Association (GAA) program that sponsored intramural programs, but the only interscholastic contests permitted for girls were archery, badminton, golf, and tennis. No one really participated in these sports with the exception of a few suburban Chicago schools that had tennis matches back and forth. At the time Ola was hired in 1967, there were five administrators at IHSA, and she was the only woman. A second woman assistant executive director was not hired until 1975. Ola was in charge of the GAA program and the Illinois League of High School Girls Athletic Associations, a division of IHSA responsible for the limited interscholastic program. With her leadership, the IHSA began the expansion of the interscholastic programs for girls with limited numbers of days allowed for sports days (one-day tournaments) in the team sports and an unlimited number of contests in individual sports beginning in 1969. When others complained about the slowness of change, Ola would say, "You have to work within the structure of the IHSA in order to be effective and to achieve something. You cannot bring litigation against IHSA and expect the IHSA to give you what you want. You will not get anyplace unless you work within the structure of the IHSA to bring about changes." In the fall of 1972, Illinois started the first girls' state tournaments in tennis, bowling, and track and field, the same year Title IX became the law of the land.

In spite of the passage of Title IX, the vote to begin these statewide competitions for girls was not a foregone conclusion, even though it had been recommended by a blue ribbon committee of IHSA. The board of directors held a meeting in the spring of 1972 during the Boys' Basketball State Final tournament. An item on the agenda was whether or not to begin girls' tournaments in any sports. Ola could tell from the way the discussion was going that the decision would likely be to postpone a decision, so she spoke up.

I said, "You know, it is very, very easy for all you men in this room to tell me no, but I want you to know if you tell me no, you are saying no to the thousands and thousands and thousands of girls who ought to have an opportunity to participate in state tournaments. You are also saying no to the women and all the schools across the state that have started these girls' programs. It's easy for you to tell me no, but I want you to know that when you tell me no, you are really telling them no." After I spoke, a motion to begin girls' state tournaments was made and seconded, and passed with a unanimous vote of the board of directors.

Ola remembers that as a defining moment in the girls' program. From then on, she continued to speak up in board meetings and the schoolmen and women paid attention.

Actually, Ola first found out about Title IX in 1973 in a used bookstore on North Clark Street in Chicago when she came across a law book about the role of women in society. It contained all the information on the hearings that had taken place before Congress before Title IX was passed as part of the Education Amendments of 1972. After reading the book, she told the other IHSA administrators, "This is now federal law and it's going to affect our whole program." They were aware of Title IX, but had not realized what its impact was to be. Between 1972 and July of 1975, public hearings were held all over the United States for people to say what they thought should be in the rules for implementation of Title IX. In 1975 Ola wrote to the Office of Civil Rights and obtained the federal rules for implementation. She made sure she gathered all the government and professional publications and articles on Title IX she could find and she mastered the meanings, interpretations, and intricacies of the implementation rules. The National Federation of State High School Associations was not exactly keeping its member organizations fully informed about Title IX, so Ola took responsibility for learning about Title IX herself, and eventually for educating others across the state.

Part of Ola Bundy's commitment to equity was to fairly enforce the policies and rules of IHSA. Elaborating this understanding, she said, "I always try to follow policies and procedures, rules, bylaws, and so forth. I'll tell you this. I was maybe insubordinate to the bureaucracy of the IHSA as to what it was thought I should do to keep things going smoothly and not rock the boat, but I was never insubordinate to the rules, objectives, or the bylaws of the association. After all, my goal was to make sure these objectives, rules, and bylaws applied equally to all the students, to the girls as well as the boys." She saw herself as doing what needed to be done even though she was in uncharted territory. Her value system was her guide and by 1975 the "system" included Title IX. IHSA provided an organizational structure for her considerable energies and the passage of

Title IX gave her the opportunity to be part of writing and implementing new statewide policies and rules to ensure equity.

In 1974–1975, after the federal implementation guidelines were published to become effective on July 1, 1975, Ola volunteered to chair an important joint committee of representatives from IHSA and the Illinois State Board of Education (ISBE). The committee, which was gender balanced, wrote the Illinois Sex Equity Guidelines, which later became the Illinois Sex Equity Rules. Although ISBE had already developed parts of the guidelines, the joint committee paid particular attention to the section governing interscholastic athletics and activities. Ola chaired the meetings, took the minutes, and made sure the job got done. The fact that IHSA worked jointly with the Illinois State Board of Education ensured that Title IX was in place by 1976 for IHSA member schools through the Sex Equity Guidelines. She was also instrumental in getting the word out about what Title IX meant, working effectively with parents and schools to bring about new athletic opportunities for girls. She educated people and built networks of support for Title IX. The relationship she built with the Illinois State Board of Education proved crucial "because it was ISBE that pushed through the guidelines that later became the Sex Equity Rules of the Illinois School Code and ensured that ISBE and IHSA would be working together whenever I was involved in working with people and the schools on enforcement," Ola explained. This was not the case in many other states, where associations and state boards of education were at odds over Title IX implementation. Even with the Illinois Sex Equity Guidelines, in the school districts the required Title IX coordinators typically wouldn't inform anybody else in their districts what Title IX was all about. So parents with a daughter who wanted to play soccer, for example, would come to Ola, she would explain their rights and advise them to work within the system, to consult the principal. Then when they left her office, she would call the principal and tell him, or her, the same thing she had told the parents. Then she would keep in touch with all parties and give further guidance and support if needed until the matter was resolved. "I guess you could call that creative insubordination because those were things I did that weren't based on any policy at the time." The relationships she built and the time she invested are examples of creatively taking advantage of an opportunity for changing the system. "I would say that was creative insubordination because I don't think anybody else had any idea of all the things I was doing in working with the schools and the state board on gender equity issues," she said.

In addition to laying the groundwork for IHSA enforcement of Title IX, Ola Bundy also fought for the appointment of women to IHSA advisory committees, for women coaches and athletic directors, for women officials, and for women as directors of state tournaments for girls. Very few women held these positions at the beginning of her career. She had to advocate eloquently and firmly with her fellow IHSA administrators to open these opportunities to women. Her leadership position in the IHSA and her fair and honest style of leadership while administering girls' athletics was very powerful. The genesis of girls' athletic competition and the passage of Title IX changed not only the lives of high school girls in Illinois but also those of women educators who had the desire to coach. Coaching gave women a taste of administrative responsibilities. They had positive experiences. The opportunity to work with parents, coaches, and officials throughout the state broadened these women's experiences and led many of them to seek higher administrative positions in schools where they could have a greater impact. Girls' athletics changed many women's lives as they had opportunities to coach, officiate, and be athletic directors and school administrators. Ola believed that having more women in high school principalships was the key to continuing change at IHSA because the principals in the member schools were the key to the decisions in all IHSA matters. She mentored other women through her 29-year career. An item in the bylaws now requires that women and minorities be represented on the IHSA board of directors.

Ola Bundy was a risk taker who looked forward to overcoming obstacles and finding solutions to problems. She was never afraid to go "head to head" with the bureaucracy. When she "rocked the boat," the outcome often put the IHSA in court. Although the IHSA was not formally involved, she served as a consultant to a district when 19 male and female coaches of girls' sports filed suit against the district for equal pay for coaching girls' sports. This was in the early 1980s. The suit was finally settled out of court and led the way for other districts to achieve equal pay for coaches of girls' sports. Her support of the plaintiffs was instrumental in the successful resolution of this case. In the court cases undertaken on behalf of opportunities for girls and women, Ola never viewed the risks in terms of herself, because she believed that if she wavered the young women of the state would be the ultimate losers. She argued for the board to require equal pay for the officials in the Girls' Basketball State Tournament. When some wanted to set the fee based on number of people in attendance or number of games played in the regular season, Ola again used the provisions of Title IX and the Illinois Sex Equity Rules and argued that IHSA must be the forerunner and set the standard. "If the fees are not the same, then you are treating the girls as second-class citizens. And you cannot do that. We have to be the leaders." If she had not been where she was, there would have been different fees. And, she explained, "If IHSA had been taken to court over it, the IHSA would have lost because of Title IX and the Illinois Sex Equity Rules." Later the executive director thanked her for taking the position she did on equity issues, and for saving the association the lawsuits and monetary costs experienced by other state associations.

Ola Bundy always stood for principle and the values and standards expressed by the founders of the Illinois High School Association. She took to heart those things written about sportsmanship and fairness in a book by the first executive director. "I really felt as if I made all kinds of decisions that maybe didn't conform to the status quo but they were the right and fair things to do. They'll keep you out of court or maybe sometimes put you in court if you need to take a stand for what's right. We were in court many times with the girls' program. If it was the right thing to do, sometimes the IHSA had to stick to its guns." A pivotal case was with Romeoville where a girl wanted to play soccer on the boys' team. When the case went to court, all the parties involved folded except the IHSA, which did not budge due to Ola's insistence. The ACLU got involved and there was the danger of a deal being made in the judge's chambers during the trial. Because IHSA did not fold, Romeoville High School offered a girls' soccer program the following spring, something they refused to do throughout the trial. The conference Romeoville belonged to settled out of court. Even with the out-of-court settlement, the case established a precedent and was important for all the girls throughout the state, not just the girls at Romeoville High School who wanted to play soccer.

Whereas the practices through which Ola Bundy pushed the bureaucratic boundaries may look different from those of others in the study, her motivation—to live and lead from her values—matches those of other leaders we studied. More than once she risked her job for her beliefs, operating more often than not as the lone woman or as the lone voice for principles of fairness and equity. A woman who always did her homework, she was protected by the *legitimacy of the justifiable*, by the relationships she had built across the state through her collegial style, and by her incredible competence. Ola acted from her absolute commitment to equity to accomplish what few others could have. She acted creatively to implement Title IX in Illinois, which at that time was a courageous act of cultural insubordination, even though it was the law of the land. The actions of Ola Bundy and other leaders committed to equity have made girls' athletics the new norm for our country. Her strong leadership within the system took IHSA and girls' athletics in Illinois to where neither could have gone without her. When she retired in 1996, the Illinois High School Association designated the entire school year as *Ola's Farewell Tour*. Her stops were at the events she currently administered: the State Girls' Volleyball Tournament, the State Girls' and Boys' Swimming Meets, the State Chess Tournament, the State Boys' and Girls' Track and Field Meets, the Boys' State Volleyball Tournament, and the Girls' State Gymnastics Meet. She received standing ovations from thousands of people at each stop. She was honored for her leadership, for being fair, honest, and passionate in powerfully promoting the cause of equity.

CONCLUSION

McPherson and Crowson (1994) commented on how the practice of creative insubordination was "remarkable for its frequency and ingenuity" (p. 58). One principal they interviewed observed, however, that "'creative insubordination may actually become less necessary over time' in a more open and less oppressive system" (p. 66). Yet McPherson and Crowson concluded about Chicago in the 1990s, "the principals who find voice here are able to use more street smarts than ever before in operating their schools" (p. 71). Whereas only one of our participants was a principal at the time of the study, the majority of the women reported that creative insubordination was at some level still part of how they got things done. In spite of the intentional transcending and transforming work of dedicated leaders, educational institutions remain more bureaucratic than many would prefer. Although perhaps outdated on one level as a way to get things done, creative insubordination remains useful in the ongoing transformation of educational institutions by providing a disruption of order, by breaking through bureaucracy's old forms and prescribed ways of doing things, by *troubling* the system. Morris et al. (1984) remarked that "the 'creative insubordination' of the principal is closely tied to the moral dimension of school district decision making" (p. 149). The moral dimension is perhaps even more important for today's educational leaders, whatever their level or type of organization, given the persistent inequity revealed, for example, by the achievement gap in schools and districts throughout the country. Getting things done in bureaucracies through creative insubordination, pushing the boundaries, is a skill, a commitment, an art, and a gift still in demand.

Chapter Five

Claiming Power Through Politics

Much of what is written about politics of education or politics in education addresses national and state contexts in which educational legislation, rules, and policies are developed. This body of literature also focuses on struggles among the federal government, states, and local authorities and private entities to administer, fund, and regulate the educational enterprise. Occasional mention is made of the impact of these political tensions on local operations, practices, and personnel. Another body of literature focuses on women and politics, emphasizing the rise of feminist politics, the impact of women on political systems, or the impacts of political systems on women.

A small body of literature examines the micropolitics of educational reform and the resulting expectations for leaders to engage communities in change. A related perspective on micropolitics examines the ways in which educational leaders interact with, leverage for advantage, or experience professional life and death at the hands of local political forces. Most of this small body of literature concerns the relationship between superintendents and local school boards. Little exists regarding the very personal impacts of local, regional, and state politics on local school leaders or on the ways in which school leaders influence political decisions. Even less literature directly addresses the dynamic intersection of gender and the local and state politics associated with successful educational leadership. Yet conversations among local educational leaders frequently cite *politics* as the reasons colleagues lose jobs.

LEARNING THE RULES AND DEVELOPING THE SKILLS

Recognizing the importance of organizational politics, and women's inexperience in this arena, Harragan (1977) authored a groundbreaking book for corporate women. Harragan's book was based on personal experience, hers and that of other women with whom she came in contact over a period of twenty-five years. Her popular press book uses military and sports metaphors to explain unspoken rules, achievement strategies, and symbolism associated with successful and unsuccessful corporate gamesmanship. Years later, despite the plethora of books, women are still getting specialized advice regarding deportment in complex organizations, in which cultural norms continue to be based on gaming learned early by boys in sports. Tannen (1990) points out how women still too often fail to read the signals of corporate culture, including those broadcast in written and spoken communications. Cantor, Bernay, and Stoess (1992) and Helgesen (1990) describe the challenges and advantages of integrating feminine strategies and principles into traditionally male models of leading. Helgesen, in particular, noticed the women she interviewed were focused on the big picture, with concern for the larger society. White (1995) argues that although there are rules, boys have learned when and how to challenge rules—even break them—but that women are reluctant to do so. Both Harragan and White note that skill in selective rule breaking is essential to *winning* in organizations. Since Harragan's book, we have seen the introduction of competition into the world of girls, especially via Title IX, opening the door for young women to learn the same lessons from sports that have been taught to boys. Rimm's books (Rimm & Rimm-Kaufman, 2001; Rimm, Rimm-Kaufman, & Rimm, 2001) exhort women to learn to compete, build on their passions, and struggle for balanced lives.

Textbooks on the superintendency are beginning to address the need for political skill among educational leaders, with most of the focus on the traditional topic of superintendent-board relations. In contrast, books on the principalship almost never attempt to teach political strategies, though emphasis on community relations has increased. A few researchers have examined the intersection of gender and conflict (i.e., politics) in school leadership. Skrla (1998) studied women superintendents hired as change agents who were subsequently released from their positions. Each experienced confrontations, bullying, manipulation, and other behaviors they perceived as reactions to them as woman superintendents and suspected would not have been occurring had men been in their positions. In a study of the micropolitical communication of three female school principals, Carr (1994) recommends that "school administrators develop not only traditional management and technical skills, but also micropolitical skills in negotiation and bargaining, problem analysis and problem solving, decision-making, and symbolic acts such as those expressed in language" (p. 22). Brunner (1999, 2000) has written about the ways in which women school leaders talk about their use of power. She concludes that women approach power as something to be gained by giving it away. Building on the work of Noddings and others, Brunner observes in her participants the use of care and relationship building, traditionally expected feminine strategies, as ways to express and develop power. Björk (2000) identifies stages of research on women in the superintendency. He concludes that 30 years of literature on the subject has confirmed that women and men superintendents approach leadership differently. In particular, women focus more on children, are more collaborative and democratic, and may even be more politically savvy than men when it comes to working with parents and community.

POLITICS AND POWER

Although this chapter focuses on politics and power, this research project was not specifically designed to explore the politics of leadership in schools. However, we did state in the section of the interview guide about discretionary decision making, "Be alert to opportunities to begin to open up the subject of politics." Then in the following section devoted to creative insubordination, we stated parenthetically, "Continue to be alert to opportunities to explore the interviewee's political awareness and how it affects her practice." Because we did not begin the project with the intent of exploring the political motives, strategies, or overtones involved in the participants' professional lives, not all interviews yielded material for this chapter. Even so, during a debriefing of the interviews and interview processes, the consensus of our interviewers was that the political stories and language should not be ignored.

Transcript analysis revealed that 17 participants described conscious decisions to engage in political acts in order to accomplish something important to them. The *something important* was nearly always externally focused. That is, participants did not talk about seeking political contacts to advance themselves professionally or to achieve greater status. Rather, political overtones crept into the interviews in response to questions about leadership and decision-making styles, discretionary decision making, creative insubordination, and the question, "To what are you unalterably committed?" Responding to an interviewer question about leadership style, one highly respected leader captured the approach of many study participants when she remarked, "You have to be in partnership with others. We have to take the lead. We have to have the courage of our convictions, that moral principle."

Repeatedly, participants talked about the strategies they used to build relationships and gain leverage. Most often their efforts resulted in success for the people involved and for the causes being furthered. Occasionally the efforts ended in betrayal, heartbreak, and failed causes. Many of the women interviewed recognized these relationship-building strategies and results as facets of local, regional, or state politics. One superintendent noted, "The reality is that there are so many other actors that enter into this level which is politics, which is really people."

DR. HAZEL LOUCKS

Dr. Hazel Loucks, who at the time of the interview served as deputy governor for education and workforce development in her home state of Illinois, is significantly featured in this chapter as an example of working politically while thinking socially. Hazel's nontraditional career began when she earned her bachelor's degree while the wife of a college professor and mother of four children. Her career as a teacher, counselor, school administrator, university professor, executive director of Illinois Women Administrators, and union leader prepared her for the daunting role of using the governor's office as a bully pulpit for doing what she thought was right for students in preschool through graduate school. Hazel told the interviewer, "I don't think politics first—it's not my background. But I have had to force myself to think of the political ramifications of my decisions as deputy governor. It's not comfortable for me. I fight it." Hazel says of her own background, "I have had so many different opportunities in life. Many of these I made for myself, and others just came to me. I couldn't have planned, however, for how well my various positions prepared me to be deputy governor of workforce and education for Illinois. It just all pieced together." As deputy governor, Hazel Loucks had the power to persuade the state legislature and various state agencies to make major changes in workforce preparation, teacher and leader preparation, and teaching and learning conditions in schools. She holds an "I want to make a difference" attitude. She said, "I'd rather take the heat for going beyond the parameters I've been given than stopping something that could really make a difference. I step over the rules line sometimes. Rules are for putting people in boxes and not for what's best." Even though she was eligible to retire at the time she accepted the position with the governor's office, Hazel was not finished when her term there was complete. She went on to a position as a spokesperson for the National Education Association.

Hazel Loucks is not the only woman interviewed who leveraged politics for power to get something done. Consequently, this chapter also includes numerous quotes from women leaders in various roles—principalships, superintendencies, elected and appointed positions, and state agency and association leadership—to explore the critical political work that must be accomplished inside organizations and communities by successful educational leaders. In addition, this chapter describes the ways in which being born female affected the ways in which the participants performed *political work*. Data from interviews emerged in four categories: collaboration as a political choice; positional versus personal influence and power; integrity, intent, and personal sacrifice; and outsider, insider, and gender politics.

COLLABORATION AS A POLITICAL CHOICE

Whether or not to collaborate with others represents a distinct aspect of discretion in leadership. A particularly politically aware participant expressed one way of looking at the dilemma of whether or not to involve others in decisions. "I think you can either be Machiavellian in your approach or inclusive in your approach. In other words, you can have an approach where it doesn't matter how I get there—the ends do justify the means. Or, you can involve other people and build a group to work together to try to get things done. The latter approach is always the preferred in my opinion." Hazel Loucks' decisions to involve others in decisions and actions as partners or teammates are emblematic of similar decisions made by many of her counterparts who agreed to be interviewed for this book. For them, collaboration was about much more than a desire to make others feel included or empowered. Collaboration was used as an internal and external political tool calculated to increase support, influence, and probability that a particular decision would be made, be implemented, and have an impact. According to Hazel, "I guess one of my major issues about decision making, is it for the better good? Is it going to make something better? Is it going to be better for children? Is it going to be better for students? Is it going to be better for adults? Is it going to be better for the community?" Early in her career, Hazel became aware of strong people skills that enabled her to bring others together and to facilitate discussions. At the same time, she realized that facilitation skills had to be backed up by knowledge. "All the difference between the positive and negative outcomes in the decision making depends on your knowledge base. The broader your vision, the more comfortable you are in making the big decisions."

Making Things Happen

Nine participants recognized that collaboration was often essential in order to operationalize a good idea. Hazel Loucks told a story about her first principalship. "When I was a school principal in another district, basically, the superintendent of the school board said, 'We can't do this because there's no money.' And I figured, 'OK, if that's the only reason, then I'm going to find the money.' So I went into the community and started soliciting and was able to get the money. Well, what could they say, you know?" Another participant told a similar story about her early experiences as a principal, reporting that she would "get some parents to come in and have a meeting and show them what you have and what you need and say, 'Is there anywhere we can work a bake sale or a whatever and raise the money for this?'" Vocalizing the sentiment of several study participants, one woman said, "A lot of good people have a lot of good ideas and then it's a matter of channeling that outer vision, like, let's get out in the schools, let's get it done. Let's get more people involved in it." This was especially true when trying to accomplish through the back door of public opinion something that had been thwarted through the front door of a bureaucracy. Back doors, in the words of one, were opened "because of who these people were."

Collaboration with external groups, including board members, community members, legislators and others in positions of influence, were blatant political moves. While a university professor, Hazel Loucks defied conventional wisdom about how to succeed in the academy by focusing her work on energy-intensive and externally focused collaborative endeavors such as parent involvement in schools. She also devoted time to traveling and building the membership of Illinois Women Administrators. In her position as deputy governor, Hazel put together constituents and groups that benefited education and the workforce in Illinois. She said, "What I have to do is get the people in the room, get them talking to each other, stop screaming and hollering at each other, pointing the finger, and then talking about, OK, what is the big picture here, what do you want to accomplish, and how are we willing to work together to make this happen?" She told our interviewer, "I have never, ever experienced anything like working in government. And that's, I think, where it's difficult, I guess, because there are so many different sets of values that come into play in politics."

Several years before Hazel Loucks was named deputy governor, Ola Bundy forced collaboration among men and women in support of girls' sports at the local, regional, and state levels. In a blatant political maneuver at the beginning of the girls' sports program, she insisted "only women were to be on the [girls' sports] advisory committees because I felt the women should have a say about how girls' sports were developed, regulated, and scheduled." Ola also insisted that women administer the girls' state tournaments and that women be considered for jobs coaching girls' sports. Sometimes she worked openly and aggressively, laying her agenda on the table and challenging others publicly to refuse to collaborate. Other times Ola Bundy worked the networks of coaches, administrators, and association officials and board members.

An urban principal described hosting legislative breakfasts and inviting community leaders to lunches and school events. A rural leader talked about keeping "in touch with the leaders of the people that are going to be able to help you and let them know what you are doing. And get their advice." Not everyone in the leaders' fields of influence believed in collaboration. Describing a case in which the attempt to collaborate resulted in resentment from subordinates, a superintendent reported employees' attitudes of "They don't like it. It's your job to make those decisions. It's your job to tell us what to do."

Being Openly Political

Overwhelmingly, our participants expressed strong preferences for open styles of collaboration over playing Machiavelli. When describing her approach to leadership, a very successful superintendent talked about a tactical decision to involve teachers during her first principalship: "I conducted building meetings the way I wished they had been run when I was a teacher. I didn't realize it but I was a forerunner to collaborative decision making and teacher empowerment. At that time there wasn't language or research to describe our leadership skills." One participant consciously chose to collaborate so that the work of teaching and learning could be reengaged following a 13-day strike. In a discussion with union leadership, she said that she "would not sign the agreement, the final agreement, unless there was a piece in there about how we were going to come together after the strike." Another participant described using collaboration to build a solid team with a shared purpose. "What a lot of men do is withhold information. And when you withhold information, you can't make a good decision. So I would spread it. I would just start passing down the information. . . . I would immediately tell my team. I would tell the faculty." A regional superintendent found that "the more you interact in our community, with our clubs, with our organizations, with our churches, and with the teacher groups, the union groups, the administrative groups, the better off we'll be." She "tried to get along very well with my unions. I always was a chili taster. I went to anything the unions ever had that I was invited to. I found occasion to just go in and talk with the head of the union and ask them what was going on in their schools, in their districts, ask how could we work together to improve conditions in the classrooms."

Creating Political Networks

Networking held the key to collaboration for at least six participants. Networking is an effective internal strategy, as described by one principal, "Having been in the district over 30 years, you do tend to know where to get things done. You do know how to speed the process along by going to talk to the person who has the ability to speed it on." Networking is also an effective external strategy, according to a regional superintendent, "I got on the JTPA board, on all kinds of charity boards, on civic boards. I must have been on 15 boards. I went to a lot of meetings. I got to know people very well and I got to know what the different organizations in my community did, because all these organizations have goals and purposes. And many of them would match up with the goals that we had in the schools for our children." Hazel Loucks networked with parents, community leaders, state business organizations, legislators, union activists, state agency officials, national leaders, university presidents, and anyone else whose interests or resources could contribute to changing something she thought needed to be changed, from the availability of too few books to accessibility of adult education in community colleges. Hazel gave the following advice, "Don't worry about the naysayers. Don't agree to the boxes people want to put you in. If it's going to make a difference for even one person—go for it!"

Collaborating for Success

Ten leaders in the study recognized that failure to involve key individuals and groups in implementation of significant organizational changes frequently doomed even excellent choices. More than one leader discovered this the hard way. One participant struggled with a key individual who missed meetings because she realized that unless he was present, any decision made would not lead to results. She said, "This person, who would like this change [being discussed], had missed two of the meetings that we had and I called him after our second meeting. And so I told him, 'If you're not at the table, chances are what you want will not be represented.' And I wouldn't have done that two or three years ago. I would have said, he wasn't there, let's just get this done." Even so, participants recognized that collaboration was pragmatic and did not require total agreement. Early in her career one of the interviewees got what she considered very wise advice about collaboration: "They told me that you just work with the ones that will work with you and be as nice as you can to the others."

Collaboration as a political act may provide a means to self-serving ends while at the same time leading to win-win solutions for sticky situations. After winning an election, one woman reported that she "became important because we had jobs to give out. And then the politics could creep in a little bit." She shared that she was able to use the political nature of the position to collaborate with county officials to move her office to a new, more accessible space, something she thought would benefit teachers and help depoliticize her office a bit. "When they built a new courthouse, it wasn't long before there wasn't enough room, and everybody wanted to be in the courthouse. So I started in, right then, saying, 'Put us somewhere else, we don't care. We don't need to be in the courthouse to serve teachers. We need a lot of parking for teachers.' And they rented an old school for us some distance from the courthouse." She reflected, "I guess I found creative ways to get around bureaucrats and work with them or give them something they want. Like when I wanted to move out of the courthouse, I gave them my space, which was a premium for them and meant nothing to me. And it was a wonderful coup because it served us both."

POSITIONAL VERSUS
PERSONAL INFLUENCE AND POWER

It is noteworthy that the majority of interviewees, all of whom hold significant positions in our schools and society, did not talk about using positional power to influence decisions or to take action, even in cases where use of their position to "do the right thing" would have been minimally challenged, if at all. The reasons for such lack of overt reference to positional power are unknown. Since we were not looking for the political aspects of our participants' work during the interview process, we simply did not ask questions that would have provided insight into the reasons they did not root the majority of their actions in the power of their positions. It may be that although most people would have considered the interviewees to hold positions of significant power and influence, the interviewees did not view themselves or their positions as being remarkably powerful or influential. It may also be that the personal value systems of most of the interviewees prevented them from wielding power simply because they could by virtue of their positions. It could be that some of the participants were very self-conscious of their gender or their personal styles. A black principal told the interviewer, "The power structure tends to be male and white. I'm just going to say, that's what it tends to be. And your status and power has to do with their perception of you. I do think longevity has helped my status and power in the district. But I'm telling you, status and power is all questionable. It's who can get the job done. So, sometimes it's perceived power, perceived status." Rebecca van der Bogert, reflecting on a complex situation, said, "I'm real good at avoiding power issues. I don't like them. I'm uncomfortable with them . . . should I have gotten pulled into the power game? . . . Then I wouldn't have liked myself."

Positional Power and Influence

The three interviewees who spoke most of positional power were, indeed, in overtly political positions, although none of them initiated their careers aspiring to become politicians. Even after nearly four years as deputy governor, Hazel Loucks spoke with wonder about her power. "Well, I look at myself now, and this is kind of surreal, because, you know, the status is the title you have." That status gave her broad decision-making powers. "In the first two weeks of my job here, I was making such astronomical decisions! I was asking, 'Where's the rule book?' I'm saying 'yes' to this and 'no' to that. Am I in the right realm? What does the governor want? I asked the chief of staff, 'How do I know this is what the governor wants from me?' He said, 'If you get too far out, the governor will pull back.' He's never pulled me back." Even so, Hazel struggled with being "naive to the extent of power, the power of money and politics. And that's been kind of hard for me. I guess I don't think politics first because that's not my background. And often times I'm expected to think whatever political ramifications go along with this decision." She talked about having "broad discretionary powers" to shape implementation of the governor's expectations.

The governor wants every child to have access to quality education. In Hazel Loucks' mind, that means a quality teacher. How are we going to make sure that there is a quality teacher? Well, with the teacher shortages, I need to be looking at the whole issue of what does the research say about how to keep and maintain teachers that we've trained in the classrooms. How to make sure that the pool is adequate. . . . Now the governor didn't tell me to do this, or the chief of staff didn't tell me this. . . . The governor didn't say, "Hazel, provide teacher scholarships. I want a quality teacher in every classroom." So, I have broad discretionary powers to make sure we address the teacher shortage by putting necessary components in place.

In the long run, Hazel Loucks discovered that positional power means having influence over others in the interest of doing what she considered the right thing. "So I've been in a position to influence a lot of decisions, not necessarily make the decision myself, but influence the decision and be sure that the background information is there so that the right decision is made." Establishing legislative and business community support for developing National Board-Certified Teachers in Illinois is an example of such a decision. "You know, in this job I've had some wonderful opportunities to change the system. I really believe in the National Board Certification. . . . I was able to go out and convince the business community, the legislature, and raise money." The privilege of position for Hazel included using her value system as the benchmark of success. "But I think that's the joy of being where I am now, being able to facilitate those kinds of things. And those efforts are based on Hazel Loucks' value system, what I value. Somebody else in the job might see something else that they thought was more important. That's the pleasure of being here, I guess." At the bottom line, Hazel's "joy came from the fact that I facilitated the process. My work was based on what I value. Yes, I have powerful connections in this position, but I am careful not to misuse that power."

A regional superintendent's awareness of positional power grew as services to schools originally centralized with the state education agency were distributed to regional offices of education.

The state pays for the regional superintendent and the assistant. So all the county has to provide is a little office in the courthouse. For years and years, that was all we had. And it wasn't too much, so we didn't have a lot of jobs to give out. We were not bothered. We were left alone. Things began to change when the offices became more, when we became regional offices, when we began providing the services that the state had once provided. My office now had a payroll of 136 people. So from when I took office, I had three employees, two paid for by the county, and when I left I had over a hundred. We became important only because we had jobs to give out.

Early in her leadership of the Illinois Mathematics and Science Academy Stephanie Pace Marshall (see chapter 8) learned the value of positional power derived from a title.

> My title was changed about five years ago. I came into this role as an executive director. . . . However, the constituencies that I connected to beyond the educational world were corporations and foundations and corporate leaders and business leaders. And they didn't have a clue what an executive director did or that it was a CEO role. So that title was not engaging enough to make my world accessible to them. As soon as I became "president," well then, of course they understood what I did. I didn't need any other language. That was the end of the conversation.

Stephanie used the power bestowed on her title to communicate with external constituencies, including those whose support was essential to the academy's future.

Three participants in less overtly political positions spoke of the instability of positional power. One woman whose career includes stints as a building principal, university faculty member, and college administrator told an interviewer, "I've said often and will continue to say, one of the most challenging jobs is being the building principal. It's like being the baloney in the middle of a sandwich; you just get it from all sides and so I think my political training really began there." She described the shaky ground on which principals find themselves when they make decisions that differ from the decisions powerful people would have them make. "I had to make a decision as a building principal about the placement of a student and at that time we had what might be considered advanced courses and traditional courses. I had to make a decision in light of the fact that the student's parent was a board member. . . . I made a decision that I thought was right for the student. And I had a price to pay to make it." A principal faced similar challenges when deciding the fate of high school students whose violations of the student handbook required expulsion for a semester. "One was a village trustee's son so I had the mayor in the house. See, there's a lot of politics that are involved in it because of who these people are." She protected both the students and herself by providing counselors, helping the families obtain correspondence courses, and supporting the students becoming eligible once again to play sports upon their return to school. A superintendent recognized that the power of her position was limited by the composition of the school board. "And I'm especially sensitive here where currently five of the seven board members are female. That wasn't who hired me. In fact, after this election, the new board members will not be who hired me two years ago. The board that hired me did not stay locked. The majority changed. So I was conscious of who the caucus might be."

Personal Power and Influence

In the absence of overt positional power or the willingness to wield it, some interview participants created interpersonal relationships and networks to get things done. In some cases, the power of personality became more effective than the power of position. When she became a college dean, one participant relied a great deal on personal strength and interpersonal relationships.

> I had to decide whether or not to say something to a department chair about what I perceived to be problem that needs a long-term solution relating to the way faculty respond to peer evaluations. I could have gone to policy and written a policy about how that should be done. And I could have done it through a collaborative group and raised the issue in a broader way. And I decided that it was important to have a one-on-one, eye-to-eye talk with the person.

Principals, too, utilized the power of personality to make changes. Referring to the need to dramatically redesign an approach to teaching reading, one said, "So I have to be very discreet when I'm talking to them one-on-one. And I would bring them in and do that one-on-one rather than say it in the whole faculty meeting." Similarly, talking about her work as a high-ranking staff member at a state organization, a longtime educator remarked, "I have found that I can usually work through bureaucracy in a pretty efficient manner because of the relationships that I have developed within the organization. And maybe that's because I know who to go to, to get things done, to expedite." She expanded on this notion with, "If you ask me what I think really, looking back and where I am right now, and watching colleagues who have been successful, or not successful, it really is about your ability to develop relationships. And I don't mean in a contrived manner. I mean in the ability to say hello to people, to ask them about their families, to listen."

Education Is Political

At least 17 study participants recognized schools and related organizations as political. Referring to her vast experience in schools, universities, a professional association, and the governor's office where she worked at the time of the interview, Hazel Loucks said, "There are politics in public schools, as you well know. There are politics in universities. Universities are very political environments. But at a different kind of level, so I guess I knew that it existed, but I just didn't understand the full extent. Almost everyone that comes here has an agenda. Almost always, it's dollars." A regional superintendent in charge of certain aspects of schooling across multiple counties talked about working with "administration that's political here." As the only female staff member of the Illinois High School Association, Ola Bundy perceived herself as having limited positional power, but as having leverage because of the visibility rendered by being different. She tested her personal power most when she openly challenged Illinois High School Association Board members at a meeting about their pending vote regarding holding state tournaments for girls' sports. She asserted forcefully that a no vote would be a vote not against her, but against all of the girls in Illinois schools, and the vote was a yes. One school leader recognized the local politics of her district and the nuances of using positional power. "If it is an emergency, if somebody needs something right now, instead of going through a lot of bureaucracy, I provide them with what they need. But if it's something that can wait, I will go through the politics. I will go to the people that I need to go to, to get the rules changed or bent or whatever to accomplish the nonemergency items." Another reflected on the nature of positional power in local schools and its limitations when faced with external pressures from the community. She said,

> I think schools are very political. What I mean by that is there are powers in the situation that whether it be a principal of a school, a superintendent, they

have a lot of power and a lot of influence. If they have a certain belief about something, it's real important to the "powers that be" to feel that we're at least willing to discuss and try to influence their thinking versus making decisions that would be unpopular to them, their board, the district. So I guess it's that political structure of the boards of our district and the communities of our district that may want something different than what we're pushing for.

Politics and Values

Positional power, according to study participants who talked about it, has limits, especially within school districts. For the most part, interviewees preferred to operate as facilitators of shared decision-making organizations in which all participants had as the goal doing the best things for children. Even so, they acknowledged that educational organizations are political organizations and that a pure shared decision-making model was not possible. The challenge for study participants who talked about the politics of education on local, regional, or state levels has been to balance their visions of what is right with the realities of how things get done in their working spheres. None took the position that the end justifies the means, though some made compromises. A few described maneuvering politically to make the right thing happen, to prevent injustice, or to fight wrongdoers. Hazel Loucks talked about "those who are unwilling to do the right thing because of somebody's political or financial influence. And that is very, very, very hard for me to stomach. And I have to say that I would far rather take the heat and go against that than have to go against my values. And so I've been in both situations: where I've decided it's not worth the cost, and where I'm going to go ahead and fight for the right thing. But occasionally I've been put in the position where I could not do anything else, and that's really been very bothersome to me." She said, "My husband says, write your resignation and keep it in your drawer and any time you feel like it's compromising what you believe too much, take it out and hand it in. I said I couldn't do that because sometimes it'd be once a day."

INTEGRITY, INTENT, AND PERSONAL SACRIFICE

Integrity is a very personal quality. Repeatedly participants in this study expressed the need to be able to look at themselves in the mirror, to make and stand by decisions that were congruent with their self-images. This is not a small statement as integrity may have a high professional price. A participant who had led many different kinds of educational organizations said, "You know, I think I come off like it's easy to do, but there's such a personal price for some of the decisions you have to make in a leadership role." She told the interviewer, "I want to be able to stand in integrity behind the decision I make. I tend to mull quietly and then present the confident front that the decision's been made and here we go and let's proceed together. But I do think it's important to acknowledge the price you pay to be a leader. And often that comes when the tough decisions have to be made." Hazel Loucks found that despite the push and pull of power politics, personal integrity mattered more to her in the long run: "I hope my gravestone says that she never stopped being a teacher. And integrity is very important to me. It's who you are and what you say you are, and our actions really do show that that's who you are." Speaking again of the value of her integrity, Hazel said, "I think some would say I have a great deal of integrity, that I'm not going to be influenced by who you are, or how much money you have, or who you know. If it's the right decision, then we should move forward." Integrity and personal values are interrelated. Describing her feelings about her work as a legislative liaison for a state education agency, one participant said,

> One of the things that I guess I would say here is that one of the most important decisions I think I made, particularly in my previous position, was to continue to speak up internally relative to public positions and policies that the agency was taking. I felt very much compelled to make sure that my colleagues and my boss had information that perhaps they didn't want to hear, but that I felt was important as it impacted the agency's image and how they were perceived by not only the legislature, but in the public arena. In that specific instance, I think it was important to me because not only is my integrity important to me, but it's important in terms of the folks that I work with. I think preserving integrity and credibility are extremely important.

Nine study participants clearly expressed integrity in terms of intent. That is, they intended to do the right thing, the fair thing, often expressed in terms of what was right for students. One said, "I would say that as a superintendent, and I guess one of the reasons to be superintendent, was I thought I had the most opportunity to impact the most people who would then impact kids." Similarly, another related intent to the well-being of children. "You know, what drives me—that's getting things accomplished and improving the quality of life for our children. We are in the business of saving children's lives and that I take very seriously. It's a serious responsibility on my part. That's why I stay in this business." Some of the people in our study felt so strongly about the importance of intending to do what was right for the children in their charge that they would make decisions based on personal professional conviction even if the students, parents, or higher authorities strongly disagreed. Referring to her decision regarding whether to place a board member's child in a general or advanced class, a participant says, "I made a decision that I think was right for the student. And I had a price to pay to make it. And I'd do it again. . . . I knew I was in a political environment and I knew there would be a price to pay. And I had to be willing to live through it. And, you know, I'm human. There were moments when I thought, you know, I could have just put her in that class, what's the big deal? But I just couldn't do it." Another went further, standing up on behalf of an entire race of students in her school district. "I decided that someone needed to take up the fight for the prejudice that I saw. And the lack of caring for minority students and lack of understanding, indifference, because you know, sometimes, it's not all prejudice. It's that other people really don't know what they're doing to people of color."

Ola Bundy, fighting on behalf of girls' access to quality, state-sanctioned sports programs tells a story about the importance of personal integrity in trying to work out fair regional tournament assignments and pairings. "You set your standards and then you follow them, because then school administrators couldn't argue with those standards." In another heated sports-related moment, one of the principals in the study challenged popular thinking when she "did not give the African American male, the only one who applied for the position of head football coach in my district, the position. I gave it to a white male and because of that he took me to the office of civil rights. And we were in litigation, and we're still in litigation. And, you know, it was the best decision I ever made because I did it based on what's best for kids. I didn't do it based on color, gender. I did it on what's best for kids."

For two other participants, integrity emanated from doing what they said they would do. One expressed that sentiment with, "And if I said I was going to do something, especially in those tenuous situations, I had to follow through." Stephanie Pace Marshall (see chapter 8) risked her position and the very existence of the Illinois Mathematics and Science Academy in order to follow through on her promise to admit students, even in the face of legislated funding cuts. She explains keeping one's word as being about integrity, about *name*.

Integrity and the Law

Seven participants who talked about integrity in relation to political realities agreed that they were willing to push the limits, but not to break the law. Hazel Loucks described her decision making as "based on the information I've put together, as long as I don't break a law." In describing how, in her view, all decisions are discretionary, one interviewee related, "I think the time I'd make the exception quite honestly is if I felt there was the potential for a legal issue. And I needed to see that I had my t's crossed and i's dotted to protect a faculty member or a student in some way, to protect the institution. And then I would honor the policies and legal expectations rather than my own opinion about them." Speaking to a question about creative insubordination, a principal responded, "I really appreciate the law and I wouldn't be flagrantly insubordinate to them and I would never do anything to embarrass them." A statewide leader asks, "And is it legal?" Likewise, from a principal, "It was always, is this first of all legal? I mean sometimes legally they would forget that this is in the student handbook. It's there in black and white. We don't want to get into a legal situation." As a principal, this participant recommended, "But if you stand and fight for what you believe in and also if you have a clearcut handbook." As a personnel director, another advised, "And you know by law, there are certain things that you have to do. And having worked in personnel for three years, I know the importance of doing that, because one decision that's done improperly can cost the district many dollars." She also said, "Rules and procedures are there to make sure that people don't get into trouble. But it doesn't stop you from doing what's best for your program." The bottom line, according to two of our participants, is that pushing the limits had limits. According to one, her boss told her, "Just go do it, but just know that I'm not going to jail for you" and another drew the line at placing herself in jeopardy, "And it assumes, however, that what you're doing you will be forgiven; you won't be put in jail."

Sometimes, interviewees found ways to use the law. Ola Bundy became an expert on Title IX. "I gathered all kinds of different materials and information so maybe that was a little bit of creative insubordination. Because I made sure I read all the professional publications, all the different information I could find on Title IX." A principal used the law to rid the district of poor teachers. "No other teacher in the history of our district, our school was built in 1955, nobody had ever been put on remediation in the district. We got bureaucratic. Don't rock the boat kind of mentality. You want to do what? Yes, I think I need legal advice. I literally worked with our district attorneys, the supervisor, the remediation plans were that thick. They were in the classroom continually."

Study participants expressed an interesting awareness of the trade-offs they made when they placed integrity over expediency, political solutions, or personal comfort. One leader talked about purposefully coining "myself in a variety of projects as a villain" in order to make the right thing happen. Referring to her preference for having women, providing they were qualified, as officials at girls' games, Ola Bundy told us, "And I took the knocks for it." For one principal, positional power also meant personal sacrifice: "Although I call my team in, bottom line, I say yes or I say no. And if it's a bad thing, then I'm the one that takes the heat for it." Another risked a close relationship to do the right thing, "I believe the person did something at a meeting that demolished the group. And I talked to her personally about it. And that damaged our personal relationship. That was OK. I mean, it was a loss to me, but I did think a person could change." One participant put it all on the line with, "You know, I believe that I am skilled enough and knowledgeable enough that I can always get a job." A university dean, whose position influenced statewide policies and practices, best expressed the sentiments of many: "And there comes a time in everybody's career—there comes a time of intensity. And it may be something small, it may be something big when you say, you're not buying my soul. You are getting me, but you will not make me do this. And I don't care what you do, I will not do it."

OUTSIDER, INSIDER, AND GENDER POLITICS

One means of trying to determine participants' motivations for the ways in which they made decisions and took actions was to ask each the extent to which she felt like an *insider* or *outsider*. The answers to this probe led to some unanticipated insights into the political savvy of the participants who, for the most part, described themselves as outsiders who moved inside. In addition, several commented on gender as a factor in the extent to which they operated on the inside. Most participants moved along a fairly traditional P–12 pathway to positions of higher authority. A few moved between systems of P–12 education, higher education, and government. Moving from P–12 to higher education made one interviewee "feel like an outsider here. I don't see the world the same way. I don't want to play the games the same way. I feel like an outsider in terms of what I can respect as a tradition that's been built up for some reasons that I haven't been privy to." A black woman who worked her way into administrative positions in a white-male-dominated hierarchy of a large school district serving primarily minority children reported, "When it comes to getting something done, I'm an insider. When it comes to social kinds of things, I'm an outsider."

Positional Authority Creates Insiders

Interviewees expressed different notions of what it meant to be inside or outside. Some characterized themselves as being insiders because they led from positions of authority in their organizations. Said one, "Well, I'm an insider. I'm an insider because my commitments are to the people that dwell inside these situations. What I do in terms of my leadership and my own work is to bring the outside world in. . . . I'm inside because my work is within institutions and within and through people, but I live in a different space." Another found that being named superintendent of a large school district led others to perceive her as having insider status. "I would say insider because I learned very early on when I was first a school superintendent, I think there were only 12 female superintendents. But because I had such a large district, and it was an urban district, I was, at least this was what I felt, immediately perceived by my peers as though I paid my dues, because many of them had jobs that required less, or say, were not as challenging as my own." Likewise, others talked about being insiders because they had worked their way through the ranks of P–12 to highly visible positions. Expressing a commonly held belief, another superintendent said, "I came from within the system. I had a support network, and the male principals were about my age." Even though a rural superintendent referred to Illinois Association of School Administrators as an "old boys' club," she counted herself at the end of her career as a superintendent as an insider: "I would have to say I was an insider because I felt welcome in the executive director's office anytime, that, in fact, he has given me references for several different things."

One former regional superintendent spent the vast majority of her career in overtly political positions, standing for election multiple times. In her case, being "tapped" for the position, and others that followed, was key. She was urged to run for regional superintendent. "I suppose because I was not political, my husband was not political, we had no particular friends high up in politics. But again, I thought about it and jumped in and I think there were seven men running against me the first time I ran, including people who had been chosen by the political party. And I think it was my ignorance at that time that made me step in and my persistence that made me stay. And I won. And then I was in for twenty years." She noted that a long career of high visibility in a position that combined educational mission and political activity resulted in increasing insider status. "I think the longer I was in leadership roles, the more accepting everyone became. I just finished two years as chairman of the Catholic Social Services diocese. That's 27 counties in southern Illinois. I don't think there was any question there. And now I'm into a lot of things, but I think now my age and my record have preceded me." She also noted that getting inside required being brought in by those already inside. "But I had so many friends all along the way and they were, often were, men, because the men were the ones who had the power. We're talking about 1970." She also talked about effective strategies for getting inside. Essentially, she persisted in developing relationships with skeptics, resisters, and enemies. "Once I became regional superintendent, those who maybe opposed me at first became very good friends. Now I have lunch once a month with one of my bitterest enemies from days gone past, a superintendent. So you have to work with them and not make them your enemy but try to make them your friend, which is very difficult."

Another participant counts herself as an insider due to her years of experience and visibility in politically active positions. "I think that coming from an educational background—I mean I have spent the last 30-some years of my life in education in one form or another—I definitely do feel like an insider." A suburban principal mixed politics and her profession to develop insider status. While serving as assistant principal and then principal of a very large high school in a progressive upper-class community, she became highly involved in the design and construction process of putting up a new building. "I was very much a part of the entire process of running a referendum and the design and assisting with the construction process. And while doing that, I was also an alderman in the same community with the experience of being the chair of finance, so working very closely with the city treasurer." These highly visible positions provided her access to community leaders and made her an influential leader in her own right.

Crossing the Insider/Outsider Line

Hazel Loucks insightfully observed that an individual can work on the *inside* even though an *outsider* due to gender, career path, position, or other legacies. Hazel elaborated,

> In organizations where I felt my presence was accepted only because of what I could do for them, I felt it was even more important to get in there, try to break down some of the barriers and look at the big picture. That's why, with women, I always say, "Don't throw up your hands and give up." Don't say an organization doesn't represent me. Get in there and make it represent you. That's what I believe. I feel like that's how you can change organizations.

Hazel's personal experiences with gender as impacting one's insider versus outsider status were confirmed by her research while a professor, "You have to work twice as hard, twice as long to show you can do the job. Our male counterparts get promoted faster and easier. Males have mentors and female aspiring leaders lack mentors. I have research to prove that. . . . Gender does make a difference. Somewhere along the line in my life, somebody gave me a backbone which tells me 'don't back down, keep going.'" Another person took a similar point of view. "I always force myself to work on the inside. Like, I made very sure that I would get a position on the Illinois Principals Association board or the

National Elementary School Association, but I always considered myself an outsider." She explained that she set herself on the path of getting on the inside because she "felt that you have to work from the inside to account for the changes that you want to accomplish." One participant recognized professional organizations as male clubs that discouraged women gathering based on gender. "And I understand that the metro area around here is a little good old boys. That you know, it's very cliquish. Any time we would want to get together as women, to get together for dinner, you know. . . . 'Well, we don't have a good old boys' club.' Well, the heck you don't. They just call it the superintendent's association."

At least four interviewees talked about playing the role of insider while feeling like an outsider. One was clear about her self-perception when she said, "You know what, I'm an outsider, but I have the role. I can play the role of insider because I've learned to do that. I've learned in order to get what I need for kids, and I know how to work the male system." Another talked about being the outsider on the inside who got on the inside in part because of the need for a "gender token" and how discouraging such a position became. She explained,

And I served on many of the IHSA advisory boards, scholastic bowls, swimming, athletic director . . . but the Illinois High School Association, I could not break that feeling. I couldn't. No matter how hard I worked for them. . . . I couldn't break through with the Illinois Principals Association. And I think it was because we were a part of the strategic planning way back 12 years ago. And we said, you've got to get some women in here. And you'd better get some minorities. Because you're not going to be respected as an organization.

Similarly, a principal who moved to a position in higher education talked about the paradox of being in a role with feelings of simultaneously being both an insider and outsider. "I feel like an insider in K–12 settings. I feel real comfortable that we are colleagues. I feel comfortable in school. I feel comfortable in school groups, professional associations, conferences related to K–12 education and some Higher Ed. I feel like an outsider in the broader context of the university administration. Not here, as much as the broader expectation of what a dean of a school or college is supposed to be." Another university dean explained that an outsider who moves inside has the opportunity to question business as usual.

My first week as a dean, I come up . . . I have no secretaries . . . I have a student worker. And I said to her, how do I get some Xerox copies made? And she said, you have to go over to that sheet, write your name down, and indicate how many copies you're making. I said, I have to do that? She said, yes. We all have to do that. I said, why do we do that? She said, well, everybody has to do that because at the end of the month we count up how many sheets people have done. And I said, why do we do that? And she said, so that we'll know. And I said, know what? And, where it was going, and this was just a little student who was just doing what she was told. And she said I guess so we know whether people are using the Xerox inappropriately. I said, how would we know that? She said, well, I guess we wouldn't know. And I said, we don't do that anymore. Now, I laughed at that because that was such an obvious one. But I think it's a good practice to ask, "Why do we do this?" rather than saying this is the way we've always done it, therefore we're going to do it this way until we die.

Gender and Political Power

Ten participants linked their gender to their experiences with political processes. Hazel Loucks reported that education's most powerful leaders in the state, all men, reacted to her as the governor's choice for deputy governor. "Initially, the governor called in the presidents of the various universities and said, 'This is my new deputy governor. If you want to talk education, you talk to her. You don't call me.' Well, for some of those gentlemen, that was a very hard pill to swallow. I think partially it was probably gender. . . . I don't think I was misreading it." One participant reported that men had trouble dealing with her during various public and private negotiations because "to begin with no one expects you to want too many of the goodies." Another person brought a significant gender-related matter she considered to be of great importance to her superintendent. He told her that she was stressed from work and from going to graduate school for her doctorate at the same time. "I went absolutely crazy. Because he pawned it all off on—which they normally do—women, you're going through this . . . and that's the picture. That's the picture he paints for women board members now, too, who don't agree with him." Another woman found that gendered perceptions impacted her relationship with males in power. "I recall once getting on my evaluation 'does an outstanding job in spite of size.' Now when I became dean I was about 118 pounds. I had that on my evaluation, 'does a good job in spite of size.' So I had to question them on that. . . . And I'm trying to make sure that people understand to evaluate people on your skills and not on your gender and your size." She recounted being excluded from social events she knew were important to developing insider status and her decision to find other ways to get what she needed. "We're talking about ball games. . . . This is for the boys, you know. . . . I don't have to be one of the good old boys in order to do a good job. If that's what the good old boys do." In similar voice, a lobbyist said, "I do have a role, obviously, as a woman in a man's world. . . . I thing the gender of being female has somewhat affected the opportunities. They've been somewhat stymied because of my sex. It's still a good old boy world, to be admitted to the cigar-smoking, scotch-drinking back room."

Eight study participants expressed keen awareness that recommendations or decisions they made would be more highly scrutinized and questioned than would the decisions of men in similar positions. Elizabeth Lewin (see chapter 6) reported that her awareness of gender and color as marginalizing factors led her to adopt stringent data-based and documentation strategies.

I have learned that based on being female and a female of color that anything, once it has been verbalized by me, is going to be scrutinized in and out. So I really don't make decisions without having almost volumes and volumes of rationale and documentation to support the decision that I have made. Because there're going to be challenges that will not be based on fact, but based on emotions just because I made the decision. There are going to be challenges, so I'm constantly and always ready for that.

Another strong leader reported, "I think my decisions are questioned differently. I think my style is questioned differently—not by everyone and again, I want to make that clear. I think there is a worry that I will be too supportive and promote too many women, but that never comes up with male leaders that there will be too many men in leadership. So I would think that it's more an issue in terms of power."

Doing Gender Work

Three individuals reported consciously choosing to do *gender work*, though they found it politically risky. Now a university dean, one former principal tried to promote gender issues in her teaching:

> I have to be honest and say that I am extremely sensitive to gender work. I can remember, I'll tell you a little story that may or may not have anything to do with this. The first class I taught, it was an intro to ed class. It was a typical survey class and we had what I would call a foundational piece of the class talking about women in administration and I was excited. I had my stuff, I had my materials. I can remember this really thoughtful gentleman in class who I really admired. He'd worked hard. We'd spent a lot of time talking ed ad [educational administration], and he struggled with making the decision to become a principal. He raised his hand in class and he says, "Do you really, are you telling us that in your career gender has been an issue?" And I said, take out your pens please and write this down. Yes, I'm telling you that. That's a fact that all of us need to put on the table so we can deal with it together. I was just amazed that people don't realize that it was an issue.

Ola Bundy spent her entire professional life doing gender work. Although she understood that being male was the political ticket to being an insider in the world of high school sports in the 1970s, she fought for the rights of girls to be *inside* high school athletics and for women officials to be *inside* the world of officiating for equal pay and respect. She also fought for women as decision makers in the political process of the governance structure of the IHSA. She told the organization leaders, "You know, there are men making all the decisions. The board of directors (IHSA)—they're all men. The legislative commission—it's all men. And I said, they are also all principals. And I said, if you want a change, if you want a change with the Illinois High School Association in terms of the decision making, then you have to have more women principals." Ola also recognized the political importance of understanding history, particularly the history of gender and administration. "I was at a town meeting and we were talking about equity in the program and talking about wanting to make sure that women principals had opportunities to serve on committees and things like that and this one woman principal, a beginning woman principal, kind of reamed me out at the town meeting and said, 'I don't think that is appropriate. There shouldn't be any favors for women administrators, you know.' And I stuck right with her and I said, 'Well, I'm going to tell you this, if it hadn't been for the efforts and affirmative action steps in some regards, you might not even be a woman principal today.'" A highly visible and activist principal reported similar responses to female principals among members of the sporting and principals associations when she said, "I worked to get women involved and represented in the state organizations. It was difficult. It wasn't easy to break through the 'good old boys' in state and local organizations . . . no matter how hard I worked for them."

CONCLUSIONS

Without a doubt, many of the leaders studied recognized their professions and their positions as political. Some were unquestionably political by the nature of election or appointment to highly visible partisan public offices. Others were political because of the ways in which people reacted to the status of the position, such as superintendent of a large school district or president of a school created by legislation and supported via annual legislative appropriation. Others became politically active because of choices they made to champion causes, primarily gender-related agendas. A few concluded that organizations are inherently political, requiring skillful communication, relationship building, and establishment of insider status in order to have influence or project leadership. For the leaders whose words contributed to this chapter, becoming political was related to developing public voice. Developing a public voice was related to the ability to behave as an insider, even if feeling like an outsider. Developing a public voice was somehow linked to integrity, intent, and even personal sacrifice, especially when politically able leaders expressed confidence in surviving the strategy of asking forgiveness after taking action. In the words of one participant, "I can move along the continuum and I can play outside the continuum. I do whatever I need to do and I think that's what most female administrators have learned to do."

Hazel Loucks used the phrase "make a difference" at least a dozen times during her interview. This phrase or sentiment can be found in the conversations held with each participant. Doing something that matters for others motivated all of the women who spoke of politics and power. These leaders wrestled with the need for and nature of becoming political in order to achieve valuable outcomes for others. Hazel reported about her own struggle, "I find that sometimes the right decision is made for the wrong reasons. And I have satisfied myself with knowing that the right decision was made. But there's part of me that's thinking, the right decision was made for all the wrong reasons. That's difficult." Even so, Hazel Loucks and other leaders, rather than not being politically involved, prefer to live with the satisfaction that the right outcome prevailed.

Chapter Six

Living and Leading From Values

Values enable us to know what to do and what not to do. Begley (1999) defined values as "those conceptions of the desirable which motivate individuals and collective groups to act in particular ways to achieve particular ends" (p. 237). Leaders whose actions align with clearly articulated values create confidence and inspire trust. Value conflicts are increasingly frequent in education as differing racial, ethnic, and religious groups intermingle in schools, and individuals and groups regularly disagree on policies, procedures, and outcomes. School leaders on a regular basis select or reject various courses of action or behavior in order to make decisions and solve problems that involve conflicting values. Those who call for change as well as those with compelling interests in the status quo are interested in and affected by the values of school leaders. Moral leadership opens up traditionally ignored social justice issues through inquiry into the purpose of schools in a democratic society (Furman, 2003; Larson & Murtadha, 2002). Moral leadership involves much more than compliance towards bureaucratic rules or authorities. Moral leadership requires thoughtful consideration of the value, meaning, and purpose of schooling to meet increasingly diverse and complex challenges in a pluralistic society.

A dimension of leadership theory that includes values and ethics of leaders centers on the moral purpose of leadership (Sergiovanni, 1992). Moral purpose in school leadership is concerned with right and wrong (Furman, 2003), serving the common good (Fullan, 2003), developing a common sense of purpose (Fullan, 2003; Furman, 2003; Sergiovanni, 1992, 1994), and developing leadership potential in others (Fullan, 2003;

Lambert, 1998). School leaders frequently face ethical dilemmas for which there are no obvious right or wrong solutions. Moral leadership may be expressed not only in response to the more obvious daily ethical dilemmas, such as justice for one group at the expense of another, but also in attention to the mundane policies and structures of schools that contain inequities and have ethical implications. Wise leaders know that every social arrangement benefits some people at the expense of others (Lashway, 1996). Assuming that schools automatically embody desirable standards is "ethically naïve, if not culpable" (Starratt, 1991, p. 187). We sought to understand more fully how the participants in our study understood their ethical calling as leaders.

The participants in our study provide a clear model for leadership defined by moral authority, derived from purpose and clarity of values (Fullan, 2003; Sergiovanni, 1999). We learned from direct responses and by implication about the values of our participants, all expert leaders and problem solvers. We asked direct and indirect questions about values. For example, "How would you describe the values behind your typical approach to decision making?" was a direct question. We asked for motivation behind the risk taking implied in creative insubordination, assuming that motivation would involve values. We asked, "Do you perceive differences in your priorities/values and those of the establishment in your district/organization?" A final question addressing values was, "To what are you unalterably committed?" Their answers to these four questions illustrate clear values that are reflected in their decision making, motivate the risks they take, and determine their unalterable commitments. These leaders live their values in ways not often compromised by the bureaucracies in which they work and lead. Chapter 4 presented evidence that values motivate their risk taking. In chapter 5 we discussed issues arising when a leader's values conflict with those of the establishment. In this chapter we examine themes in the participants' responses to the questions about values in decision making and their unalterable commitments. How the leaders in our study live their values can be understood through exploration of five themes: valuing people and relationships, making decisions to benefit children/students, maintaining personal integrity/doing the right thing, honoring diverse perspectives, and expressing spirituality.

DR. ELIZABETH LEWIN

Dr. Elizabeth Lewin's story and ideas about leadership will be shared in this chapter to give a deeper meaning to how values shape professional lives and leadership practices. Elizabeth, or Liz as she prefers to be called, is superintendent of schools in Carbondale, Illinois, a college town located in southern Illinois where she was born. Speaking of her parents, she said, "Both were first-generation college graduates and they shared a vision of making a good life for their children and wanting to make a major contribution to their community." When her parents met at Southern Illinois University, her mother was "an artistically gifted farm girl" and her dad was an "idealistic, smooth-talking, ambitious Marine recently home from Korea." Liz and her three sisters grew up in this talented and educated family that provided a strong foundation for values. Her father, a minister, was active in the Civil Rights Movement during her childhood. In her acceptance speech for the *Dare to Be Great* award in 2004, Liz said,

> My practical, sensitive, and nurturing Mom and ambitious, passionate, and crusading Dad immersed me in opportunity after opportunity to discover and exercise the skills and values I inherited. Before I started school, Dad took me to several Civil Rights marches. I remember holding on to his pant leg as we both watched KKK members in their sheets holding burning torches outside our home when it was rumored that the black and white schools would be merged and Dad would be the principal.

Liz tells about driving her father to preach and to Civil Rights speaking engagements when she was 14. As she drove along, he would practice his sermon or speech, asking Liz for her point of view. When they arrived, Liz often was responsible for collecting the offering. Liz's mother, who did not work outside the home, provided strong support when Liz was one of the first African American students to attend the Southern Illinois University Laboratory School. Liz described how her father "worked two jobs while serving as pastor of a church to pay for my tuition." She remembers that she would "help Dad mow the grass, clean the church, and assist the deacon with repairs before Mom would supervise my piano and flute lessons, then drill me on schoolwork." She continued, "When I shared some of my unpleasant experiences at school, with classmates or teachers who felt blacks were to go to their own schools, Mom and Dad would sound like a harmonious choir as they would say, 'You are there to learn. You are smart, you are strong, you are only responsible for your actions and more importantly you are who we say you are.'" While in college Liz decided to student teach in a town in southern Illinois with a reputation for racial intolerance—in fact, the last town in Illinois to have lynched black people. She was the first African American to student teach or teach in the school. When Liz's mother called to see how her first day of student teaching had gone, she heard a heart-wrenching account of actions of racial bigotry that had been aimed at her daughter. When Liz finished a tearful account of the day, her mother's response was, "I am so proud of you." Her mother's quiet strength and encouragement supported Liz's courage to achieve her goals in spite of obstacles. She always kept in mind her parents' veritable chorus, "Knowledge is the key to success and our purpose on Earth is to spread goodwill and enlighten others. Do the right thing and the right thing will happen." Raised with a strong sense of values based on religious beliefs, as well as moral outrage at racial or any other kind of injustice, Liz learned at an early age from her father's example how to *trouble* the bureaucracy.

Elizabeth has spent a lifetime courageously doing the right thing. Her first teaching job was with the East St. Louis schools. While a volunteer poll watcher for board elections, she was assigned a location where most of the elderly lived. She said,

> I witnessed young men intimidating potential voters to keep them from entering the polls to vote. Appalled that no one was doing anything about it, I went outside and lectured three men like they were my junior high students even though they all stood over six feet tall and were in their thirties. I proceeded to escort those older people with enough spunk inside the polls. I later learned that those young men were carrying guns and were overhead discussing how they were going to deal with me. I learned this when the FBI came knocking on my door one morning shortly after to interview me about the incident.

After she and her family moved to Edwardsville, Illinois, Elizabeth continued community volunteerism along with her career. She accepted an appointment to become the first female alderman and chaired the public safety committee and the finance committee. Viewing political challenges as adventures, she told this story of one tense situation:

My first adventure came after receiving a terrifying call at 1:00 a.m. from an old woman with emphysema. Her neighbor was burning leaves and she could not breathe. She explained that for years she had complained to those men and none of them would do anything. She was pleading and crying and said that now that a woman was on the council she was hopeful. Fortunately for her, my second child had just taken my husband and I through a scare in dealing with asthma-like symptoms that were brought on by environmental factors. So I was motivated to take on this one. I introduced a no-burn ban inside city limits and immediately became public enemy #1 of every hauler, farmer, tire business, and so forth in the town. After the meeting when the ordinance passed, I entered the parking lot to leave and found my car surrounded by trucks and men leaning on them. I took a deep breath and with authority walked toward my car with my teacher look that dared one of them to stop me. They parted and I got out of there as quickly as possible.

Married for 30 years, Liz has two grown children. She has extensive experience as an educator, having taught for 17 years before she became the first African American administrator in the Edwardsville school district. She served as a principal and assistant principal at the large high school of 1,800 students for seven years in Edwardsville, located close to St. Louis. The high school was in need of a new building during her tenure. She was part of the entire process of making that happen, "including running the referendum, working on the design, and assisting with the oversight of construction." She said, "I really believe that it was my background and my cumulative opportunities at financial and leadership positions that prepared me for the superintendent's seat." She moved from being a high school principal to being a superintendent when a board member from Carbondale called and said, "Little Liz, we've been hearing about you." He asked her to come back home to lead. At the board's invitation, she interviewed for the position and became the Carbondale superintendent in 1995.

VALUING PEOPLE AND RELATIONSHIPS

Moral leadership emerges from the values and ethics of leaders themselves (Furman, 2003). An ethic of care opens up possibilities for leaders to "deal with individuals with whom we have relationships, not as representatives of social groups. Leaders who adopt an ethic of care are more likely to see themselves in relationship with others" (Grogan, 2003, p. 25). "Caring is a way of being in relationship, not a set of specific behaviors," Noddings wrote (1992, p. 17). Leaders develop communities of learning with others when they build relationships, and develop shared values of caring, knowledge of and attention to teaching and learning, and inclusiveness (Lambert, 1998; Senge, 1990; Sergiovanni, 1999; Wheatley, 1999).

In articulating values behind decision making, all 18 of the leaders in our study spoke directly to the importance of caring about people and relationships when making decisions. Elizabeth Lewin speaks clearly about the importance of relationships, beginning with family: "I've always felt that women were basically natural team builders. I think our experience of holding families together has given us the skills to lead and to get things accomplished." Her experiences as a mother and her professional life are merged. She insists that educators in her district maintain a clear perspective that their own families come first. When Liz talks about the importance of family, she is clear to educators in her district not only about her values, but also that it is permissible, indeed expected, for them to express and live by what they hold most precious. She said, "I believe that family must come first and that is emphasized whenever I've interviewed for a position. I would not work for a board or in a situation where there was not going to be sensitivity to the parent part of me. If ever a family situation occurred that required my immediate attention, that situation would take precedence."

Three themes emerged from participants' discussions about relationships: nurturing the talents of others, honoring and respecting others, and connecting with others. Care was manifested in their direct statements of values and in the ways they approached decision making. "Caring leadership builds a learning community that includes everyone involved with a school. . . . We must each care in ways that are uniquely our own, realizing that caring emerges from the ground of who we are, moves from inside out, or else it moves no one" (Lyman, 2000, pp. 11, 14).

Nurturing the Talents of Others

Twelve participants specifically talked about the importance of nurturing and developing talents of others. This included the importance of involving others in the decision-making process, especially those who will be affected by the decision. They often deliberately developed the leadership potential of others by involving them in decision making. For example, one person said, "I like people, I want them to succeed and solve their own problems. I value people and want them to feel good about themselves." Others regarded development of others as a leadership responsibility. An assistant superintendent said, "A true leader is when you are grooming people. I'm always grooming people to take my position. I love people." A former superintendent said she hoped to be remembered as a woman who helped other women develop their leadership potential. Five other participants talked directly about nurturing the leadership talents of others. Leadership that consciously nurtures the potential of others is needed in contemporary schools and organizations (Fullan, 2003; Kouzes & Posner, 1997). Empowering others develops competence (Kouzes & Posner, 1997), is based on mutual understandings of the mission of the school (Lambert, 1998), and reflects love and respect for others (Collins, 2001).

Honoring and Respecting Others

Five persons in the study mentioned honoring others as a way of valuing people and relationships. A superintendent summarized the importance of care and respect in saying she believes that people-centered schools align the system to accomplish all that needs to be done. Elizabeth Lewin spoke to honoring and respecting others when she described what had been her most difficult decision, the termination of a building principal involved in a conflict with faculty. She said, "I think the difficulty in it was because I saw the value and understood the position of both, the principal and the faculty. I really think that the differences they had were insignificant, but neither seemed able to get beyond the little things. I valued both points of view." Speaking of the work she did prior to the termination, Liz spoke of investing time in conflict resolution with both parties and in trying to build a good relationship with the principal. Even though the principal was terminated, "the faculty learned that I value everyone's contribution and will work hard to solve a problem. They learned that I value treating each person in the manner I want to be treated." Another leader articulated her mission of respect for others when she said, "I as a leader, I am conscious of needing to honor the people to whom I'm speaking, and so I choose language very specifically." When making decisions that affect others, two respondents articulated a practice of respecting the feelings of others. For example, a dean said, "Decisions involve people and their lives and careers, and I approach those decisions thoughtfully." A former principal spoke of always working in ways that safeguarded the dignity of those with whom she worked. For each of these leaders, honoring others through respect and care was part of their being. Respect for others lays the foundation for relationships that support the moral purpose of schools.

Connecting With Others

With a genuine sense of caring for others, several of the participants talked about the importance of connecting with others for a common purpose. Their thoughts illustrate values that make relationships of equality possible. One former principal said, "I believe people need to connect personally to perform at their best professionally." Others discussed the difference that relationships can make in difficult times. For example, a former superintendent described tenuous times in her district during and after a strike. She said that it was her relationship with the union president, their mutual respect for one another, that allowed them to create healing processes in the district. Another former superintendent described the importance of strong relationships when she said, "You can take people to a whole different level if they respond to you beyond the formal authority [of the position]." Elizabeth Lewin told of personally connecting with staff experiencing anxiety during the process by which the district restructured and implemented grade-level centers. Liz said, "Uprooting individuals who have been in buildings for a lot of years is difficult because it creates high levels of anxiety. In order to minimize that anxiety, I held periodic building meetings as well as individual counseling sessions with those experiencing the most anxiety."

MAKING DECISIONS TO BENEFIT CHILDREN/STUDENTS

What is best for children/students, *what is best for kids*, is a guiding value that resonates with many educators. At the same time, what is best for stu-

dents can also be used in schools and agencies to justify multiple and con-
tradictory courses of action. It is not uncommon for different factions on
a given issue to claim they have the *right* solution because what's best for
students matches the values that *they* hold near and dear. The issues confronting school leaders when individuals or groups conflict based on different conceptions of what is best for students illustrate complexities of
the moral dimensions of leadership. Conversations and conflicts reveal
different views of right and wrong and, in the best of circumstances, create dialogue where members of the community seriously aim to develop
shared beliefs about what is best for all. Clearly articulated, shared beliefs
are critical for the development of a school guided by moral leadership
(Sergiovanni, 1999). Ongoing dialogue can clarify what is most important
to a particular group (Kouzes & Posner, 1997; Lambert, 1998; Senge,
1990). Effective leaders respect group values as well as the organization's
integrity, developing in everyone a clear understanding of the sacred center of the community where those values that everyone holds paramount
reside. At the same time, leaders see what must change and then work to
get others to reframe the problems and formulate solutions based on commonly held values (Goleman, Boyatzis, & McKee, 2002; Lambert, 1998).

Making decisions that benefit children/students was mentioned by 16
of the leaders in our study. Their stories demonstrate how they actualize
the value of *what is best for kids* in many ways, in diverse institutions, and
through multiple roles. Their responses also illustrate how they identify
and make explicit the values and beliefs that define the center of their
school communities. They balance disciplined ongoing inquiry about decisions that benefit children with action toward those ends (Fullan, 2003),
thereby revealing their values to others. They model strong communications skills that value and respect differing perspectives, while at the same
time holding themselves and others to high standards. They seek practices
proven to benefit children as opposed to practices that in actuality benefit
adults, or simply perpetuate the system.

To be more specific, 13 of the participants in our study articulated
what's best for students as a standard they use particularly in making decisions. In speaking of how she makes decisions, Elizabeth Lewin said, "I
take a look at who will be impacted and how they're going to be impacted.
But I think the value that I use most in drawing a conclusion or decision

is fairness. It is important to me that my decisions be fair, and ultimately what's best for the majority of the children, long term." Holding oneself and others accountable to the standard of what's best for students is not simple, as Liz's comment illustrates. Reflecting the commitment and responsibility to children that were expressed by many in the study, one leader said, "I just think the work we do is critical. And I think we're at a critical point for our profession that requires serious inquiries, our best effort for the children." Also developing the theme of what's best for students was the expectation that opinions and decisions be explained and justified. For example, a leader described the process by which she and her staff at the Illinois State Board of Education make decisions related to large grants. She said her priority is always to "get the biggest bang for our buck. They know I'm going to ask them what the priorities are, what's the benefit for kids?" The difference between values articulated by an individual or group and the values to which they actually commit through actions can vary considerably. Two subthemes emerged in the interview data relative to decision making and what is best for students: taking risks in the interest of children/students, and consideration of who will be affected by a decision.

Taking Risks for Children/Students

Conflicts arise from cultural pluralism if school leaders simply reflect the culture and interests of the dominant class in opposition to the culture and interests of nondominant groups. Bringing the opinions, culture, and interests of nondominant groups into the conversation is important to creating schools that value all students (Reitzug, 1994). Eight leaders in our study talked about risks associated with making decisions based on the best interests of children. For example, one principal described the process by which she led her teachers to abandon the district reading curriculum to meet the needs of the students in her school. "I think that taking the risk is something you have to do. If I feel I'm right, or if I feel that it's going to make a difference in the lives of my students, my staff, my family, then I'm willing to be forceful." Elizabeth Lewin gave an example of a risk she took when bureaucratic rules did not allow her to do what was best for children, given the circumstances presented by their Hispanic families. Liz explained,

No one could show proof of being in the area or the country legally. There were several small children clearly in need of school, but because of a statewide focus on residency, every district made sure that students were legally enrolled. Basically I assisted the Hispanic students by labeling them as homeless individuals. They had moved from shack to shack to work area apple orchards. These were individuals who were in our area wanting to be in our schools because they knew we had services that would meet the needs of their children in terms of language.

In choosing the homeless category, she gave the family time to get proper documentation together. "We started providing them services—getting the little ones in school, providing them with some health services because they were badly in need of medical care." The risk was that what she did could have been challenged by anyone in the community, and that could have been embarrassing for the family and for the district. "But to me," she said, "the bottom line is that children come first. And if we were the only ones willing to provide the services, it was worth the risk to me personally to do that. I take risks to do what I need to do to help children."

Who Will Be Affected?

Five of the leaders in our study mentioned regularly considering who will be affected by their decisions. Processes of shared decision making reflect commitments to relationships rather than strategies to get people to do work. One person said, "I believe in shared decision making, because I respect the integrity of the people I work with and I feel they have a lot to offer." Sharing her method of arriving at decisions, one leader talked about the benefits of including those affected by decisions in the process. She said, "It's really hard, long, and arduous at times, but having done it both ways, sometimes you can 'eke' through without getting stakeholder involvement, but later on you have to redo everything you've done because you left out a core constituent group. When I chair or lead a task force or meeting, I think it's real important that relationship issues are addressed." Consideration of the greater good was another aspect of making decisions based on what's best for students. One leader reflected optimism in making decisions, describing how she asks, "Is it going to make something better? Is it going to be better for children, students, adults, and the community? If it is beneficial for the greatest good, then I just say, go for it. If it's the right decision (based on greater good), then we should move forward." When making decisions based on children, she continued, "I'm willing to take the fallout. Whatever it takes, I'll take the guff."

MAINTAINING PERSONAL INTEGRITY AND DOING THE RIGHT THING

Many women go into education because they believe they can make a positive difference for children. If a particular course of action is not right for children, many women will risk their jobs and reputations to do what they believe to be right. "Honest, high values are counter-cultural (in some situations); surviving takes some skill. The playing field is complex and not for the faint of heart. Integrity can require courage to proceed under heavy fire" (Gupton & Slick, 1996, p. 56). Values play a critical role in a leader's integrity or credibility. Covey (1990) defined integrity as behavior that "honestly matches words and feelings with thoughts and actions, with no desire other than for the good of others, without malice or desire to deceive, take advantage, manipulate or control; constantly reviewing your intent as you strive for congruence" (pp. 107–108). Goleman, Boyatzis, and McKee (2002) defined integrity as congruence between values and behavior. Maintaining personal integrity or doing the right thing was expressed as a value in the words of 16 of the leaders in our study. Four themes emerged from their responses: fairness, a willingness to leave or move on, admitting mistakes, and credibility.

Fairness

Seven participants talked about the importance of making the right and fair thing happen by listening to their consciences or inner voices. For example, Ola Bundy, in her role as a dogged advocate for young women athletes in Illinois, described the tension of conflicting values when she said, "Maybe sometimes [your sense of what is right or fair] can put you in court if you need to take a stand for what is right." Bundy described taking a stand after painstaking research on the rules and regulations and, ultimately, making decisions that were the "right and fair things to do." A retired high school principal expressed her sense of fairness and compassion this way: "You tell me, who are the good kids and who are the bad kids? I treated them all the same." Her values and sense of fair play prevented her from labeling or stereotyping high school students. Rebecca van der Bogert talked about her long-standing penchant for standing up for what she believed was right. "Even when I was in high school, if I felt there was some injustice, I just felt like it was worth the risk to stand up and find a way to help the right things to happen." Becky reflected on ways that her values guide her decisions when she said, "You just have to make the right thing happen. Not that I always know the right thing, but I think that if you have a sense of compassion, or fairness and equity, that you just have to step out." Another leader related fairness, credibility, and risk when she said, "You must always do what's right. And you have to live with yourself, but you have to weigh the risks. Is winning the battle more important than winning the war? You have to ask yourself, is this my fight? What are the consequences of what I do?" Elizabeth Lewin emphasized fairness as the value that she uses most in coming to a decision. She said, "I am passionate about my work and have been since I began my career in the classroom. Throughout educational history, many children have been let down by adults. It is my desire not to be among that count of the adults who failed our children. Frankly, I refuse to be among that count." From her perspective, letting the children down would be an ultimate unfairness.

Willingness to Leave or Move On

In certain circumstances, leaders can find themselves in positions where their values conflict unalterably with those of their organizations. While we didn't ask the participants how they would ultimately handle incongruence between their values and the organization's, seven persons volunteered that they never worried about leaving a situation that might cause them to compromise their values. For example, one person described a difficult situation when her values guided her to make an unpopular decision, saying, "I thought if it means my job, it means my job. I made a fair decision." A dean described a difficult "time of intensity" when she said, "You're not buying my soul. You can fire me, but I'm not doing it. It was liberating." Elizabeth Lewin said, "When I am taking a risk I have already prepared myself for a worst-case scenario even if it means my job. . . . When people say, well, you could have risked your job, I remind them that there are a lot of opportunities to make money. I am motivated by opportunities to get things accomplished and improving the quality of life for our children."

Admitting Mistakes

Another difficult aspect of integrity involves handling mistakes. Four participants discussed their attitudes about mistakes. They regarded mistakes as opportunities to learn. In describing one of the most difficult situations in her career as a high school principal, one leader talked about a situation where the misbehavior of a group of students had serious implications for their futures. She stressed with others in the school that it was important for the students to take responsibility, forgive and be forgiven, and then everyone needed to move on. A retired regional superintendent said about decisions and mistakes, "I don't worry about my decisions after I've made them. I evaluate them after a period of time, and certainly I've made mistakes. And then I want to make a point to go back and tell those others who wanted to do it a certain way they were right and I was wrong. But I don't worry about it. I just change my ideas when needed." Each has a strong sense of being open to the possibility of mistakes, taking responsibility, forgiving and forgetting, and then making the future better.

Credibility

Credibility involves clear convictions and the will to stand up for one's values. One participant expressed the importance of credibility when she said, "People have to be able to count on us, that our value system will influence all decisions." When those values are clearly articulated and behaviors match values, others perceive leaders as honest and trustworthy (Kouzes & Posner, 1997). Elizabeth Lewin's credibility shows in the effectiveness of the process she uses to share decision making:

> I do a lot of thinking out loud with colleagues. Basically, I bring people along with me in my decision making. Very often I've been able to help others to reach a desired conclusion, or to verbalize it before I do, primarily because I have made them privy to my values, my information, and my thought patterns. Through questioning and information gathering, I can ba-

sically lay things out, almost like putting together a puzzle, I engage in this process for everyone to see.

Stephanie Pace Marshall (see chapter 8) expressed her commitment to integrity: "I think I have a reputation that when I put my name on something you can take it to the bank. What I say is what I mean." Describing the importance of honoring one's word, sense of integrity, and self, she said, "The only thing that defines an organism is its sense of self—its core, what it is, who it is, what it represents, its essence." Another person described her sense of self and credibility in these words, "I'd like to be remembered as someone who is helpful, and follows through on what I've been asked to do. That's very important in terms of credibility."

HONORING DIVERSITY BY RESPECTING OTHERS

Leaders address issues of diversity and equity through agendas and leadership practices that are inclusive. Values of inclusion and connection are valuable to leadership (Dunlap & Schmuck, 1995; Gupton & Slick, 1996). Often, women's unique perspectives are based upon their historic status as outsiders within the ranks of school administrators. Minority women in particular may bring to their roles a sense of difference that has instilled in them compassion toward children and others (AhNee-Benham & Cooper, 1998). Elizabeth Lewin understands from personal experience what it feels like not to be respected because of race. She was the first black person to student teach or teach in a small southern Illinois town. Her grandparents lived there and she was eager to spend the student-teaching quarter with them, save the expense of an apartment, and eat her Grandma's cooking. She told how on the first day of school, "My Granddad had dressed in his Sunday suit and pulled out the Sunday car and proudly dropped me off in front of the junior high on my first day with the students." When she walked into the faculty room for the first time, the whole room of teachers filed out. That was one of the quieter insults she endured on her first day. As a superintendent, she still understands that "as a female of color, anything, once it has been verbalized by me is going to be scrutinized in and out. So I really don't make decisions without having volumes and volumes of rationale and documented support for the decision that I have made."

New concepts and practices of leadership premised on social justice will create schools that serve all children (Grogan, 1999). Grogan explains one such practice, the desire to encourage debate and dissensus, is at the heart of feminist poststructural approaches to leadership. Encouraging open dialogue that uncovers different perspectives contrasts sharply with leadership practices that require consensus at all costs. Twelve persons in our study expressed the importance of honoring diverse perspectives as a value in decision making. Two themes emerged from these responses: the importance of appreciating different perspectives and recognizing the potential of others.

Appreciate Different Perspectives

The importance of appreciating differing perspectives was clearly recognized by 10 participants in the study. Voices of dissension provide greater insight into issues and open up possibilities for solutions or courses of action previously not considered. A superintendent values the opinions of others and particularly those with whom she disagrees, because she wants "a full breadth of opinions, all the diverse views brought forward so that we can do the best analysis." Another person spoke of what she does at the end of a decision-making process, when she has gathered information, opinions, feelings, and reactions, and "connects them all to make meaning." Continuing to honor relationships when in disagreement with others was specifically mentioned by five of the participants. For these leaders, the relationships they nurtured were based on mutual respect that endured through disagreements. They told stories of disagreeing openly with others, but doing so in a way that maintained the dignity of all. A former principal said she was always careful to safeguard the dignity of others because she did not want them to look foolish or to embarrass them. A superintendent expressed her respect for the integrity of others this way, "Well, my core values are a genuine respect for the integrity, the ideas, and the viewpoints of others. I truly believe even with those who strongly disagree, and as misguided as I might think their conclusions are, that there's always a grain of truth in their viewpoint. So I definitely have a healthy respect for the views of others. . . . I want a full breadth of opinions." A former superintendent explained, "I like surrounding myself with people who see things differently. It [respect] doesn't come by doing everything people want. It comes by treating them fairly and with dignity and looking at the issues and trying to use what tools you have to come to sound decisions." Strong relationships with others based on common values, but also open to dissent, are critical to the processes of leadership.

In the process of listening to the viewpoints of others, several participants mentioned openness to being influenced by others. One person said, "I respect the integrity of those I work with and I feel they have a lot to offer." A former superintendent expressed the idea in these words, "All people have valuable input. They have a different perspective that can help you view a problem from a different angle, from different life experiences. Rarely ever is input worthless." Stephanie Pace Marshall (see chapter 8) elaborated, "I am as interested in how people felt or reacted, what they sensed, what their heart tells them or what their intuition says, as I am about the research they might have done. I take it all in. Then I synthesize. I look for patterns and connect them. I connect them all."

Recognize Potential in Others

Eight of the participants in the study communicated a strong commitment to belief in the potential of others. Rebecca van der Bogert described her early years as a principal, when she changed the format for building meetings to make them more collaborative and professional. She said, "I demonstrated my strong belief in the staff as competent, intelligent, and articulate participants in this thing called school." She develops and builds on the talents and ideas of others and lives by the philosophy, "If it was your idea, you get the credit; it doesn't diminish me in any way." A university dean said, "You don't know what's going to cause the big things to happen. So if you see people doing good things or somebody comes to you with a good idea, fan it. . . . People's talents are amazing to me. . . . Faculty operationalize a vision with their ideas." Relative to recognizing potential and nurturing the talents of others, Elizabeth Lewin takes seriously her role as a role model. "I realize that I'm one of a few African American females in a chief executive officer position to serve as a role model for young ones out there. So I watch very carefully what I do and that's why I lean so heavily on my own personal values in making decisions. I did not get here by modeling what I saw that 'successful male' do to get where he is." Liz explained how when someone expresses that they want to go into administration, "I start immediately providing them with some guidance, even to the point of helping them select courses. . . . When I advise an aspiring administrator, I ask why it is they want to do what I do, knowing that they have little knowledge of what I do. When I hear answers such as 'to reach more children' or 'to better serve the families in our community,' then I am pleased to offer my support and counsel."

EXPRESSING SPIRITUALITY

To interpret the data, we defined spirituality as the diverse ways individuals answer their longings to be connected with the largeness of life (Palmer, 2000). Spirituality was considered in the universal sense as an aspect of being human that transcends sectarian boundaries. Spirituality included expressions based on religious practice, creativity, intuition, wisdom, beliefs, appreciation for others, and compassion. When asked about the values that guide their decisions, participants in this study expressed their spirituality in several ways. For some, spirituality was manifested in their religious faith. A question about values naturally led them to talk about faith. Others expressed spirituality in terms of intuition, mission, or soul. Eight persons responded from a spiritual perspective to questions about values in their decision-making processes. The participants' responses include both secular and religious expressions of spirit. Keyes, Hanley-Maxwell, and Capper (1999) define spiritually guided leadership as resting on three dimensions of relationship: a relationship with self, a relationship with a power or force greater than oneself, and relationship with others (p. 229). All three dimensions are interrelated and can have many varied expressions.

Relationship With Self

Relationship with self involves a journey of the soul, often resulting in an encounter with both light and shadow aspects of life and oneself. Ethics that are rooted in soul guide individuals and organizations to better understand deeply held identity, beliefs, and values (Bolman & Deal, 2003). One participant has learned the difference between "wearing your heart on your sleeve and leading with your heart." She reveals soul when she explains, "Leading with the heart is leading with the passion about making decisions for the children. . . . That's who we are about," an insight arrived at through processes of reflection. Stephanie Pace Marshall (see chapter 8) relies upon her sense of self within the context of the whole to make tough decisions. "If there are decisions that impact my own life, I go back to the principles and commitments and 'story' that matter to me. I give myself an opportunity to listen, to pay attention, and notice my own voice. What is my heart telling me? What is my intuition telling me? Does this honor who I am?" Valuing credibility also reflects valuing the relationship with one's self or soul.

Relationship With a Power Greater Than Oneself

Four participants expressed spirituality in terms of reliance on a power greater than oneself. Their remarks reflected their religious practices. Three of the four were African American and one was Caucasian. Hazel Loucks said, "I have a very strong Christian background, and I know the difference between right and wrong and I believe that everyone is created equal. We are all important, we just have different-shaped shovels to dig with." This response testifies to her religious faith and its influence in her daily life. The journey of spirit for African American women often reflects the cultural experience of lives affected by the intersecting forces of racism, sexism, and poverty. According to Murtadha-Watts (1999), confronted with challenges brought on by these cultural realities, African American women respond with a deep spiritual strength through individual efforts, community activism, church alliances, sisterhood, and fraternal organizations to provide hopeful action for change.

> African American women in leadership positions often draw upon profound historical traditions of inner spiritual strength as well as an activist ethic of risk/urgency. Through forms of God-talk, moving and acting in conversations with 'God,' 'asking of the good Lord,' 'the Spirit,' 'Providence,' and the many ways of relating to spirituality in their lives, they are strengthened to set goals, to see hope and possibility, and to love—despite gains and losses in life (hooks, 1994, p. 3). (Murtadha-Watts, 1999, pp. 155–156)

Turning to our participants, an African American principal expressed her reliance upon a higher power in these words, "I'm always praying. I'm always seeking higher guidance. And so, therefore, if I say or do anything, I'm not expecting it to turn out wrong. And I'm not expecting it to be something that would make everybody else around me uncomfortable." An assistant superintendent said, "I keep saying the Lord is making a way for women to take over the world. I believe that women are very compassionate, we're caring, we're nurturing." Accepting that her decisions may not be successful by worldly standards, Elizabeth Lewin said, "I am comfortable . . . because I've decided that it is what's right and I answer only to myself and my God. Whenever I believe something is right, whatever risk may exist from a bureaucracy, board, or any tangible body, it is pretty low priority to me because I answer to something much higher." For these leaders, decisions of daily life and work flow naturally from the guidance of their religious beliefs and practices. Each is a risk-taking activist.

Relationships With Others

Three participants in our study expressed spirituality in terms of their relationships with others. Leaders with soul bring spirit to groups of people who then create meaningful change (Bolman & Deal, 1995). Spirituality, in this sense, requires leaders who are capable of connecting with others by interacting within larger and larger circles of participation and meaning. Through inclusiveness, as groups work through similar dilemmas, a leader acknowledges each individual's struggles with questions of meaning and purpose, power and assertiveness. A central office administrator talked about her mission in life, "Love of what we do for others, love and relationships are valued. . . . And I think everybody has a gift. We have to find it. I think that's what we're supposed to do—help people find their gift." A dean expressed how others inspire her and how she has learned to connect particular talents to the needs of the group: "People's talents are amazing to me. . . . We have to have the courage of our convictions."

Finding the sacred center of a group requires searching for the patterns of complexity and multiplicity, guiding people towards a sense of purpose and connection to something more powerful than themselves. A leader's role in that process is to provide the avenues of dialogue and possibility (Bolman & Deal, 1995; Briskin, 1998; Issacs, 1999). A leader's role is to provide opportunities for others to create and realize their own potential to make a difference. Telling a story about a difficult decision, Stephanie

Pace Marshall (see chapter 8) said, "So I'm always looking for ways to offer people that possibility. . . . It was really important for me to say, this is not about image. It's about something much more important [the purpose of the organization]." Helping others to find meaning and a higher purpose is important to her. "It's all about consciously creating conditions, having conversations, using language, and inviting people into possibility," she said.

ETHICS OF CARE, JUSTICE, AND CRITIQUE

A focus on the moral and ethical dimensions of education leads to questions about purposes and moral dilemmas in contemporary schools. Starratt (1994) proposes a multidimensional ethical framework that includes an ethic of care, ethic of justice, and ethic of critique. The ethic of care focuses on relationships. The ethic of justice provides a blueprint for social order through governance by observing justice. The ethic of critique questions the efficacy of bureaucratic structures in schools and the status quo. Starratt argues that the three ethics complement and enrich one another, that no one alone is sufficient for the creation of ethical schools in contemporary society, and that each ethic requires the strong convictions embedded in the other.

We looked at participants' responses based upon Starratt's three ethics: the ethic of caring (What do our relationships demand of us?), justice (How can we govern ourselves fairly?), and critique (Where do we fall short of our own ideals?). Analysis at this level revealed new levels of complexity in the blending of leadership practices with values. Responses of all 18 revealed an ethic of care; responses of 16 reflected an ethic of justice; and responses of 17 revealed an ethic of critique. Their abilities to live their values yet function from multidimensional frameworks may explain the leadership successes of the participants in our study.

The ethical foundations upon which leaders in our study made tough decisions were not confined simply to the ethic of care, discussed earlier in the chapter. The ethic of justice was a critical aspect of their leadership. Responding to interview questions about making tough decisions, 10 said explicitly that they would never go against rules or policies in their institution. Troubling the organization did not mean breaking the rules. Determining the ethical course involved fairness and careful consideration of whom the decision might affect. Ola Bundy put it this way: "I was honest to my own detriment sometimes. I would tell them the truth, you know, if there was a situation with the violation of rules or ethics or whatever, or with the bylaws of the association. I would tell them the truth, or if I made a decision, you know, like the selection of officials, I always told the officials exactly what my decision was based on. I always thought it was important to be honest."

On the other hand, when dealing with bureaucratic rules or policies, the leaders in our study were quite clear that they would not blindly adhere to a rule if it violated their values. A former superintendent addressed the core of ethical leadership when she said, "There is not a rule to cover everything. That's what leadership is all about. Otherwise you would just have someone read the rules." Along the same lines, an assistant superintendent said, "Work within the system and still do what needs to be done based on what's best for kids." The leaders "worked within the system" by knowing the rules. "I was never insubordinate to the rules, objectives, or bylaws of the association. . . . I always did my homework. . . . I never supported anything I hadn't thoroughly researched the reasons for and against," said Ola Bundy.

Starratt's ethic of critique is displayed in participants' values guiding them to question the system. As stated before, decisions based on clearly defined values of caring and justice provided the participants with perspective to understand when organizations or practice fell short in terms of mission. Eight leaders in the study articulated clearly answering to a higher standard. They shared how they developed capacities to critique or *trouble* their organizations. For example, six persons mentioned seeking out and respecting differing perspectives. One person who believes strongly in the importance of respect for differences said,

I think that if two people are in a room and they both agree, one of them isn't necessary. I think it's real important that we honor difference and seek it out so that we can stretch our minds to new ways of thinking. And sometimes it's really painful and messy. And I'd really just as soon not do it sometimes. But my experience tells me that it's just real beneficial, that we have to think differently in the ways we see the world. And through that we can create different kinds of synergy.

A passion for justice and equity motivated our participants to question practices or policies in their schools and organizations. Hazel Loucks said, "Really, to deal with an issue (of injustice) I ask myself—can I get around this issue or is confrontation the best way? But sometimes, confrontation won't do any good whatsoever. Then I have to be very creative and think about how I can make happen what needs to happen. I believe it is well worth the risk." Questioning the status quo is at the heart of the ethic of critique. Unfortunately, the debate between care and justice in particular has often polarized opinion on which is more important. Arguments abound. For example, some say the justice orientation prescribes formulaic remedies (Noddings, 1999). Noddings, however, is careful to emphasize that polarization is not required, saying, "Care theorists usually seek out ends compatible with justice, but we try to achieve them by establishing conditions in which caring itself can flourish" (p. 19). The values and actions of the leaders in this study illustrate how each ethic informs and intertwines with the others.

CONCLUSIONS

Leithwood and Steinbach (1995) have studied the role of values in problem-solving processes of school principals and superintendents. They found that dominant values play an explicit role that directly impacts leadership behaviors at key points of decision-making processes. The more expert administrators use principles (values) to interpret the problems, frame long-term goals, and provide a context within which choices could be made by all involved in solving the problem. Experts more frequently draw upon principles and values in solving ill-structured problems and give greater attention to consequences for students. The expert leaders in our study demonstrate unwavering commitment to clear values consistent with the moral imperative of school leadership. The participants in our study asked *why* and *why not*; they based actions that troubled the bureaucracy upon their values and strong convictions about justice, equity, and the potential of all constituents. Fullan (2003) cautions leaders to maintain a moral compass by continuously reexamining the status quo. Values, acting as a perceptual screen, enable leaders to focus attention on what matters in difficult situations and everyday decision making. Those who lead well use principles and values routinely in problem solving. Clear values arise from integrity, enhance an educational leader's credibility, and contribute to bonding and shared vision in a community. Concern for community and caring, often seen as women's values, in fact are central to moral leadership in the service of all children, whatever a leader's gender.

The participants in our study may or may not identify themselves as feminists. We did not ask that question. Nevertheless, embedded in their decision-making values is an ethic of care that has been an emphasis in feminist writing about leadership. How they spend time, the responsiveness they show to others, how they value connections and community— all reveal an affinity for relational leadership practices. The values they express center around respect for self, others, and the students they serve. Similar values resonate with many. What distinguishes these leaders is their capacity to see injustice clearly and work within the system to create changes to remedy injustice in this increasingly diverse society. They clearly are expert problem solvers who know how to trouble their organizations. Their stories show us the way to trouble our own schools to serve all children in our contemporary postmodern communities of difference (Shields, 2003). What these leaders have in common, what caused us to select them for our study, is an uncommon understanding of how to bring about change, in part through living and leading from values.

Chapter Seven

Redefining Leadership:
New Ways of Doing and Being

In this book we have been about the serious work of redefining leadership. The work is serious because the critical needs of children, families, and the global interdependent world call for educational systems in all countries that will teach us what we need to know as a species to survive and live into our full humanity. Past understandings of leadership from a paradigm of power and dominance are not equal to the challenges of today and have in fact contributed to the challenges of today. Three themes in our data speak to new ways of *doing* leadership, including new understandings of power in the practice of leadership. These themes are the developing of collaborative decision-making processes, pushing the bureaucratic boundaries, and claiming power through politics. A final theme, living and leading from values, implies new understandings of what leadership is *for* (Furman, 2003), and speaks clearly to integrating one's *being* into the work of leading. One point is clear: there is no agreed-upon definition of the concept of leadership (Leithwood & Duke, 1999). We contend that the leaders in our study are living out a redefinition of leadership that emanates from a constructive postmodern paradigm aimed at social reconstruction.

The concept of postmodern leadership, called post-heroic leadership by some, offers a new understanding of what leadership is and implies new ways of doing the work of leadership. Just as there is no agreed-upon definition of leadership, neither is there a single definition of postmodern leadership (Chapman, Sackney, & Aspin, 1999; Furman, 2002; Willower & Forsyth, 1999). A critical-theory perspective infuses moral and ethical dimensions throughout all categories of leadership practice; so too, by extension does postmodernism. Postmodernism implies resistance to the status quo, including deconstructing the injustices and impersonal hierarchical bureaucratic leadership practices that still characterize too many schools. Postmodernist leadership rooted in a critical perspective moves us away from certainties and toward social justice, including alternative images of leadership. Emphasis on social justice is an aspect of critical postmodern thinking about leadership. Writing about leadership for social justice, Larson and Murtadha (2002) explain that one strand of social justice theory is about "deconstructing existing logics of leadership" (p. 136), clearly also a postmodern claim. They stand with those critical scholars who "have shown that an enduring allegiance to theories of leadership oriented toward maintaining stability through universal theories and hierarchical visions of schooling has maintained inequity in education" (p. 137), including inequity of opportunity for women who would lead. In a second strand, Larson and Murtadha discuss new images of leadership emerging in the work of feminist scholars and African American scholars and leaders for social justice. These images include "an ethic of care rooted in concerns for relationships rather than roles" (p. 140), and leaders who allow spirituality and love to have a place in leadership. Larson and Murtadha's third strand focuses on constructing theories, systems, and processes of leadership that promote social justice. Scholars who advocate and leaders who create multicultural communities of difference through democratic leadership are important to this third strand, and to increasing equity and social justice in schools. Leaders for social justice, including many of the leaders we studied, are about the work of social reconstructionism.

Furman (2002) has written, "Clearly there is no agreed-upon definition for 'postmodernism.' Giroux (1992) has called the term a 'shifting signifier' (p. 51)—dynamic rather than static in its meanings" (p. 54). This notion of the meaning of the term as something that shifts is helpful in sorting out different strands of thinking about postmodernism. Furman presents an analysis that is helpful, categorizing the scholarship into three facets of postmodernism as it relates to the social world: descriptive social theory, constructive social theory, and oppositional/deconstructive social theory. According to Furman (2002), descriptive social theory clarifies a picture of this contemporary age, characterized by rapid advancement and globalization of technology, one of the major factors leading to a global culture. The theorists in this category make real the multiplicity and interdependence of the global culture. She writes, "Descriptive postmodernism gives us some inkling of the changes that are occurring in *how we think* as humans in society" (p. 55), including that "it becomes necessary to give up the certainties of the modern era about our own cultural (and racial) superiority, the rightness of our value systems and of our religious beliefs" (p. 55). Descriptive postmodernism offers a worldview that differs from the parochial views we tend to have when we view reality only from the perspective of our own culture.

Furman describes oppositional/deconstructive social theory as an approach to "deconstructing the modernist paradigm" (p. 57), particularly the modernist/positivist certainties of knowledge, including belief that processes of reason through objective and disinterested inquiry can lead to any certainties at all. According to Furman, "It is this negating aspect of postmodernism that is troublesome to many educational analysts and has been critiqued as nihilistically denying the positive contributions of 'modernist' theory and research in education without offering constructive alternatives" (p. 58). Additionally, deconstructive postmodernism seeks to take apart the pieces of the educational system that marginalize students through "epistemic arrogance . . . rigid forms of testing, sorting, and tracking" and curricula that "privileges the histories, experiences, and cultural capital of largely white, middle-class students" (Giroux, 1994, p. 353).

Moving to constructive social theory, Furman (2002) emphasizes that "constructive postmodernism seeks to build a new worldview, a way to live in harmony with nature and with each other as the postmodern age unfolds" (p. 56). These theorists incline towards advocacy for cooperation rather than competition or coercion in human relationships, and for regarding the world as a living organism rather than as a machine. A goal of constructive postmodernism is a "more balanced and ecologically sustainable global community" (Slattery, 1995, p. 31). Valuing and cooperating with those who are different is implied. This facet of postmodern thought echoes the social reconstructionists' beliefs that education is a vehicle for transforming culture, rather than for passing it on.

Although the influence of postmodernism on the field of practice has been limited, it is a topic of considerable interest among academics and points the way to a new age in the field of educational administration where for decades passing on the culture through preserving the status quo has been an expectation, a norm, and an art form. Some of the scholarship associated with postmodern leadership focuses on redefining the essence or meaning of leadership, given the world's pluralism and new scientific understandings of the nature of reality; other scholarship focuses on implications for practice. Constructive postmodernism, as defined by Furman, is influencing the practice of educational administration. This evolving worldview, emerging in part from the rising level of diversity or pluralism, makes *one-best-way* hierarchical leadership difficult to justify (Shields, 2003). Another postmodern influence on educational leadership is Wheatley's (1999) popular analysis of the implications of the new science for leadership. She has provided a different way of thinking about organizations and leadership that is clearly postmodern, even if she does not use that term in either the original (1992) or the revised editions of *Leadership and the New Science*.

THE *DOING* OF LEADERSHIP

The patterns of meaning in our data will be examined in terms of the developing images and practices of postmodern leadership, or what could be called the new ways of *doing* leadership. We will also look at the data in terms of authenticity, or bringing one's whole *being* into leading. The data from this study emphasizes the importance of *both* the doing and being of leadership. Three of the major themes in this book relate to the doing of leadership and echo ideas of constructive postmodernism. In a postmodern world, the traditional views of leaders and the doing of leadership are changing. Senge (1990) wrote,

> Our traditional views of leaders—as special people who set the direction, make the key decisions, and energize the troops—are deeply rooted in an individualistic and nonsystemic worldview. Especially in the West, leaders are heroes—great men (and occasionally women) who 'rise to the fore' in times of crises. Our prevailing leadership myths are still captured by the image of the captain of the cavalry leading the charge to rescue the settlers from the attacking Indians. (p. 340)

Senge advocates for a new view of leadership for learning organizations where leadership "centers on subtler and more important tasks" and "leaders are designers, stewards, and teachers" (p. 340). In developing collaborative decision-making processes, pushing the bureaucratic boundaries, and claiming power in the political arena, all of the leaders we interviewed were bringing about change. They were bringing about change in how leadership is perceived by their very presence and also by their practices, which are changing perceptions of how leadership is done. Blackmore (2002) argues, in fact, that there is "a postmodernist script that characterizes women as good change agents in organizations. Women are seen to be more flexible and to cope with change better than their male colleagues" (p. 59). Their marginalized status as outsiders gives them less investment in preserving the status quo, whatever that may be. "Their power is derived from their difference, their capacities as women to facilitate change" (p. 59), she writes. Speaking also to leadership of women, Heifetz (1994) writes, "Leadership without authority has been the domain to which women have been restricted for ages" (p. 184). Recognizing women's experience as change agents, he states that "women have headed social reform movements dating back more than 150 years, but only recently . . . have their accomplishments been chronicled" (p. 184). Having been denied formal authority roles in most societies, women have had "more latitude for *creative deviance*" (p. 188), Heifetz asserts.

Developing Collaborative Decision-Making Processes

The doing of leadership blends attributes of authority, ambition, and ability. The strongest theme in our data about decision making was the commitment to collaborative decision-making practices by 14 of the 18 participants. Constructive postmodernist leadership implies not a single all-powerful leader making all the decisions, but leaders who build community and meaning through collaborative decision-making practices. Data in chapter 3 suggests most of our participants would agree with Fullan's (2003) words: "It is the combined forces of shared leadership that make a difference. School leadership is a collective enterprise" (p. xv). Recognizing the complexity of shared decision making, the leaders in our study are nevertheless establishing collaborative decision-making practices involving people and information sharing as the new norm. Almost all are comfortable with discretionary decision making, defined as making decisions based on one's own judgment rather than arbitrary bureaucratic rules and policies. Timing, politics, a sound knowledge base, and trusting your instincts were seen as important for productive outcomes. The participants recognize that the outcomes of discretionary decision making can become problematic when people and collaborative processes are not honored.

In a groundbreaking book about the facilitation of individual and organizational change, Heifetz (1994) revisits concepts of leadership, influence, authority, and power. He takes a systems approach, understanding the value of disequilibrium to a living system. He sees asking questions, rather than giving answers, as the role of the leader. His image of leadership is not of a person who gets others to follow a vision, but that "leaders mobilize people to face problems" (p. 15). He addresses both the ends and the essence of leadership. "Tackling tough problems—problems that often require an evolution of values—is the end of leadership; getting that work done is its essence" (p. 26). He distinguishes between two types of problems: technical problems are those to which we already know how the respond, and adaptive problems for which learning is required. Heifetz writes,

> This study examines the usefulness of viewing leadership in terms of adaptive work. Adaptive work consists of the learning required to address conflicts in the values people hold, or to diminish the gap between values people stand for and the reality they face. Adaptive work requires a change in values, beliefs, or behavior. . . . Leadership, as used here, means engaging people to make progress on the adaptive problems they face. Because making progress on adaptive problems requires learning, the task of leadership consists of choreographing and directing learning processes in an organization or community. (pp. 22, 187)

Talking about her leadership beliefs and practices, one of our participants said, "I think most decisions need an adaptive process and I've become a real fan of Ron Heifetz, and what he describes as adaptive leadership. And so I try to model it as best I can." Elaborating, she continued,

> If you believe in adaptive leadership, you don't give answers, but give guidance or support or resources so they can arrive at that themselves with supervision along the way. I don't think you can build or give leadership opportunity unless you believe and value a more problem-solving approach because in that value you're saying that there may not be only one answer to this. There may be several answers. You may not know the answer. I think that is what leadership is all about.

Her description of her own process and Heifetz' theoretical ideas illustrate a clearly postmodern approach to leadership and decision making using collaborative processes to cocreate approaches to solving adaptive problems within a community.

Grogan's (1999) analysis of how collaboration ties together the interrelated themes in qualitative research that she and Brunner conducted with women superintendents is relevant to our work:

> Analysis of the data identifies three dominant themes that recur in all of the discussions: (1) concepts of power; (2) beliefs about decision making; and (3) notions of leadership. These themes are interconnected and often merge with one another. But what becomes clear upon close inspection is how collaboration connects all three. In other words, for the superintendents in the study, power, decision making, and leadership all depend on collaboration. . . . They describe collaboration as their preferred mode of operation, and they seek collaboration on as many issues as possible. (p. 203)

This analysis can also be applied to our data. We also documented that commitment to collaboration in decision making permeated beliefs of our participants about leadership as well as their attitudes toward power and authority.

Pushing the Bureaucratic Boundaries

In chapter 4 we explored attitudes of our participants toward getting things done in bureaucracies through practices of creative insubordination, particularly when conflicts existed between their personal values and bureaucratic rules and policies. In the words of one participant, "I am not stopped by rules that need to be changed. If people are stopped by rules perhaps they are proponents of the status quo." We discovered that counterbureaucratic practices associated with creative insubordination in the classic Morris et al. (1984) study were still alive. Strongly motivated to live and lead from their values, those who claimed creative insubordination were willing to live with the sometimes considerable risks because their personal values had a higher claim than bureaucratic rules or policies. Perhaps of more importance, we also found that five persons were committed to transforming and transcending bureaucratic systems rather than being content with occasional acts of creative insubordination. The leaders in our study not only had personal ambition but also the determination to get things accomplished for children. They were willing to create disequilibrium. They took risks and pushed the boundaries of the largely bureaucratic organizations in which they worked. This work required all of their abilities; in fact, it was strong relationships, their own competence, and the legitimacy of the justifiable that maximized their accomplishments and minimized their risks. They not only pushed the bureaucratic boundaries in their organizations but dared to cross boundaries to new possibilities in their personal and professional journeys.

Hazel Loucks was definitely a boundary crosser. She said, "Never in my life did I envision myself in this type of position. I am the first deputy governor for education and workforce in Illinois and I am the only one in the country. There's nobody else who preceded me to write a rulebook to prepare me or give me a road map." In her words, "Politics has been a different world—sometimes power makes it impossible to do what I believe should be done." Others in the study have also daringly ventured into politics or political positions. Several crossed boundaries when they moved from one type of educational organization to another, making significant career changes where they had to learn all over again how to get things accomplished. Still others were among the first women superintendents, or were the first female or first African American in high-level positions in their organizations. Many returned to school to pursue the degrees that would open doors in their careers. One person, in particular, was aware of getting a doctorate as a boundary-crossing experience, saying it "opened up new parts of her mind." Rebecca van der Bogert has crossed and recrossed boundaries in a career that has never been about position. She said, "I never intended to be a superintendent and have not moved up any ladder. I have been all over the place. Neither my career nor how I do things fits the mold. I can't think of too many instances where I just followed bureaucratic rules." Clearly she enjoys pushing the envelope. "People have an expectation for the [superintendent] role. I do things differently," she said. That so many of the leaders in our study have crossed boundaries in their own lives may be the source of their determination to prevail against the system and the odds to accomplish things for children.

Success with either collaborative decision making or creative insubordination does not happen in the absence of strong relationships. Both of these practices imply the importance of relationships to leadership. By definition, political success is about relationships, such as building networks and coalitions, and engaging in productive negotiations. Drath (1996), from the Center for Creative Leadership, wrote that the beginnings of a relational model of leadership could be seen in the leadership literature. The idea underlying a variety of versions of the model is this:

> Leadership is a property of a social system, an outcome of collective meaning-making, not the result of influence or vision from an individual. Leadership is being created by people making sense and meaning of their work together, and this process, in turn, can bring leaders into being. We could call the idea that leadership is created by a single person *individual leadership*. We might call this idea that leadership is a property of a social system *relational leadership*, pointing to the way it arises in the systemic relationships of people doing work together. (p. 2)

He continues by saying that if leadership is "a property of the relationships that people form when they are doing something together," then leadership is affected by the "quality and nature of those relationships. Good sets of relationships constitute good leadership" (p. 2). This approach to leadership would minimize the prominence and eventually the reality of the leader/follower language so prevalent in this culture. He is among many who believe we need a new language of leadership. He believes that increasing diversity in organizations is calling forth this relational model. "If our organizations are going to embrace differing cultures, they will need to be able to embrace differing values, philosophies, attitudes, ideas, and feelings" (p. 3). Interestingly, he believes that naming the model can help extend the new practices, but that it is the world of leadership practice, such as what we are describing in this book, that is calling this new model into being.

Claiming Power Through Politics

When it emerged in the interviews, we explored the political work of the educational leaders we studied, providing a look at another facet of the doing of leadership. Although not an initial focus of our inquiry, the extensive political activities and awareness of 17 of the 18 participants called for attention. Participation in politics for these participants was typically a conscious decision for the purpose of accomplishing something important to them. In addition to overtly political activities or positions involving collaboration with external groups, many viewed collaboration within their organizations as a political choice. Most participants did not speak of positional power; in fact, some spoke of the instability of positional power. Those who did acknowledge positional power were in overtly political positions. Many relied on networks of interpersonal relationships to accomplish things. For each person who discussed politics, integrity was a concern. They were willing to push the limits for their values and goals, but not to break the law. For the most part, the participants described themselves as *outsiders* who had moved *inside*. For the leaders considered in chapter 5, becoming political was related to developing a more public voice and the ability to behave as an insider even if feeling like an outsider.

In moving to political action, the women in our study traveled beyond what Chase (1995) calls a more typical political pathway taken by women, that is, individual solutions to the collective problem of inequality. This is not to say that their political actions were entirely addressed to remedying inequality, but by virtue of stepping into public life in the political arena they join together with others hoping to lead public policy decisions in new directions. They become part of a collective approach to solving problems. Chase writes, "Because [power] has been declared unwomanly . . . accomplished women have often suppressed or disguised ambition and success in recounting their experiences" (p. 9). The stories recounted in chapter 5 make a particular contribution as counternarratives by revealing how women's actual experiences can differ from the culture's metanarratives about women. One role of postmodernism is to challenge these grand or metanarratives. What Chase says about the women in her study could also be said about the women in our study, particularly those who have engaged overtly in political action, "While they are certainly aware that their success violates the persistent cultural expectation that men should hold positions of power, these successful women do not disguise or mute their accomplishments" (p. 9). Chase states, "A woman who describes herself as a leader, as powerful, sounds arrogant in light of conventional gender ideologies" (p. 149). The stories Chase tells and the stories of our participants about their political successes violate "the ideology that women are not suited to positions of power" (p. 149). Women

willing to become engaged in political action make a particular contribution to closing the leadership gap between men and women. Consider this
statistic: "Internationally, the United States ranks sixtieth in women's political leadership, behind Sierra Leone and tied with Andorra" (Wilson,
2004, p. xii). Women educational leaders willing to become engaged in
politics make a double difference given their proximity to students; their
examples directly influence the next generation.

THE *BEING* OF LEADERSHIP

According to Bolman and Deal (1997), studies conducted in the 1980s
and 1990s of leaders in corporations found no single universal characteristic, but vision came the closest. They wrote, "Beyond vision, the ability
to communicate the vision with passion, and the capacity to inspire trust,
consensus breaks down" (p. 298). When Bennis and Nanus (1985) wrote,
"Vision is the commodity of leaders, and power is their currency" (p. 18),
they were speaking from an interest in what they called a leadership strategy. The context was "strategies for taking charge," and *management of
attention through vision* was one of those strategies. Their analysis required a leader not necessarily to have the vision, but to be able to synthesize vision within an organization. Their work popularized the idea of
transformational leadership articulated by Burns (1978). The transformational leader was able to influence or inspire commitment to the purposes
or goals of an organization. Transformational leadership, described as el-
evating purpose to the level of what is now called moral leadership, was
among the approaches to leadership referred to as the new leadership paradigm in the mid-1980s (Leithwood & Duke, 1999). Transformational
leadership, however, is still about getting others to do what you want them
to do. For many leaders both language and practice have moved beyond
strategies for taking charge, moved from a leader synthesizing vision to
visioning as a group process.

Living and Leading From Values

According to Furman (2003) moral leadership is just one of several
strands of scholarship converging in the 21st century in a new focus.

"Traditional scholarship tends to focus on what leadership *is*, *how* leadership is done, and by *whom*" (p. 1), she writes, with transformational leadership belonging to the *how* category. She claims instead "that educational leadership as a field is focusing more and more on what leadership is *for*; that it is the moral purposes of educational leadership that are emerging as the central focus" (p. 1). Furman analyzed the convergence of four theoretical strands: moral leadership, critical-humanist leadership, constructivist leadership, and distributive leadership, claiming that "these moral purposes and theories converge in an 'ethic of community'" (p. 1). From an international perspective, Blackmore (2002), an Australian, has similarly advocated a shift in the research on women's leadership from focus on style to focus on substance. She writes, in language that matches Furman's, "We need to ask what we are leading for" (p. 64). Both Furman and Blackmore believe that strong values incline leaders to actualize visions, to focus on what matters. Clear values contribute to shared vision in a community, to leadership with a moral imperative (Fullan, 2003). Values-based leadership, benefiting children, maintaining integrity, honoring diversity, and expressing spirituality are themes from chapter 6 that convey the clear values base from which our participants lead. Elizabeth Lewin said, "I work at being a visionary, one who sees down the road to guarantee that everything we do will benefit our children." Whereas the leaders interviewed may not be described or describe themselves as visionary, most do describe their decision-making processes in terms of values. They understand that leading is about visioning, or meaning making, to use more contemporary language.

Further evidence of the values-based leadership of our participants can be seen in the adjectives they chose as descriptive of themselves from the perspective of others with whom they work. During their interviews, participants were asked two questions about themselves as leaders. Early in the interview they were asked, "What three adjectives do you think others would use to describe you as a leader?" Then at the close of the interview each was asked, "What three adjectives would you use to describe yourself as a leader?" These questions resulted in a total of 96 descriptors. A total of 38.5% of those words related to either being focused on purpose or having qualities that gather others around purpose. The specific words offered were passionate (4), visionary (3), fair (3), honest (2), energetic (2), ethical, creative, innovative, proactive, provocative, risk taker, positive, optimistic, dynamic, confident, persuasive, motivator, dedicated, courage of our convictions, advocate for children, stand up for my beliefs, creator of learning environments, growing, lifelong learner, change agent, storyteller, integrative, and seeker. Two other thematic clusters emerging in the words included a nurturing and process-oriented people focus (32.3%) and an assertive task focus (27.2%). There were two other descriptors (2%): don't like to categorize myself and wonderer.

Often leadership inspired by moral purpose is about righting a perceived wrong. In fact, Freeman and Bourque (2001) report that "for many women leadership begins with an intensely experienced wrong" (p. 5). This seems to have been the case specifically for seven of the participants, and at some level for others. Three dared to fight overtly for equity for women and girls during the 1970s. As has been described, Ola Bundy's story played out in the field of athletic opportunity. She was among the courageous women around the country who took Title IX and made it a reality that changed the lives of women and girls. Another woman, a former principal, sued her school district with 19 complaints for equal pay for coaches for girls' sports in 1978 when girls and boys swim coaches were not paid the same amount of money. These actions opened up many new coaching and competitive possibilities for women and girls. A university dean fought for equity in salary and to have assignments reflect qualifications, an issue related to salary and status, when she was with the Illinois State Board of Education. A special education director continues to fight for equity for students with disabilities. When interviewed she said, "I feel strongly about certain systems change—the flexible service delivery model, kids being included and not segregated." Continuing, she elaborated, "I would like to have every child in our schools have the same advantages to learn as much as they can and be able to learn how to access what they don't know. . . . I just feel really badly for the kids that don't have that."

Three of the four African American women told stories of personally confronting the wrongs of racial inequity and discrimination. One remembers as a third-year teacher having a car accident on a stormy night, and not being allowed into a home to use the phone because she was African American. When they arrived, the police left her to stand in the cold, but invited the man who was driving the other car to sit in the police car. She heard the children inside the house saying, "Nigger go home." She had heard such taunts regularly driving into the neighborhood where she taught. She describes handling the pain and rage by resolving that "one of these days I am going to be principal of this high school and then what are you going to say?" Another, who had dropped out of school at age 13 when she had a child, was motivated in her return to school in her thirties by what she saw as a volunteer in her own children's schools. For her, that so many African American children could not read and no one seemed to care was an intensely experienced wrong. That sense of outrage was the source of her determination to become a teacher. As a superintendent, Elizabeth Lewin took creative action to get newly arrived migrant workers' children the schooling and services they needed. When bureaucratic rules did not permit enrolling the children, she categorized their families as homeless and was able to get them into school where they belonged. These seven leaders confronted barriers of inequity for themselves and/or others in these examples. Undoubtedly countless other examples could have been shared by our participants, as each in her own way has advanced the cause of social justice.

The values of our participants are reflected in the responses they gave to the question about what they wanted to be remembered for. All but two were asked and answered the question. Several identified their hopes for children: "My focus was always on what was best for kids." "That I got things accomplished for kids, not to be among that count of adults who failed our children." "Advancement of the children, opportunities." "All children can learn. We have to learn how to teach them, help them find their gifts." Several other responses focused on more specific accomplishments: "Making equity a reality for so many students." "Someone who helped other women develop into good administrators." "As a person who is helpful and follows through on what I've been asked to do." "Turning around the schools in my district." "That I cared enough about the children and the community to put a new school in place."

One category of responses emphasized integrity: "That I always loved kids. I never sold my soul." "Integrity, that she never stopped being a teacher." "That I made a difference for kids in a way that was fair and had integrity to all the people with whom I work." Another set of responses centered on facilitating learning: "Helping people think outside of the box and be supported for taking risks, so that every child in our schools has the same advantages to learn." "I hope to be remembered for trying to open a structure so that all learners grow and thrive." "That everywhere I've worked I've left a healthy environment behind, where everybody can be everything they can be—for giving to others." And finally, one response defies categorization: "When they asked what I came to do, I answered . . . I came to live out loud." Creating opportunities for kids, making a difference through specific accomplishments, being authentic, facilitating learning—these leaders are redefining leadership as they live into their legacies.

Integrating Doing and Being

Collaborative decision making integrates doing and being in a leadership practice that grows out of a constellation of values. Pushing the boundaries in bureaucracies integrates doing and being when leaders refuse to have their doing artificially constrained by bureaucratic rules and choose instead to find a way to do what they believe. Claiming power through politics integrates doing and being when leaders with integrity publicly put their lives on the line for their values. Integrating doing and being results in authentic leadership. Bringing one's being into leadership is about authenticity, bringing the whole of who you are to your work, not leaving any aspect of yourself at the door. Authenticity is defined in multiple ways. Terry (1993) explains that authentic leadership is being "true to ourselves and true to the world, real in ourselves and real in the world" (p. 139). Being authentic could also be called having integrity. Without using the word *authentic*, Bolman and Deal (1995) express the concept this way: "Leading is giving. Leadership is an ethic, a gift of oneself. It is easy to miss the depth and power of this message. The essence of leadership is not giving things or even providing visions. It is offering oneself and one's spirit" (p. 102). Authentic leadership as Shields (2003) understands it "is incomplete unless it is also leadership with a clear focus on ethics and morality" (p. 27). Authenticity can have a cost. A superintendent talked about how, as a direct reflection of her values, she built a collaborative approach to decision making in a district.

> This is what I was unofficially doing by involving a lot of people in discussion and decision making. It does change the definition of leadership and there were some board members who said that I was not being a leader

because I would not tell the staff to do something and get it done. Instead it would take a while for things to get done and so I ran into issues with the board, which is why I left. I chose to leave. *But had I not chosen to leave I would have been fired.* I would much rather work for commitment from staff and not compliance.

For her next superintendent's position, she chose a district that was a better match for her leadership approach, and in that district "we became a true learning community." She explained, "I've tried to make any system I've worked with a place where people know I value ideas, and I value different ways of looking at issues. I ascribe to the leadership values of compassion and commitment. I believe in empowering people and collaborating to arrive at a richer decision."

Sometimes language hinders integration of doing and being. Postmodernists attend to language and how historically situated discourse shapes and limits our conceptions of abstractions such as leadership. Grogan (2003) combines theoretical frameworks, feminism, and postmodernism to offer a theory that is "a combination of the espousal of social change fundamental to feminist critical theory and the focus on language and discourse offered by postmodernism" (p. 26). As an example of understandings that emerge when one pays attention to discourse and how it shapes thinking and reality, she writes, "For instance, although it is quite common to hear the term *woman superintendent*, it is not at all common to hear of a *man superintendent.* The idea that superintendent is synonymous with man has emerged in the discourse of educational administration, due to the overwhelming number of men who have held the job and the association of traditional male leadership attributes with the role" (Grogan, 1999, pp. 201–202). Brunner (2002) focuses on new images of the doing and being of leadership when she writes, "Recommendations grounded in feminist postmodern perspectives—such as the idea that relationships and the inclusion of multiple perspectives form the foundation for the superintendency—require proactive listening, which includes hearing things that one does not want to hear" (pp. 425–426). She views feminist postmodern perspectives as providing the tools needed to change the language used within the field. Some women leaders, when caught in inhospitable environments, do not have or do not exercise the option to leave, but choose a gender script to follow, according to Blackmore (2002). These gender scripts are ways to cope and survive when authenticity does not seem possible, or if the cost will be too high. It takes self-knowledge and ego strength to sustain leaders in the daily work of leadership, according to Curry (2000). Unable to arrive at authenticity, some women in Curry's study of women who were presidents or chief executives of colleges, universities, and state central administrative offices for education maintained a *leader persona* that functioned as a gender script by requiring compartmentalization of certain features of themselves as persons, partners, or parents. For others, arriving at a leader persona was an achievement of wholeness or identity congruence, and that congruence became a source of power. Such a level of authenticity, or wholeness, seems also to describe many of the women we studied. Interestingly, for 13 of the participants, there was absolute congruence between how they said others would describe them as leaders and how they described themselves.

Perhaps the ultimate integration of doing and being could be called leading with soul. Bolman and Deal (1995) offer their understanding of what it means to *lead with soul* in the form of a story. They moved to storytelling to help leaders understand how to restore the heart, too often missing from leading. Their *Leading with Soul* (1995) features conversations between a sage (a woman) and a leader (a man) who has lost heart. They argue in the introduction that images of leadership dominant today—the heroic visionary leader and the analytical "policy wonk"—both miss the essence of leadership. "Both emphasize the hands and heads of leaders, neglecting deeper and more enduring elements of courage, spirit, and hope" (p. 5). In a series of conversations over time, the sage reintroduces the lost leader to his spirit, "the internal force that sustains meaning and hope" (p. 20). "The heart of leadership," she insists in their first conversation, "is in the hearts of leaders. You have to lead from something deep in your heart" (p. 21). She introduces him to nature as a teacher and conversations with her reveal other lessons that gradually loosen his heartsong. He learns to offer to others four gifts of leadership: authorship or participation in decision making, love, power, and significance. In the end, he becomes real again, grows into a more integrated and authentic self. Bolman and Deal conclude, "The signs point toward spirit and soul as the essence of leadership. There is a growing consensus that we need a new paradigm to move beyond the traps of conventional thinking" (p. 39). They offer the magic of stories, encourage leaders to work with the power of stories in their own lives and the lives of others. Stories are one of the oldest forms of meaning making.

Leadership as Meaning Making

Drath and Palus (1994), from the Center for Creative Leadership, sum up the cultural transition underway in both the understanding and the practice of leadership. They claim we are moving away from leadership as a dominance and influence frame, and toward "leadership as a social meaning-making process that occurs in groups engaged in some activity together" (p. 1). From the old frame or worldview, the belief is that an objective reality exists, is "something that can be more or less directly known" (p. 2). From the social meaning-making perspective, knowledge and reality are constructed in our minds, a concept central to postmodern thinking. We make meaning individually, as well as socially, as we arrange our understanding of experience into something coherent. From this constructive postmodern worldview, "Leadership in organizations can likewise be seen as more about making meaning than about making decisions and influencing people" (p. 4). Meaning making includes both cognitive and emotional frameworks. Although most views of leadership still "begin with the assumption that leadership is a dominance-cum-social-influence process" (p. 5), Drath and Palus assert that "When the making of such frameworks [cognitive and emotional] happens in a community of practice (people united in a common enterprise who share a history and thus certain values, beliefs, ways of talking, and ways of doing things), then we can say leadership is happening" (p. 4).

In the Drath and Palus (1994) reformulation of leadership, meaning refers both to the way words and symbols stand for something, and to the substance of people's values and commitments. Language becomes important to leadership because "naming something categorizes it, which puts it into a certain context and relationship to other things. . . . Because of the power of language to shape our very understanding of what is real, these contexts and memberships in categories bring things into existence for us" (p. 7). They use the example of *civil disobedience* as a name created by Thoreau for something that carried with it "whole ways of being in the world" (p. 7). Our individual meaning making is deeply affected by cultural beliefs. "Culture provides people with givens in the form of names for things, ways of classifying and thus interpreting things" (p. 10). Drath and Palus summarize by saying,

We refer to leadership as a social meaning-making process that takes place as a result of activity or work in a group, instead of referring to leadership as a social influence process in which individuals get others to engage in activity or work. . . . We speak of leadership as flowing from meaning instead of meaning as flowing from leadership. We refer to leadership as that which creates commitments in communities of practice. We view leadership as that which connects people to work and to one another at work. We refer to leadership as a social process in which everyone in the community participates. (p. 13)

From this formulation, influence is the outcome rather than the essence of leadership. Rather than figure out how to take charge, from a meaning-making frame, the question for one who would lead changes from the old paradigm "How do I take charge?" to "How do I participate in an effective process of leadership?" (p. 19). Part of the confusion existing around evolving concepts of leadership is that we have layered the older concept of leadership as dominance with the idea of leadership as influence, and a third layer that might be termed *participative leadership*. As demonstrated in this study, all these ideas about leadership coexist and interact with cultural gender norms to put us, whether women or men, into a time of sorting out what we want leadership to mean for ourselves, organizations, and the world. Drath and Palus offer an image to entice us to reconsider the old views. "Leadership may be much more than the dramatic whitecaps of the individual leader, and may be more productively understood as the deep blue water we all swim in when we work together" (p. 25).

CONCLUSIONS

Without the writings of Margaret Wheatley (1992, 1999), many of us in education would have no inkling of how new findings from the world of science require us to view reality differently if we are to see clearly. Reading Wheatley, one understands that the objectivist Newtonian worldview is dead, albeit having a slow passing. Her writings have introduced leaders of all types of organizations to the idea of chaos, or disequilibrium, as a disruption in living systems that leads to reordering at a higher level. "Disorder becomes a critical player, an ally that can provoke a system to self-organize into new forms of being" (p. 12), she writes. She has encouraged us to understand that information must flow throughout an organization from all directions just as it does in the universe. She challenges us to regard vision as an invisible field that permeates everything. Most importantly, she calls us to understand implications of a central finding from quantum physics: "In the quantum world, relationships are not just interesting; to many physicists, they are *all* there is to reality" (p. 34). At the subatomic level, elementary particles do not function as the basic building blocks of matter they were once thought to be. "Matter can show up as particles, specific points in space; or it can show us as waves, energy dispersed over a finite area. Matter's total identity (known as a wave packet) includes the potential for both forms—particles and waves" (p. 36). What it shows up as depends on the observer, upon what is measured. The universe is not a finely tuned machine but a living organism of relationships. If relationships *are* the universe what are the implications for organizational realities? Wheatley writes,

> To live in a quantum world, to weave here and there with ease and grace, we need to change what we do. We need fewer descriptions of tasks and instead learn how to facilitate process. We need to become savvy about how to foster relationships, how to nurture growth, and development. All of us need to become better at listening, conversing, respecting one another's uniqueness, because these are essential for strong relationships. The era of the rugged individual has been replaced by the era of the team player. But this is only the beginning. The quantum world has demolished the concept that we are unconnected individuals. More and more relationships are in store for us, out there in the vast web of life. (p. 39)

The call to redefine leadership in terms of new ways of doing and being is clear. It comes from many perspectives, including postmodernism, the new science, the figuratively shrinking and physically vulnerable Earth, the millions of children living in poverty, and nations and peoples beset generation after generation with the violence of war. Our collective existence is fragile. We are living in what is being called the sixth mass age of extinction, with species disappearing annually at an unprecedented rate, last seen when the dinosaurs became extinct. In the words of Granoff

(2004), "We are the first generation that must choose whether life will continue."

As Wilson (2004) reminds us and the women in this study show us, we must understand anew that leadership of women matters. We must claim our authority and ambition, lead from our ability with authenticity. Each of us is incredibly powerful when we are clear about what we are leading *for*. The future depends in part on women taking their rightful places alongside men as equal partners in the leadership of all major institutions. Our growth and survival as a species depend upon a new language of leadership and widespread participation of women in meaning-making processes at micro and macro levels. Collaboration in a global context is no longer optional. In all the institutions of our society, we need leaders of both genders who will take a global perspective, build a productive global consciousness. Educators in all countries, but particularly in the United States, must be part of this movement to expand how the world is viewed, to focus the new lenses, and to take the long look. Addressing a joint session of Congress in 1977, Václav Havel said, "Without a global revolution in the sphere of human consciousness, nothing will change for the better . . . and the catastrophe toward which this world is headed, whether it be ecological, social, demographic or a general breakdown of civilization, will be unavoidable" (Palmer, 2000, p. 76). Palmer elaborates, "The power for authentic leadership, Havel tells us, is found not in external arrangements but in the human heart. Authentic leaders in every setting—from families to nation-states—aim at liberating the heart, their own and others', so that its power can liberate the world" (p. 76).

In the next chapter, we present Stephanie Pace Marshall, a leader who integrates her total *being* into her *doing* of leadership as the president of the Illinois Mathematics and Science Academy. Her redefinition of leadership speaks to her practices of collaborative decision making, dissolving bureaucratic boundaries, operating powerfully in the political arena, and living and leading authentically from her values. She frames stories and pushes the language of leadership, using new language to call to life new possibilities. She turns the kaleidoscope of people, processes, and concepts to reveal patterns that connect people to each other and to the needs of the larger interdependent world. Her leadership work reaches across the world, touches us all. We invite you to meet Stephanie Pace Marshall and learn about what she calls "her work on the planet."

Chapter Eight

Visionary, Provocative, Integrative

by Madeline Hafner

Dr. Stephanie Pace Marshall brings her entire self, the core of who she is, to her leadership work. A leader who maneuvers in and out of many different worlds, she remains true to her identity as "a seeker, a wonderer, and a storyteller." She is as comfortable working with teachers, administrators, governors, and legislators as she is with research executives, foundation heads, Nobel Laureates, and aboriginal healers. Founding president and founding board member of the Illinois Mathematics and Science Academy, Stephanie Pace Marshall is a prime example of a leader who dares to live into new possibilities.

In her 36 years of experience in the field of education, Stephanie Pace Marshall's work has taken many forms: teacher, district administrator, university faculty member, and superintendent. For the past 18 years, her role has been as president of the Illinois Mathematics and Science Academy. In addition, Stephanie served as president of the Association for Supervision and Curriculum Development (ASCD), one of the largest international associations of professional educators in the world. She continues to consult and speak nationally and internationally.

Recognizing that her specific role in education does not necessarily describe her life's work, Stephanie Pace Marshall describes herself as a *designer of learning environments*. The fundamental characteristics of who Stephanie is as an individual—"visionary, provocative, and integrative"—are the essential design principles that form the core of her leadership and invite her and those around her to create learning environments for children and adults alike that "invite all of who we are to our work." In order to more fully understand how Stephanie Pace Marshall's leadership invites her and those around her to grow into new possibilities, it is necessary to know who she is within one context of her leadership work, as president of the Illinois Mathematics and Science Academy.

THE ILLINOIS MATHEMATICS AND SCIENCE ACADEMY

Traveling west on the interstate, it is difficult to believe there is an extraordinarily innovative learning community nestled between the on and off ramps and large corporate buildings that seem to blur together. The Illinois Research and Development Corridor, home to several of the nation's largest research laboratories, has expanded further and further west as the suburbs of Chicago have grown and developed. A large working dairy farm and a few fields of tilled soil provide remnants of a past before urban sprawl.

Once off the interstate you make your way through corporate office buildings, distribution centers, and a subdivision or two, to recognize a school, differentiated from the surrounding buildings only by a large grassy playing field. The Illinois Mathematics and Science Academy, or IMSA as it is known, is a rather unassuming building. The tree-lined walkway, the sunken cement work areas, the residence halls for students, and the unusual slant of the walls tell visitors in a subtle yet visceral way they are entering a unique educational environment.

Although the space is very open and inviting, inside the main building (built in 1978, long before IMSA was created) IMSA first looks very much like a typical U.S. high school, with trophy cases on the walls, students milling around, and artwork in the hallways. Yet, as you take a closer look, you begin to realize that typical is not a word to describe the learning environment at IMSA. Two trophy cases stand across from one another. The student trophy case is divided into four equal sections. One displays sports awards while the other three exhibit academic honors, including textbooks and research projects collaboratively written by IMSA students and scientists or research experts from across the United States. The staff trophy case spotlights work by faculty and staff, including journal articles, book chapters, and textbooks. Students sit casually on benches or the floor engaged in heated debate, analytical discussions about research projects and class assignments, or quiet conversations with friends. They may also be talking to resident scientist and Nobel Laureate Dr. Leon Lederman. There is vibrant artwork and sculpture everywhere, ranging from small paintings framed on the walls to installation pieces measuring two stories in height. But what catches your eye mostly as you move from the main corridor to other wings of the building are the bold banners hanging on the walls and from the ceiling. Everywhere you look there are larger-than-life reminders of the vision of IMSA: "Liberating the genius and goodness of all children for the world." A banner draped from the ceiling nearest the main staircase denotes a proclamation provided by an early visitor to the academy, Dr. Carl Sagan: "The Illinois Mathematics and Science Academy . . . a gift from the people of Illinois to the Human Future."

Located in Aurora, Illinois, 35 miles west of Chicago, IMSA is an "educational laboratory" where learning is "competency driven, inquiry based, problem centered, and integrative." Created in 1985, IMSA was charged by the Illinois General Assembly to "offer a uniquely challenging education for students talented in mathematics and science." A three-year public residential educational program for students in grades 10–12, IMSA currently serves 650 Illinois students. Course offerings range from multivariable calculus to microeconomics, from topics in modern physics to ceramics. Of the students attending IMSA, 50% are female and 50% male. Ethnic representation of the student population includes 9% African American, 37% Asian American, 5% Latina/o, less than 1% Native American, 5% no race or mixed, and 43% white. Conscious of the gender and achievement gap in the areas of science and math, IMSA works diligently to recruit, prepare, and support female students and students of color. The advanced program focuses its resources on ensuring that the next generation of leaders in mathematics, science, and technology research and education are representative of the broader population of students in Illinois.

In addition to providing residential students with a personalized academic program, IMSA also serves as a "learning laboratory" for educators and younger students across the state of Illinois and beyond. Through its professional development center, IMSA provides teachers, students, researchers, and other educators with opportunities to explore state-of-the-art curricular and instructional processes. IMSA faculty members (45% of whom hold Ph.D.s) are nationwide experts in various areas of education, including mathematics and science education, gifted education, problem-based learning, integrative curriculum development, and educational change and transformation. The innovative content and the inquiry-based nature of the professional development programs demonstrate how IMSA serves the larger Illinois educational community.

MEETING STEPHANIE PACE MARSHALL

Stephanie Pace Marshall is a striking woman, tall, with dark hair and kind, gentle eyes. She has a presence in a room. She is not imposing or threatening but invites you into conversation. Her demeanor is simultaneously calming and invigorating to those in her presence.

The office of the president of IMSA offers insight into Stephanie's leadership. It is a space that radiates and invites hard work and a strong sense of self, a gathering place for purposeful administrative tasks as well as reflection and introspection. It is a warm work environment painted in deep blues and maroons and filled with dark cherry wood furniture. Every wall is covered with artwork. Brilliant colors jump out as the light and movement in the room changes.

Stephanie's desk faces the wall opposite a large conference table that seats six or so. Along the wall between the two are a couch and a rocking chair, anticipating visitors. Windows line this wall, providing a constant source of energy. Bookshelves and low file cabinets are organized along the wall across from the windows, interrupted only by the entrance to the room. Framed pictures and distinctive objects fill the room. There are snapshots from different events and people who have informed Stephanie's work. These include framed congressional letters of support, photographs of children, and pictures of current and past IMSA board of directors. Each offers visitors a brief overview of the work Stephanie has embraced in her 18 years as president of this institution.

Nestled in between these more standardized representations of leadership are more intimate reminders of Stephanie's ever-integrated work life. On shelves, cabinets, and tables rest various talisman-type figures as well as kaleidoscopes by the dozen—an image Stephanie regards as a symbol and metaphor of her leadership and work. When a kaleidoscope is initially peered into, the various colors and shapes appear random and disordered.

But when illuminated by light, a view that was once considered random and disordered is transformed into holistic and constantly evolving patterns of intricate connections and complexity.

As we sat down at the conference table in her office, I was struck by how unrushed Stephanie seemed to be. As the president of an organization that operates more like a small college than a typical high school, I anticipated this office to be a hub of fast-paced decision making and information sharing. To the contrary, the office, and Stephanie herself, radiated a sense of introspection and stillness that invited us gently into conversation.

Throughout our time together, it became clear to me that several underlying ideologies guide Stephanie Pace Marshall's leadership work. These ideologies can be best summarized by the descriptors she feels others would use to describe her leadership: "visionary, provocative, and integrative." Stephanie operates as a visionary leader; every decision she makes is rooted in principles and values, even decisions that perturb or provoke the organization she leads. Living an integrated life, intellectually and spiritually, is a fundamental prerequisite for her leadership work. These ideologies are the basic beliefs, or design principles, that inform Stephanie's leadership.

VISIONARY

Vision is an essential aspect of Stephanie Pace Marshall's leadership work. In the words of one of her colleagues, "Stephanie is so visionary. And that's *not* rhetoric. It's in her heart and soul." Her ability to synthesize various perspectives assists Stephanie in maintaining a visionary leadership focus. She describes herself as a "quintessential integrator and synthesizer." She elaborates:

I learn by listening to other people. I can go into a meeting or a conversation with an idea formulated and emerge from a conversation with a completely different view. Scientists change their minds all the time. You put on multiple glasses so you're seeing things differently. That's what I think makes someone a visionary. It's about vision. It's about insight. And it's about noticing and paying attention to what "wants" to emerge.

Flying at 50,000 Feet

Stephanie shared a metaphor that offers keen insight into how she perceives her role within the larger leadership team at IMSA. The One IMSA Management Team, a group of 35 individuals including Stephanie as president and chief executive officer, meets five times throughout the year for the purpose of "sharing information, building relationships, and looking for connections." This group focuses on strategic issues impacting IMSA—for example, the direction of the academy or the goals of the institution. Stephanie uses the following altitude metaphor (created by John Allen) to describe how leaders must view their work and the work of their institutions from multiple perspectives and priorities.

~ At 10,000 feet are the tasks you do every day.
~ At 20,000 feet are your roles and the accountabilities of your work.
~ At 30,000 feet are what you want to accomplish in the next 12–18 months.
~ At 40,000 feet are what you want to accomplish in three to five years.
~ And at 50,000 feet—leaders ask, "What's my work on the planet?"

Stephanie admits that an essential part of leadership is being able to navigate at each of these levels; however, as the CEO she pays particular attention to her work and accountabilities at the 30,000 to 50,000 feet levels and she never loses sight of her work on the planet. As Stephanie referenced "flying at 30,000 to 50,000 feet" to describe where she operates as a leader, she added, with a smile and a deep laugh, that at times members of her leadership team utilize this metaphor to remind her of the 10,000-foot operational tasks that require her attention. She explains how "I'm generally at 40,000 to 50,000 and my team asks me to come back down sometimes. We use the altitude metaphor because it's a clear way for them to say to me, 'The air is quite thin up where you are—you need to come down here.'" Given the altitude metaphor, Stephanie acknowledges that she can operate at the 10-, 20-, and 30,000-feet levels but believes leaders must hold the context—the story—of why the institution is doing the work and why it matters. This question of identity and meaning resides at the higher altitudes.

Enacting Vision

The development of the IMSA vision statement is one tangible example of the impact of Stephanie's visionary leadership. Several years ago Stephanie and a small group of Western leaders spent two weeks in the outback of Australia camping with aboriginal spiritual leaders and healers. This experience had a profound impact on Stephanie's life. As a result of these two weeks, Stephanie returned with a vision statement of her life's work. She describes: "My work in the world is to do whatever I can to create conditions by design, whether it's through my leadership, writing, or speaking, to liberate the goodness and genius of all children and to invite and nurture the power of creativity of the human spirit for the world." Recognizing the transformative power of this experience to her and the clearness of her vision, Stephanie engaged her leadership team in uncovering their visions for the organization.

She began by asking them to connect to the deepest part of themselves that they felt comfortable accessing at this point in time. She continued, "What are you passionate about—what matters to you? What is your work in the world? What is your work in this place? If you were going to leave here, what would you be leaving for? What do you want on your tombstone? Why do you care so much about IMSA? What are you caring for?" Each member of the leadership team shared their personal vision for their work. The conversation concluded with Stephanie sharing the vision statement she had created for her life's work. After this discussion the leadership team decided that Stephanie's articulated vision statement represented their collective "passion," their collective "life's work on the planet," the reason why they care about their work—and it did so in a way that honored each person's individual response. Stephanie's personal vision for her life's work was then offered to IMSA.

As Stephanie shared this story about how the vision statement for IMSA developed, she noted how she came to think about the concepts of vision and mission within her leadership work. Ben Zander, a conductor for the Boston Philharmonic and a friend of Stephanie's, once defined for her the essential differences between the vision and mission of any organization. He described the vision of an organization as "a possibility to be proclaimed and lived into" while the mission is "a purpose to be articulated and achieved." Given these descriptions, Stephanie has come to understand the operationalization of the vision and mission of IMSA in the following way:

> If our vision is liberating the goodness and genius of children for the world and our mission is the transformation of math and science, then the question is how do we, by design, create a learning environment that will more likely enable us to transform teaching and learning and math and science so that we invite children to liberate their goodness and genius by inventing a new mind? I think that's what schools must do. They must create opportunities for kids and learners of all ages—to invent a new mind.

Transformation and liberation are at the core of Stephanie's leadership work—for herself, the educators around her, and the students they support. Her ability to "fly at 50,000 feet," asking how we, as educators, invite students to "invent a new mind," is only one example of how Stephanie Pace Marshall's visionary leadership invites all of us in education to live into new possibilities.

Principle-Based Decision Making

The vision Stephanie has articulated is one of the fundamental lenses she and her colleagues employ when they make decisions in their work at IMSA. As I asked Stephanie to describe how her decision making is informed by the vision she has created for her life's work, she explained how the vision is translated into principles and values that are enacted in the everyday work of the IMSA organization. By design, IMSA is a highly participatory and inclusive community.

Stephanie differentiates between different types or "constellations" of decisions she makes in her leadership work. The first constellation of decisions she describes as "personal and strategic" and the second "structural or procedural." Stephanie defines "personal and strategic" decisions as those leadership and institutional "decisions that only I as the leader can make based upon strategic considerations, values, principles, and the integrity of the academy." She defines "structural" decisions as those organizational decisions that are "procedural or tactical" in nature. Many leaders are responsible for "structural and procedural" decisions, allowing her to focus time and energy on the principle-based decisions that influence the long-term value, health, and sustainability of the organization—

decisions that she describes as requiring thinking from the "40- and 50,000-foot levels."

Gathering Information

As a first step in her decision-making process, Stephanie gathers as much information as possible and in as many ways as possible. She describes the initial stages of decision making in this way: "I seek, generate, and gather abundant amounts of information, from as many people as possible and in as many different forms as possible. I am as interested in how people felt or reacted, what they sensed, what their heart tells them or what their intuition says as I am about the research. Then I look for patterns and connect them. I connect them all."

In addition to gathering information from as many sources as possible, Stephanie considers her own intuition as a valuable "data point." She shares, "I go back to the principles and commitments and 'story' that matter to me and to us. I give myself an opportunity to listen, to pay attention, and to notice my own voice. What is my heart telling me? What is my intuition telling me? Does this honor who I know I am and who I know we are? Does this honor what I know IMSA is striving to become?"

Once she has gathered a wide range of data points, including "hard data," Stephanie sifts the information through the shared values and beliefs that guide the organization, those values and beliefs that resonate with the vision and mission articulated throughout the organization.

Considering Shared Values and Beliefs

As a visionary leader, Stephanie steadfastly asks how each decision reflects and advances the vision and mission of the IMSA community and its unique work. Stephanie explains how her decision making is intimately guided by the collective "design principles" of the organization. She defines a design principle as a set of beliefs, competencies, and relationships that guide people's thinking and actions in order to reach a desired outcome. She elaborates,

> When I'm making decisions here, I am guided by our beliefs, goal, and core learning competencies. I am also guided by our vision and mission. I hold

that vision in every pore of my being—liberating goodness and genius of children for the world, inviting and nurturing power and creativity of the human spirit. It's a screen to me. It's a filter. Are we in transformative conversations? How bold are we? How brave are we?

Stephanie provided an example of how IMSA's vision and mission are translated into design principles that in turn shape the curriculum and instruction utilized with students. Given that the vision of IMSA is "liberating goodness and genius for the world" and the mission is the "transformation of science and mathematics," one design principle developed by teachers to guide their actions includes "designing experiences that are competency driven, inquiry based, problem centered, and integrated." Examples of curriculum and instruction rooted in this design principle include problem-based learning and IMSA's Student Inquiry and Research Program. Problem-based learning is a pedagogical technique that focuses each facet of the teaching and learning process on real-life, ill-structured problems, such as the impact of automobile emissions on global warming. The Student Inquiry and Research Program is a self-directed and inquiry-based experience that places a question an individual student is passionate about exploring at the center of the research process. Students work with peers and IMSA teachers as well as researchers and scientists knowledgeable in a particular field to investigate their problem. Utilizing design principles is one way each member of the IMSA organization shapes his or her practice to achieve the mission of "transformation" and lives into its vision of "liberating the potentials of students."

Stephanie readily admits that this type of principle-based decision making requires a tremendous amount of time and energy. She offers a reminder that not everyone in an organization feels this type of decision-making process is necessary, noting that she has been criticized by colleagues who believe she makes decisions too slowly. Although she acknowledges she could speed up the decision-making process, Stephanie feels the quality of her decisions is enhanced when speed is not the primary design principle informing the decision. In addition, Stephanie points out leaders must recognize that some principle-based decisions might disrupt or perturb the organization. She notes that uncertainty and disequilibrium are not the antithesis to healthy and effective decision making, but necessary elements in any living system.

Discerning, Creating, and Interpreting Stories

After she gathers information, considers personal and institutional values and beliefs, and reflects on the "design principles" impacting the decision, Stephanie describes how it is at this point of confluence that organizational *stories* may emerge. As different stories become visible through patterns of conversation and behavior, the role of the leader becomes one of storyteller. She explains,

> Something I have learned about leadership and decision making that has stayed with me, and I use frequently, is the responsibility and opportunity of the leader is to listen for, discern, and identify the patterns of the institution as they are unfolding, and then to verbalize and play these emerging stories back to the community. This enables the community to see that within a community there is no such thing as a random comment; every comment contributes to a part of the story. One of the fundamental roles of a leader is to connect the comments within a community and name the patterns (stories) they are creating. When stories are named and made visible, a community then has a choice of which one they want to live into. This is where vision comes in. You offer people a chance to "choose a story of possibility" that is worthy of their lives. The stories that we have created so far in most schools, are in my view, far too small for our children's imagination and for our own.

Through her visionary leadership Stephanie helps the academy shape next generation's stories. She shares: "Stories are choices. And most institutions do not understand that they are living a story. We are always making it up. That's the point. Our strategies, goals, visions, and mission are created by us; we make them up. And that, I think, is one of the fundamental roles of a leader. It is to be very clear that every community can choose the future it wishes to embody."

PROVOCATIVE

Stephanie Pace Marshall describes herself as a provocative leader and believes that an integral and natural role of a leader is to perturb or provoke the system at the deepest levels in order to engage the imagination and inventive genius of people. This has been her experience across her 36 years of work in public schools. Stephanie views disequilibrium as a natural and healthy element in any organization. It is during times of disruption that an organization has the opportunity to reevaluate who they are and what they believe. The following story that Stephanie shared during our time together personifies the power of the storytelling role of a leader. This experience would perturb the IMSA organization in ways even Stephanie could not have imagined. Nonetheless, in order to grow into the vision she held for herself and the organization, Stephanie made a decision rooted solely in the values and principles espoused by IMSA. The decision illustrates how principle-based decision making is part of her core identity as an educational leader. This is but one of the many ways Stephanie Pace Marshall challenges herself and others to grow into new possibilities.

Perturbing the System

As a public residential educational program, IMSA accepts approximately 200 new students every year. The enrollment is limited by space and the funding provided by the Illinois General Assembly, which impacts every facet of the academy's operation, residential as well as academic. In the late 1990s IMSA sent out congratulatory letters to its new students. In error, however, 32 additional students who were actually on the waiting list for admission to the academy were also sent acceptance letters. This error was not discovered until two weeks before the school year was to begin.

Several of the staff proposed that IMSA call these 32 students immediately and apologetically "uninvite" them. Stephanie explained how "many of the staff said, 'We've got to get on the phone right away and call people and say we just feel horrible; we apologize, we made a terrible mistake, but your child's on the wait list and has not been invited.'" To this proposal Stephanie responded, "Absolutely not. Our name and word are on this [letter]. We will admit these children. They are now ours." Stephanie listened attentively to all the different perspectives regarding the positive and negative implications of accepting these students, but was firm in her decision. The integrity of the organization was at stake.

Although many of the staff members were "supportive and proud" of Stephanie's decision to admit the students, others felt the decision "threw the organization into turmoil." As she considered this decision, Stephanie readily admits that the logistical issues impacted by this decision (for example, "not enough beds, not enough mattresses, and not enough staff") were not the most critical issues. She explained her thinking in this way: "You can secure beds. You can secure mattresses. You can secure all of those things. You can add a couple of kids to a class. To me, its [this]— IMSA gave its word and IMSA was not going to go back on its word." She explained how "from the institution's perspective, relative to our integrity and our name, it was the only thing we could do."

Recognizing the impact this decision would have on the organization, Stephanie assured her colleagues that she recognized how her "50,000-feet" decision would influence the "10- and 20,000-feet" decisions that would need to be made. When she informed her staff of her decision to accept the 32 extra students, she clearly articulated her support of them.

I'm not abandoning you in this decision. I'm not being cavalier. I know you've got to redo class schedules, give placement exams, increase class size, redo roommate assignments, and purchase new furniture. And I know you've got to call parents. I believe that my decision deepens the integrity of the institution. So if we need additional resources, we shall have them. If we have to start classes maybe a couple of days later because you can't get the schedule done, then that's what we do.

Stephanie worked diligently with her staff to prepare for the additional students.

As the opening of the school year approached Stephanie recognized two very different "stories" taking shape regarding the admission of the additional students. Immediately she began asking staff members to tell her all the comments they heard (positive and negative) about bringing these students to campus. After synthesizing all the comments, Stephanie noticed two distinct patterns or stories emerging. She reflected them back to her staff as two "choices" they needed to consider. She recalls,

At the opening session of the academy that year, I had created two transparencies. One I called "The Firestorm." In the center I had drawn a blazing fire and around the edges I had written every negative comment that was heard. And, the other transparency, I called "The Gift" and had drawn a large gift box with a bow, and I had written every positive comment that was heard. I projected these two images and emergent "stories" and said this is what I heard in the last two weeks. Each of these two stories is equally plausible. Which story do we want to live into?

In her role as leader, Stephanie walked her staff through the process of recognizing that each of their comments and conversations collectively created an organizational story. Through her visionary leadership, her ability to "fly at 50,000 feet," and her provocative nature, Stephanie was able to demonstrate how only one of the stories being created reflected the shared values and beliefs held by the organization. She describes the leader's role in this process of creating and interpreting organizational "stories" in the following way:

It's all about consciously creating conditions, having conversations, using language and images, and inviting people into the possibility. The leader has already made the choice of what possibility she wants to live into. I had already made the choice that embodied our values, but I was doing everything I could to create conditions that made it so invitational that the community intentionally chose to live into the story—they were going to live into the gift, because it was the most congruent with our identity—with who we are.

Stephanie was able to hold up for her colleagues the story that was "a possibility worthy to live into." In retrospect, she believes that as an organization "we lived into a much more positive story than I think we would have lived into, had we not been aware of the negative story we were starting to write."

As demonstrated through her provocative leadership style, Stephanie Pace Marshall is challenging each and every one of us to live into new possibilities—in particular, new possibilities that arise from embracing organizational perturbations as natural and essential occurrences within our leadership work. Stephanie recognizes disequilibrium within an organization as an energizing force that provides the opportunity to rely on and reaffirm the vision and mission around which we have established our policies and procedures.

INTEGRATIVE

As a scholar steeped in contemporary leadership theories, including the implications of chaos theory, quantum physics, and self-organizing systems on the practice of leadership, Stephanie embraces the concept of an organizational "sense of self" as a fundamental design principle through which to comprehend and guide her leadership work. She explains,

> You know—and Meg [Margaret Wheatley] has said this in her book *Leadership and the New Science*—what defines an organism is its sense of self—its core. What it is. Who it is. What it represents. Its essence. The essence of any living system is its identity, its self. And Meg Wheatley says . . . most of the time you can go into organizations and you notice they suffer from multiple personalities. When you try to find the self, there isn't one, there are multiple selves. So one of the challenges of leadership is that you must always create, articulate, and embrace your institutional identity. In our environment, there are so many things going on. I could not possibly keep track of all our programs and initiatives and the work. But, there are some things I have to hold and have to expect the institution to hold and this is the institution's sense of self.

Stephanie believes that IMSA's "sense of self"—the core around which it operates—consistently guides the decisions she makes as a system leader. One story Stephanie shared during our time together personifies the significant role an organization's "sense of self" plays in guiding leadership decisions, even when those decisions are highly political in nature and have the potential to incur negative consequences.

IMSA's Sense of Self: "It's About NAME"

The concept of the Illinois Mathematics and Science Academy was developed by Dr. Leon Lederman, a Nobel Laureate in the field of physics. At the time, Dr. Lederman was director of Fermi National Accelerator Laboratory in Batavia, Illinois, and chair of the State of Illinois's Governor's Science Advisory Committee. In 1985 Stephanie heard Dr. Lederman speak about the development of an institute of learning focusing on talent development in mathematics and science. Her response to the idea was immediate and impassioned. The day after hearing him Stephanie phoned Dr. Lederman and said to him, "You don't know me and I don't know you, but if you're serious [about the creation of this type of institution] I will help you. I'm not a scientist or a mathematician but I know how to design innovative learning environments." Stephanie and

Dr. Lederman soon developed a formidable partnership as they worked together with local and statewide corporate leaders, legislators, educators, and scientists to craft the legislation that would give birth to the Illinois Mathematics and Science Academy.

Stephanie described how "the first year of the academy . . . was a fascinating time. The institution was created in a climate of both high expectations and doubt. Let's just say not everybody embraced the creation of this institution." Although the bill was defeated the first time it was proposed to the Illinois General Assembly, Stephanie, Dr. Lederman, corporate and legislative leaders, and other IMSA supporters "came back a year later—much smarter . . . a little bit bloodied, but much wiser" and proposed the legislation again. Stephanie described how "key legislators . . . and key leaders in the community" were involved in the legislative process and how "lots of decisions were made extremely quickly. Agreements were made behind closed doors, agreements of honor, handshakes, and [the underlying message] 'we're going to make this happen' and 'Illinois is going to have a math and science academy.'"

After the bill successfully passed, the board of trustees was appointed and Stephanie became vice president of the board. The board then began organizing the academy's first school year. Stephanie described the startup process the legislators had agreed to: "The agreement was that we would start slowly with one class and we would add a class a year and then our funding would commensurately increase." She continued,

> And so we admitted the first [class]. [Stephanie was now IMSA president.] We had 200 kids and then, as per our agreement, in March of the first year we added another 200. We sent out the invitations and started the process of doubling the staff, and modifying the curriculum. We asked [the General Assembly] to double our appropriation. And we were told "No. Continue with the money that you have, 'uninvite' the kids and staff and we'll give you the money for next year, but run one more year with 200 students."

Although surprised by the General Assembly's decision to alter their original agreement to fund a new class of students for the second school year, Stephanie knew intuitively what the board's response to the General Assembly must be. Her belief that "there are some things we have to hold and have to expect the institution to hold . . . the institution's 'sense of self'" was at the core of her response. Stephanie describes her thinking,

I recommended to the [IMSA] board that we do not ["uninvite" the kids and staff and run one more year with 200]. I recommended that we make it really clear to the General Assembly that we would not go back on our word and that we would operate for six months and seek a supplemental appropriation. If we did not receive it, we would close on December 31st. And the board agreed with my recommendation. And I knew that . . . there was a strong possibility that of course the institution would close. All the students and all the staff but one returned.

Although Stephanie was confident in her recommendation to reject the General Assembly's proposal, she was well aware of the risk of the academy closing mid-school year.

Cognizant of the political fallout of this decision, Stephanie felt that to uninvite students, faculty, and staff would contradict the core values and beliefs IMSA had established for itself as a teaching and learning organization. Stephanie continues,

It was a decision about our NAME, our credibility, our word, and our identity. The most important decisions are always about your NAME. And . . . I put name in caps. It's always about your NAME—who you are, what you stand for, where is your stake in the ground. Those are almost always the decisions that really, really, matter. The other ones don't really matter as much. But the decisions about your NAME are the most important ones.

Committed to upholding the idea that IMSA's name represented "who they were" and "what they stood for" as an organization, Stephanie shared the decision with faculty, staff, and parents to elicit their feedback and plan their next steps.

I had to go to all the faculty and staff and say you have a job until December 31st, but if you leave there is no school so I'm asking you to stay. Because it was spring, they could have left in the summer and had jobs. Everybody stayed except one. We had to go to all the parents and say please send your kids back, but I'm only guaranteeing them a program until December 31st. They may be going back to their home schools. And then we got on every radio station and television station and took all 400 kids and the faculty to the capital and set up classes in the capital rotunda and the General Assembly passed a supplementary appropriation bill. This was a decision on principle. It was a decision about NAME and integrity.

The overwhelming commitment of faculty, staff, and parents to support Stephanie's recommendation and the board's decision is testimony to the power of an organization's "sense of self." However, Stephanie acknowledged that several people disagreed with her decision, many phoning her and pointedly asking "Have you lost it?"

When asked what it was about IMSA's "sense of self" that garnered such trust and commitment from faculty and staff, Stephanie reflected:

> Many of the people [who stayed] are still here, so we're talking 18 years ago. Some had young families. Some had college tuition, and some knew they could be out a job by the end of December. So what was it that made them stay? [brief pause] Because people are deeply yearning for a sense of purpose, something to believe in and feel proud about—something, some purpose—that will enable them to transcend who they are alone.

As she elaborated on this idea of people "yearning for a sense of purpose" Stephanie described how faculty and staff responded to what she considers one of the fundamental and often disregarded aspects of a leadership—inviting yourself and others to bring all of who you are to "your work on the planet." She continues,

> People are deeply yearning for a sense of purpose they can connect their lives to, something to feel proud about and something to be connected to that is bigger than they are. We all want to make a difference, and I think that's also part of it. . . . The other is this notion of [cynicism]. Cynicism is an interesting thing to me because it's not that cynics are not hopeful. They're just afraid to hope again. So, you need to give them a reason to hope one more time. Maybe it can be different. I believe that's partly what IMSA represents.

Emphasizing the importance of both our intellect and our personal sense of self, Stephanie rejects the myth of the superhero leader who is emotionally disengaged and removed from the organization. She focuses on the more subtle and intimate qualities of a leader's sense of self noting that,

> IMSA is not "who it is" . . . because there is one charismatic leader. But it's because I try to invite everyone's goodness and genius. I also remain personally open and vulnerable. I encourage everyone to bring all of who they

are to our work. We just don't know how to do it in most organizations, because most organizations don't invite all of who we are. Most organizations say bring your intellect, bring your expertise, bring your talents, bring your computer skills, bring your writing skills. But don't bring your soul. Souls are very messy and undisciplined!

Stephanie's decision to keep the doors of IMSA open to all invited students is one example of how her leadership emanates from and is integrated with the core values and beliefs of IMSA. This story illustrates Stephanie's belief that one of the most important roles of a leader is to ensure that the organization is honoring and acting on its sense of self. Stephanie emphasized that although there is no predetermined formula for making decisions with politically volatile outcomes, one guiding question she continues to utilize as she engages in her leadership work is: "When it is all said and done, what is the decision that affirms who we are and what we stand for?"

As we wrapped up our conversation, I asked Stephanie to describe what it was she felt she personally "stood for" when she made the decision to reject the Illinois General Assembly's recommendation, a decision that carried incredibly high levels of political risk for both the IMSA organization and her personally. She responded:

It's interesting to hear yourself reflect on your own patterns of behavior. [brief pause] To me, it goes back to name and integrity—the name of the institution and what it stood for. If I had "un-invited" 200 kids and dismissed new hires, no matter what I would ever say again, I believed IMSA and I would never be trusted. I believe I have a reputation that when I put my name on something you can take it to the bank. What I say is what I mean. . . . Your honor, your word, your sense of integrity, and self, that's what makes the difference.

Stephanie roots every aspect of her leadership work in IMSA's sense of self—its name. As demonstrated in this story, IMSA's name—its sense of self—is its mission and vision, core values and beliefs.

A New Language for Leadership

As noted earlier, Stephanie draws much of her information and insights about leadership from contemporary leadership theories. Throughout our time together, Stephanie spoke passionately about the need of a "new language for leadership." She considers language to play a fundamental role in how both individuals and organizations think about their work. She explains, "I spend a huge amount of time on language because I believe that language creates pictures, stories, and images. So I pay attention to words." Maintaining that using "a new language for leadership" can assist leaders in conceptualizing their work in a more integrated manner, Stephanie continues,

> We have to use a different language. For us to get out of the reductive, algorithmic, mechanistic, linear, objective world in which we live, we need a new language. And . . . the language has to come from nature. Because the current lexicon, by virtue of its . . . fragmentation and constraints, will not even allow us to think holistically. And we don't have the language yet. We're . . . slowly embracing it through nature and through ecology. If you look at someone like Fritjof Capra, he's working on how we view institutions as ecosystems; how we look at their relationships, their networks, and their diversity. . . . Because it's all about relationships. I also view organizations as living systems so I focus on relationships. It is about organizational identity, information, and relationships. So those three constructs are the domains of living systems. We must understand the language to allow us to get into new conversations.

As a leader, Stephanie invites the community into "new conversations" in order to "reveal and explore their best selves." Two examples, one relating to the nature of leadership and the other relating to the nature of schooling, illustrate how Stephanie utilizes "new language" to invite others into "new conversations."

The Being of Leadership

Stephanie recalled a time when a dear friend offered her some insights about the work in which she was engaged. Specifically, Stephanie was struggling with a writing project. She shares how the conversation with her friend began.

> [I said] I have this *task* ahead of me and it's on my shoulders all the time. My friend asked me what it was. I said, well I'm trying to write this book and I have a day job and I can't seem to get it all done. My friend said, well,

don't worry about it. You'll never write *this* book. I said, well what do you mean? She looked at me and said, "The soul doesn't do *tasks*. You'll write it when it becomes your soul's work."

As she summarized the importance of this conversation, Stephanie reflected, "So what does all of this have to do with leadership? To me, here's what it has to do with it. Leadership is not about doing. Leadership is about being. We lead who we are." Encouraging Stephanie to surrender to her soul-work invited her to "be different" not only in her writing but also in other elements of her leadership work. This integrated notion of "being" and "doing" very much shaped how Stephanie has come to think about her leadership work. It has provided Stephanie with a new way of both thinking about and speaking about the integrated nature of her leadership.

Inviting Grace

A second example of how articulating a "new language for leadership" is a natural part of Stephanie's integrated approach to leadership invites us to "think differently" about the nature of our work and about the nature of schooling itself. Stephanie reflected on the hope that a "new language for leadership" brings to her work. She shares,

> I'm a member of a board that is giving about eight or ten million dollars over the next couple of years to five or six high schools that we have identified. I spoke with the principal last night about the opportunity that these resources provide for them . . . to think boldly and bravely. And said, "You know if we had set out to design an institution that dishonored children and asked them to do unimportant work, and did not give them the flexibility and freedom to find out who they were, we would have designed the American high school. So, we've gotten exactly what we designed for. You now have a chance to bring a different set of values and principles to the design of something else."

Stephanie paused for a moment, and then continued:

> I made those comments at the beginning [of the meeting], and at the end [of the meeting] the chairman of our board was saying goodnight, and he said, I'm going to ask David just to say a prayer for us before we leave. David's a retired minister and another member of our board. I turned to the person

next to me who is the leader of this initiative. And I said, "We're starting a story—a five-year journey. When was the last time you ever began a professional venture with a prayer?" And he said never. And I said, "Remember this night. We have called in grace, and it will matter."

As evidenced in these stories, an essential component of leadership is reminding individuals and organizations of the integrative and sacred nature of our "work on the planet." Through employing a "new language of leadership"—language that allows both our mind and our spirit to speak—Stephanie challenges each of us to think "boldly and bravely" about the integrated nature of our work as school leaders.

CONCLUSION: LIVING OUT LOUD

As represented by the stories shared in this chapter, Stephanie Pace Marshall is an educational leader who is challenging herself and others to live into new possibilities. When asked to describe herself as a leader Stephanie responded with unassuming conviction: "I am a seeker, a wonderer, and a storyteller." I have been blessed to hear the stories she has gathered along her journey.

When I asked Stephanie how she would want to be remembered long after her work on Earth is done, she paused and then replied with an excerpt from a poem by Emile Zola: "When they asked what I came to do, I answered . . . I came to live out loud." In addition to her noteworthy leadership work at the Illinois Mathematics and Science Academy, another example of how Stephanie "lives out loud" is through her writing. As a scholar Stephanie shares her visionary, provocative, and integrative approach to leadership with the broader educational and leadership communities. I conclude the chapter with a recent example of her thinking and writing about leadership.

The New Work of Elder-Leadership
    We now need leaders who evoke spirit, invite soul and empower the fullness of our community's intellectual, emotional and spiritual potentials. We can no longer pretend that our interior lives are separate from the "real world" and our rigorous pursuit of deep learning. Our system of schooling has lost its connection to life and deep learning and this has severed its abil-

ity to evoke the wholeness, meaning and connectedness and creativity our children so desperately seek. This enormous hunger for learning and for a transcendent story of meaning, purpose and belonging is not being fed in the old places. If we want to unleash the intelligences, creativity, and adaptive capacities of our systems and our children and if we want to increase their individual and collective knowledge, vibrancy, inventiveness, and shared sense of purpose, we must be engaged in new work. Our system's capacity for openness, exploration, creativity, and connectedness, depends upon the conditions we create by design that enable life and deep learning to flourish.

Chapter Nine

Concluding Reflections

Conducting the research and writing this book took place over four years, and involved countless hours, much persistence, and the generous investment of time and energy by 18 Illinois Women Administrator interviewers and 18 impressive women leaders. We took an innovative, participative, essentially feminist approach to this research project by involving IWA members at the grass roots level as collaborators (Olesen, 2000). The interviewees, as well as interviewers, became collaborators in the project when the interview transcripts were sent to both for corrections and clarifications. Finally, each woman quoted by name reviewed chapters and provided clarification and feedback. This was a safeguard for preserving the authenticity of the voices of those interviewed. A goal of the book has been to give voice to both the interviewees and the interviewers as we have woven the themes. As Olesen articulates so well, "How to make women's voices heard without exploiting or distorting those voices is an equally vexatious question" (p. 231). We are aware of the caution against "taking individual voices to reflect group ideas" (p. 232), although we have used the technique of representative quotations to build our themes.

The previous chapters have presented what has been learned about the *how* and *why* of leadership through this research. Our four themes—developing collaborative decision-making processes, pushing the bureaucratic boundaries, claiming power through politics, and living and leading from values—suggest that redefining leadership requires a new integration of *doing* and *being*. In the spirit of postmodernism, we end not with conclusions but rather with reflections about the process, content, and meaning of the book, beginning with the voices of the persons involved in the project as interviewers.

INTERVIEWER REFLECTIONS

Interviewer reflections are focused on both the process and content of the book, as well as the project's effect on them as persons and leaders. Interviewer reflections were collected at three points in time. At the end of the initial training on September 9, 2000, reflections were submitted from 13 of the 24 who attended. Then in March 2001, the 18 persons who had completed an interview were invited to a debriefing meeting. Reflective comments in response to questions we asked were made orally at that meeting by the 10 who attended. A transcript of the meeting was prepared to capture the comments. Finally, 16 of the 18 interviewers wrote and submitted reflections after completing their interviews.

Reflective comments by 13 interviewers at end of the initial organizational and training meeting reflected much enthusiasm for the project. Nine women explained how the collaborative nature of the project was important to them. Six described how energized they felt by the project, with *excited* being the word most frequently used. For example, one wrote, "I am so excited about participating in a project that will allow me to work with women who are dedicated to the celebration of women leaders, to meet a woman who has shown exemplary leadership qualities, and to ultimately find my fit in a leadership role. I look forward to being a user of the final product." Comments from seven others focused on content, either on the topic of creative insubordination, or women's ways of leadership, or the potential usefulness of the book. One interviewer spoke of the book to come in terms of its "potential for furthering women's preparation for educational administration." Another person said, "Very often in our everyday lives as educators/leaders we are in male-dominated arenas that are not always the most conducive to the exchange of ideas and information important to women." Someone else wrote, "It has been a bonding day." Another wrote, "This is an exciting relevant project, one which I feel can greatly benefit all who choose to lead. I learned so much, just sitting, listening, asking questions—just spending time with women, speaking our minds directly (like a male, I guess) but always spoken with or to in a connectedness (like a female, I guess)." Another commented, "The collaborative nature of this project seems really appropriate. I believe that this research could serve to legitimize 'women's ways of leading' in a way that previous work has not been able to achieve."

The debriefing meeting in March 2001 was conducted like a focus group. Two questions elicited rich reflections. The first of these questions was "How close was the experience to what you expected?" Several mentioned that there were no real surprises. Three were surprised by the emotion of the experience, however. One said, "I was surprised about how much this interview impacted and changed me." Another person said that the interview "exceeded her expectations." She continued, "I am still emotional about the time we spent together. I came to know her humanness." The third person articulated a thought that generated widespread agreement: "I discovered that even though I knew her story, I didn't know it."

A topic that came up in the discussion of this question about whether the experience was what you expected was a perception of a *mask* by three of the interviewers. For example, one person said, "There were a few moments when poise dropped away and she revealed a little bit about her struggles with the male bureaucracy, but she wouldn't stay there long." Another used the word *mask*, saying, "Some things I expected, but I did not expect the mask piece. It seems to be part of the way she has gotten to where she is—that effective mask. It was disappointing not to be able to get to the heart of it." A third interviewer referred to her sense of the participant being "armored," perhaps wanting to give the right answers. This perception of a mask interested the persons at the meeting, and discussion ensued about possible reasons. The perception itself, however, was not widespread.

The second question discussed was "Has what you experienced or learned made any difference to you?" Two spoke of having new insights. One of these two talked of having more awareness, especially with regard to creative insubordination. The other shared this realization: "It's important to listen to everyone's stories, their wisdom." Two spoke specifically about being different, while three others described a sense of renewal. In one woman's words, "I am doing something different. Her insight that women tend to wait until they have learned enough to take on more spoke to me. I am allowing myself to take the time I need for learning." A second person said, "I am building on the good woman/smart woman piece. I am becoming more creatively insubordinate as a result of this experience. I am wondering about whether I am being too careful, in fact, and if it is hampering me from getting done what I want to do." The statements by the three who had experienced renewal were powerful. One said, "The

interview made me realize that I am not done. It is not time for me to retire. It helped me decide to run for the high school board. I have too much
energy. My story is not done." Another said with admiration, "I said to
myself that I wanted to be like her—have that kind of a spirit and a heart.
I said to myself 'get back on that path, that's the way to go.' The interview
renewed my values and aspirations." Finally, one woman was completely
in agreement with those expressing renewal, and described her experience
of the interview as lifesaving. She said,

> I identify with you who say "I was reminded again of what I am about." I
> had been broken by who I had worked with, did not consciously realize that
> I didn't care anymore. I am no longer jaded. I have a purpose again. I care.
> I will never not care again. She gave me permission to be creatively insub-
> ordinate. In losing my purpose I had begun to believe that I was wrong. I
> left the interview thinking that I was right. I went into a room and cried. A
> piece of me was dead and I didn't even know it. I don't know where I would
> be today if I had not had this experience.

Finally, reflections written by 16 of the 18 after their interviews provided the richest source of data about how the interviewers had been personally affected by participating in this research. Several themes from the
March focus-group discussion were extended. Each person was asked to
write a reflection on the process and content of the interview, as well as to
reflect on how they had been affected as leaders. A few wrote of surprises,
extending that theme. For example, "I was shocked to find out that gender had never affected her opportunities in any of the districts where she
has worked." Another said of the person she interviewed, "I was surprised
by her openness, frankness, candor." One person used the word energized,
extending that theme. She wrote after the interview, "I was energized
hearing that she had started her career late in life too. I had wondered if I
had started this leg of the journey too late."

Also extending a theme in previous reflections, several interviewers described inspiration and renewal. For example,

> I learned that I could be a superintendent if her leadership style becomes in
> demand. Her understanding of an educational leader is different from most
> superintendents I know. It was an encouraging personal and professional en-
> counter. Nicest outcome was the validation of many of my beliefs and un-

derstanding of leadership. This experience has increased my confidence in my leadership abilities. I believe that I have what it takes to be an outstanding superintendent.

Another wrote, "I learned that strong leadership gets things done; that people are what matter. I learned that it is okay, if not necessary, to have values and beliefs/principles that you live by, that impact your leadership style. It was refreshing to listen to someone who lives what she believes and follows her guidelines/principles first and the institutional ones second." Another interviewer expressed being inspired in these words:

This was a very rewarding experience. I had a block of quality, uninterrupted time to talk with an admired professional woman who has climbed many mountains and risen to the top through hard work and commitment. I felt inspired and in awe of her demeanor and her wisdom in choosing words carefully and articulating so clearly. I was absolutely blown away with her professional, perfectly couched responses to what must have been very difficult questions. Her professionalism showed throughout the interview. Will I be different? I hope so.

Still another interviewer experienced renewal, a sense of not being alone. She wrote, "Through my interview, I have seen my manner of leading reinforced. I have learned that I am alone in the decision-making process, but not really alone in that there are others practicing discretionary decision making and creative insubordination and using integrity and honesty for the benefit of the children."

Finally, an interviewer wrote of being moved to tears at one point in her interview by the "passion with which she [the participant] spoke about her life's work; the genuineness with which she shared her thoughts and feelings—these all moved me." She continued,

I was inspired, excited, disheartened, and hopeful all at the same time. The statement that brought me to tears was "It is not about doing but about being." I cannot begin to describe to you the visceral reaction that came over me as I heard these words. For years I have searched to integrate these two parts of myself into my work as an educator. I have felt in my bones forever that there has to be a way for me to do and be at the same time. But I am young. I have a difficult time assuming my belief/my idea/my hypothesis/my intuition/my voice could be right. So my initial response was one of hopefulness for the practice of administration and self-deprecation for me. Eventually after several days of reflection and analysis of the interview I was able to see myself as a fellow leader working in my own way to put into practices the beliefs/values/ideas we share in common.

Taken as a group, these layers of reflections suggest being on the interviewing team was a meaningful experience that had strongly positive and some profound effects. The learning took many forms, ranging from learning to do an interview for some, to validating and renewing core beliefs for others.

AUTHORS' REFLECTIONS

We have been personally strengthened by the collaborative process of this research and what we have learned. We have experienced both the complexity of collaboration and the *wisdom of the group* from start to finish of this project. We have changed our minds, and our direction more than once. We have alternated between wanting to present current scholarship and wanting to feature voices of practitioners, hoping to arrive at a balance. We view the content of the book as a contribution to knowledge about women's leadership, but more importantly to understanding of educational leadership as a field of practice, of what is required from women and men who would lead education in the 21st century. We anchor our reflections to those two arenas of scholarship and practice.

Studying Women's Leadership

In chapter 2 we raised four contemporary issues in the study of women's leadership: resolving cultural tensions, essentializing, honoring diversity, and the role of feminism and feminist research. It seems fair to say that most participants adopted an individual as opposed to collective approach to resolving cultural tensions at a personal level, including redefining roles. Certainly our participants, particularly those whose leadership interfaced with the political arena, were aware of cultural tensions surrounding their leadership roles. The participation in political activity by the participants suggests openness to collective approaches to getting things done. A desire to redress wrongs could involve them in collective action with regard to gender inequities (Chase, 1995). We did find examples, in some participants' responses to questions about gender, of what Chase has called a *discursive disjunction* between women's experiences of professional success, and their "subjection to gender and racial inequalities" (p. 11). Although several interviewers sensed a mask in place during the interview situation with participants, this was not prevalent across the interviews. Interviewers did not spend enough time with the participants to identify their leader personas, although transcripts suggested that several participants did seem to lead from transcendent themes (Curry, 2000). The importance given to integrity by well over half the participants suggest them to be leading and living authentically, including their *being* in their *doing*. All the participants seemed comfortable with authority and the positions to which their ambitions had taken them. Several have achieved comfort through redefining roles, in particular the role of the superintendent. Through their stories we have presented "images of female power that can inform notions of leadership" (Conway, 2001, p. xix).

We have kept in mind feminist concerns about the study of women's leadership. We have paid attention to the "'micropolitics' of power" (Arnot, 2002, p. 258) in our analysis of data revealing how the participants claimed political power. We have avoided essentializing, making any generalizations about *all* women as leaders, even though the beliefs of the majority of our participants do reflect an essentialist view of women's leadership practices. We have included views of diverse women in the perspectives of the four African American participants. We have noted when the views of this group differed and when they were similar. Their stories and experiences clearly illustrate why it is important, as discussed in chapter 2, to include the views of diverse women when studying women's leadership. If not *alternative* visions, each did have strong values and clear visions of what she wanted to accomplish as a leader (AhNee-Benham, 2003; Dillard, 1995; Mendez-Morse, 2003). Each of the four leads from a deep spiritual reservoir, bringing her whole *being* into her *doing* (Atlas & Capper, 2003; Murtadha-Watts, 1999). Finally, their stories suggest strongly that the intersection of race and gender in barriers to leadership opportunity still confronts minority women who would lead (Alston, 1999; Brunner, 2003).

We believe this book makes a contribution in terms of the new questions and emerging themes in the study of women's leadership that we identified in chapter 2. Ideas and practices from chapters 4 and 5 illustrate how some women are reshaping the prevailing definitions of leadership and power. In chapter 7 we elaborate on their redefining of leadership through the integration of doing and being, and connect their ways to newer understandings of leadership and the postmodern worldview. We believe taking the examples of our participants seriously could enable us to "change the face of educational leadership" (Gardiner, Enomoto, & Grogan, 2000). The deliberateness with which the leaders in this study brought their values into every aspect of their leadership practices contributes to the emerging literature on "the meaning-making practices of women leaders" (Blackmore, 2002, p. 55). Our intent in this book as expressed in chapter 1 has been to approach what Shakeshaft (1999) describes as Stage 5 research, that challenges traditional leadership theories, and contribute to Stage 6 research that will eventually document how theory has been transformed or reconceptualized to include experiences of women.

Educational Leadership in Theory and in Practice

There is no agreed-upon definition of leadership, but there is agreement that the leadership required in the organizations of today is not the leadership of yesterday. The traditional ways of thinking about school administration are inadequate for educational leadership in the 21st century (Murphy, 2002). In the words of Senge (1990), we no longer need "the captain of the cavalry leading the charge" kind of leadership (p. 340). Instead, we can consult an array of theorists who offer other views of leadership. For example, Heifetz (1994) encourages us to focus on leadership as *doing*. He writes, "Rather than define leadership either as a position of authority in a social structure or as a personal set of characteristics, we may find it a great deal more useful to define leadership as an *activity*" (p. 20) that involves "choreographing and directing learning processes in an organization or a community" (p. 187). Drath (1996) points to the emergence of a relational model of leadership. Drath and Palus (1994) write that "leadership is a social meaning-making process that occurs in groups engaged in some activity together" (p. 1). Furman (2003) directs us to consider "that educational leadership as a field is focusing more and more on what leadership is *for*, that it is the moral purposes of educational leadership that are emerging as the central focus" (p. 1). Wheatley (1992) writes, "What leaders are called upon to do in a chaotic world is to shape their organizations through concepts, not through elaborate rules or structures" (p. 133). Bolman and Deal (1995) address leading as *being* in these words, "Leading is giving. Leadership is an ethic, a gift of oneself. It is easy to miss the depth and power of this message. The essence of leadership is not giving things or even providing visions. It is offering oneself and one's spirit" (p. 102).

Leadership theory and practice are responding to societal changes by shifting focus from what leaders do and how they do it to what leadership is for, with a resulting emphasis on values. The data and the major themes identified in our research suggest that the leaders we studied are leading from contemporary, even postmodern, understandings of leadership. They are focused on what leadership is *for*. As we discussed in chapter 3, an overwhelming majority of the 18 leaders we studied understood the power of collaboration, of relational leadership (Drath, 1996). For 14 participants, collaborative decision-making processes associated with meaning making were the norm (Drath & Palus, 1994). As documented in chapter 4, 12 participants had a high comfort level with creative insubordination, troubling, pushing, or simply going around the bureaucratic rules and structures that stood in the way of valued ends. Another five participants were inclined to transcend and transform bureaucratic structures in order to get things done, to shape their organizations through concepts (Wheatley, 1992). As illustrated in chapter 5, the leaders we studied had a clear idea of what their leadership was *for*, and all but one described conscious decisions to engage in political acts in order to accomplish something important to them, which in every case had to do with their values (Furman, 2003). As displayed in chapter 6, the leaders in our study understand leading as "an ethic, a gift of oneself," as seen in their commitments to caring relationships, their integrity, and their willingness to take risks to benefit children (Bolman & Deal, 1995). Their leading integrates *being* and *doing*. We believe their leadership practices redefine leadership as they bring emerging leadership theory to life.

Leadership must be redefined because schools can and must do a better job of educating every child. Educational failure is no longer an option in this country or anywhere else. Educators across the globe face inadequate funding, issues of accountability, and growing numbers of children and families living in poverty. The problems seem insurmountable; they are not, however, impossible to confront. Antrobus (2000) writes, from her perspective as an feminist activist in the Latin American and Caribbean region for over twenty years, "As my first case-study shows, transformational leadership is possible within bureaucracies" (p. 55). Change is possible but we must be asking the larger questions. Heifetz (1994) eloquently asserts, "One may lead perhaps with no more than a question in hand" (p. 276). From the United Kingdom, MacBeath (2002) asks important questions,

> Within a political context, increasingly global in nature, increasingly hegemenous, what is truly "effective'" leadership? How can it be genuinely learning-centered? How can leaders help to create the conditions in which their students and their teachers can "live finely," can give their attention to the things that matter, can be the building blocks of a better more democratic social order? (p. 104)

Yet as Blackmore (1999), an Australian, makes clear, "One is rarely encouraged to ask: leading to what end and for whom—for the national interest, for individual students, for social justice in a democratic society?" (p. 5). To name only a few, global challenges include ongoing violence, lack of clean water, growing numbers of refugees, unprecedented species extinction, nuclear proliferation, global warming, widespread injustice, and the search for sustainable ways of living. "The key to ending violence between cultures and advancing to global cultures of peace, nonviolence, and mutual flourishing is our individual and collective advance as beings who live in patterns of deep dialogue" (Muller, Lazlo, & Singh, 2004). Through meaningful dialogue, we can build communities of difference, find unity within diversity, and create schools that are democratic, just, empathetic, and optimistic (Shields, 2003).

Leaders, including those in education, must address the tragedies of war, hunger, and disease that daily decimate populations around the globe. We address them through providing students in our schools and universities with the best possible education of their hearts and minds. As a species, we are facing great adaptive challenges or problems for which the answers are simply unknown. Heifetz (1994) defines adaptive challenges as those that require adaptive work, meaning a "change in values, beliefs, or behavior" (p. 22). We cannot simply apply some sort of technical fix or carry on with business as usual; if we are to meet adaptive challenges, learning is required. Learning implies engagement with the unknown. "The inclusion of competing value perspectives may be essential to adaptive success," Heifetz writes (p. 23). The voices of women and men need to be at the tables where decisions are made during these challenging times. It will take well-educated compassionate leaders throughout the world, women and men, to make progress on these and other issues that threaten life as we know it. We must pass on to the future generations the best of what is known and we must teach them to ask and keep asking the important questions. It is time to treat future generations as we would be treated. We must learn to move from a monocentric modernist lens to be able to dance between worlds, to see reality differently, to lead differently. We must move beyond dualistic thinking, one expression of which is gender inequity.

FINAL REFLECTIONS

In a book about the leadership gap between men and women, Wilson (2004) has identified four contemporary scarlet A's that intertwine with women's aspirations and opportunities to participate as equal partners with men in the leadership of government in the United States at all levels, including the White House. Reminiscent of the scarlet letter the fictional Hester Prynne was forced to wear for stepping outside cultural norms for the mid-19th century, the contemporary scarlet A's Wilson (2004) identifies for women who would lead are **a**uthority, **a**mbition, **a**bility, and **a**uthenticity. She calls these "the ways we [women] are minimized and defined, ways we are kept in our place, and ways we keep ourselves from the life we might lead" (p. 29). The media supports the perception that women neither have nor can handle authority. Women are often required to cut down their ambitions to what is considered appropriate. Wilson traces how perceptions of women as having less ability than men have developed historically over time, in part by the devaluing of women's work in the home. Finally, she looks at issues associated with authenticity that emerge for women who would lead with their whole *being* rather than imitating stereotypical male approaches. Looking at the cultural disconnect between leader and woman, she advocates hanging on to authenticity and emphasizes the importance of refusing to imitate men as a pathway to authority. She considers the cost to men and boys, as well as to women and girls, of keeping one's caring side out of the public sphere.

In fact, a leadership gap between men and women exists in all the institutions of contemporary society. Wilson's argument that women's leadership matters places the ongoing struggle for gender equity in educational leadership into its rightful larger context: equal numbers of women in school, district, and university leadership will contribute to transforming not only these organizations, but also American culture, and ultimately the world. Wilson's premise is "that our future depends on the leadership of women—not to replace men, but to transform our options alongside them" (p. x). Wilson believes that as a country we remain in denial about the cultural barriers to women's leadership. "Americans tend to ignore the societal and cultural foot dragging at the root of the matter, often failing to recognize deeply embedded gender roles that, for all our advancement, have kept our nation from realizing its potential" (p. 18). Because "male assertiveness and control continue to be in higher demand" (p. 21), Wilson advocates for a redefinition of culturally accepted definitions and perceptions of leadership and who leaders are. This book and the leaders we portray contribute to that overdue cultural redefinition.

We interviewed women who have emerged as recognized authorities within differing educational settings, women who have claimed and developed their abilities and have been ambitious. They have not only survived but thrived, with their authentic selves and their integrity intact. They have confronted the cultural scarlet *A*'s courageously and their stories contribute to transforming each *A* from a constraint to a component of possibility. Wilson calls for a post-heroic understanding of leadership as "relational and collaborative" (p. 107). Unfortunately, she writes, "Traditionally, our culture sees leadership as men's work; when it is executed by women (or nontraditionally by men), it is often not acknowledged as leadership at all" (p. 106). She concludes, "When we finally assign value to the assets of women, when we encourage men to lead relationally, when we merge our public and private selves to create strong bonds at work and at home, we will alter the meaning of leadership" (p. 115). It is time to close the leadership gap and alter the meaning of leadership in education. Our hope is that this book will contribute to the ongoing redefinition of leadership, that *leaders who dare* will move themselves and our culture closer to gender inclusive perceptions of what leadership is and who leaders are.

Biographical Sketches
of Leaders Interviewed

DR. MARY JAYNE BRONCATO

Mary Jayne Broncato retired from the position of deputy state superintendent at the Illinois State Board of Education (ISBE) in 2003 to become an educational consultant. Her educational background includes a bachelor's in literature from Lewis University in 1961, a master's in educational administration from Northern Illinois University in 1969, and a doctorate in educational administration from the University of Illinois in 1996. She began her career teaching literature at St. Francis High School in Wheaton, moving from there to teach in Romeoville, then joining the Joliet Public Schools #86 in 1967. She taught for a total of 13 years. She was in charge of instruction for nine years and served as superintendent of the Joliet Elementary District for seven years before moving on to ISBE. Joliet is a large urban district with a thousand employees and 24 schools. Dr. Broncato served the Joliet district from 1967 until she joined the state board staff in March 1990 as associate state superintendent for programs and accountability, one of six senior staff positions.

At ISBE, Dr. Broncato led the agency's instructional programs over a 12-year period in Springfield, including serving as interim state superintendent in 1994. She is the first and only woman to date to hold the position of state superintendent in Illinois, interim or otherwise. Dr. Broncato's main responsibility as an assistant to the superintendent was to supervise the creation of a new accreditation process for schools and students. The General Assembly passed legislation in 1991 (P.A. 87-559) establishing accreditation of schools based on performance. Under the new plan, Dr. Broncato oversaw input from over 13,000 people who were affected by a new way to accredit schools. Another major accomplishment of her career was providing leadership for the Flexible Service Delivery System (FLEX) in 1995 as an option for Illinois districts to use in addressing a number of ongoing problems in the delivery of special education services. She was actively involved in expanding the state-funded early childhood program. She continues as a consultant to work with Illinois school districts on improving curriculum and instruction. Her interviewer described Mary Jayne as a most amiable, easy-to-talk-to person, saying, "She laughed at herself, readily shared stories, and is notably committed to doing what's best for children." Mary Jayne described herself as tending to be a "hands-on, face-to-face, walk-around administrator." Asked for what she would like to be remembered, she replied, "that my focus was always on what was best for kids." To describe her career in one word, she finally settled on the word *"fun."* Mary Jayne received the *Dare to Be Great* award from IWA in 2005.

Interviewer: Jeanne Bodnar

Jeanne Bodnar is principal of Whittier School in Blue Island, Illinois. She has over 30 years of experience in education, 20 of those in administration. Her educational background includes a bachelor's from Loyola University in 1971, and a master's in educational administration and supervision from Chicago State University in 1984. She was the Illinois D.A.R.E. Educator of the Year in 2000.

OLA MARIE BUNDY

Ola Bundy retired in 1996 after 29 years as assistant executive director for the Illinois High School Association (IHSA). At IHSA she was responsible for developing interscholastic athletic competition for girls in Illinois. She is recognized as one of the pioneers of girls' athletic competition. She implemented Title IX, and was instrumental in the formulation of the Illinois Sex Equity Rules. Her responsibilities included the administration of state series tournaments in a variety of sports for boys as well as girls. Bundy's career also included a year of teaching at Champaign Central High School, six years of teaching at Lansing (Thornton Fractional South) high school, and half a year at Homer High School. She taught physical education and was Girls Athletic Association (GAA) advisor at all the schools where she taught. She earned a bachelor's in physical education in 1958 from the University of Illinois, Urbana, and later completed some graduate work at the University of Illinois and Northern Illinois University. Administrative experience before accepting the position at IHSA included assistant director of two Girl Scout camps, and serving as assistant director and then director for five years at Northern GAA Leadership Camp conducted by IHSA.

Her interviewer wrote this about Ola Bundy: "Her standard that women coaches should coach and officiate girls' sports whenever possible, that women should be selected for the girls' sports IHSA advisory boards, that women should assume athletic director positions, and that women should be high school principals affected the entire education arena in Illinois." Highlights, to name only a few, from Bundy's distinguished career include the National Distinguished Service Award, presented by the U.S. Volleyball Association for leadership in Illinois and nationally; the Pathfinder Award, presented by the National Association for Girls and Women in Sport; she was inducted into the Illinois Basketball Coaches Hall of Fame; she was the first person inducted into the Illinois Girls' Coaches Association Hall of Fame; she was inducted into the National High School Sports Hall of Fame; she was a recipient of the Diamond in the Rough Award, presented by the Willye White Foundation on the occasion of the 10th Annual National Girls and Women in Sports Day; she received the Special Recognition Award from the Illinois State Board of Education for contributions toward gender equity in Illinois schools; and she received the *Dare to Be Great* award from Illinois Women Administrators in 2001.

Adjectives Ola Bundy thought others would use to describe her included the word *responsible*. When asked to what she was unalterably committed, she answered, "I think equity in everything, whether it's equity for the girls or for the boys, or completely throughout the entire IHSA program and operation." Asked for what she wanted to be remembered, Ola replied, "Equity in the schools. I feel I made a contribution in making equity a reality for so many schools and for their students, and not just because it was the law, but because it was the right thing to do."

Interviewer: Dr. Vita P. Meyer

Vita Meyer is a retired high school principal. Since retirement, she has been an adjunct professor at Governor's State University, a consultant for

Illinois state board of education, trainer for the Gates project with Illinois State University, and president of the board of education for Bremen School District #228. She describes herself as one of the many women whose positions in administration were a result of the mentoring of Ola Bundy. In addition to being an interviewer, Vita is one of the leaders interviewed for this book and received the *Dare to Be Great* award in 2002.

DR. ANN DUNCAN

Ann Duncan had almost 30 years of administrative experience before retiring. She served as superintendent for two districts, Giant City District #130, from 1989 to 1992, and Carlyle U.S.D. #1 from 1992 to 1998. She had been a principal in Carterville Unit #1 from 1973 to 1989. She received a bachelor's degree (1960) and master's degree (1961) in rhetoric and public address from Southern Illinois University–Carbondale. Her doctorate in educational administration was earned in 1982, also from Southern Illinois University–Carbondale. Dr. Duncan was accidentally an educator, with neither her bachelor's nor master's degrees in education. She obtained her first teaching job in Arkansas when walking her daughter in a stroller past the superintendent's office. She wondered if they needed a teacher, went in to inquire, was interviewed and hired on the spot. She taught English in the junior high that fall before she and her family moved to Illinois. Again, she secured a teaching job almost accidentally after learning from a friend that the district needed a kindergarten teacher. After teaching kindergarten for three years, Ann took steps to earn a teaching certificate.

Dr. Duncan was teaching and serving as the teachers' union representative when Unity Point expressed displeasure with the superintendent. Because Ann had a master's degree, she was recruited to do the work of the superintendent and given the title of curriculum director. In addition to her work in the central office, Ann went back to school to begin classes in administration. She continued in that central office position from 1968 until 1973, when she left to become a principal and curriculum director in Carterville, a position she held for 16 years before becoming a superintendent. Since retiring as a superintendent, she has served as a consultant to the Regional Office of Education #50.

Ann Duncan served as president of IWA for two years from 1990 to 1992. As president, she encouraged members to "look on the 1990s as the decade to reach out to other women." At the time, she was one of only 35 women superintendents among the 950 superintendents in Illinois. The membership of IWA expanded greatly during her tenure as president and she was honored by IWA with the *Dare to Be Great* award in 1992. An underlying value for Ann is that "all people have valuable input," a belief that undergirds her commitment to shared decision making. The three words she picked to describe herself as a leader were *decisive*, *open*, and *flexible.* Her answer to the question "To what are you unalterable committed?" was brief and to the point: *kids.* When asked what she wanted to be remembered for, Ann replied, "I would like to be known as someone who helped other women develop into good educators."

Interviewer: Dr. Pam Floit

Pam Floit earned her doctorate in educational administration from Illinois State University. At the time of the interview, she was an assistant superintendent for Collinsville Unit #10. She is currently superintendent of Belle Valley School District #119 in Belle Valley, Illinois. Pam served as IWA president from 1998 to 1999.

BRENDA J. HOLMES

At the time of her interview, Brenda Holmes had just begun serving as an educational consultant/lobbyist for the Illinois Statewide School Management Alliance. Her previous positions included 13 years as a special assistant to the state superintendent of education, Illinois State Board of Education (ISBE). In that position she oversaw and directed federal and state governmental relations, public affairs, the legal department, internal audits, and human resources. She was a member of the ISBE executive cabinet. She served most recently as deputy chief of staff for education, appointed by and reporting directly to the governor, and she is serving as a member of the Illinois state board of education. Brenda earned a bachelor's degree in education from Eastern Illinois University in 1969, followed by a master's degree in history in 1972 from Sangamon State University, now the University of Illinois–Springfield. She has additional hours of postgraduate studies. After teaching social studies at Pawnee High School Unit District #11 for 13 years, she decided she really wanted to pursue a career in government working with the legislative process. First she spent a year in the Illinois legislative internship program, for which she was selected by a competitive process. Then she moved onto the legislative staff for the Illinois State Senate, where she served for three years in a position that included staffing the Senate Education Committee.

Brenda Holmes was characterized by her interviewer as "an admired professional woman who has climbed many mountains and risen to the top through hard work and commitment." The interviewer also spoke of Brenda's "professional demeanor and her wisdom in choosing words carefully and articulating so clearly." Brenda described herself as impatient, hard working, and with high expectations. She called herself "unalterably committed to sharing information about how the legislative process works" because she believes that "people have misconceptions and are somewhat cynical about the process." Brenda said, "I would really like to be remembered as a person who is helpful, and as one who follows through on what I've been asked to do. That's very important—*my credibility*." Brenda received the *Dare to Be Great* award from IWA in 2005.

Interviewer: Dr. Frances Karanovich

Fran Karanovich has been a superintendent in Illinois for 12 years, currently serving the Macomb Community Unit District #185. She began her administrative career in Georgia, where she served for five years as an assistant superintendent for curriculum and instruction. She earned her doctorate in science educational leadership from Georgia State University, has served as president of Illinois Women Administrators, and continues to serve on the IWA board. In 2004, Fran was named Superintendent of the Year by Illinois Association of School Administrators (IASA).

DR. GWENDOLYN LEE

Since 1999, Gwen Lee has been associate superintendent of schools in Thornton Township High School District #205 in suburban Chicago, where she is in charge of curriculum and instruction. Except for two years as principal of Hillcrest High School in District #228 from 1992 to 1994, her career has been in Thornton Township. She was hired to be a social studies teacher at Thornridge High School in 1971, where she taught for 10 years. Her administrative positions in Thornton Township have included four years as dean of students, seven years as assistant principal, and six years as principal, all at Thornridge High School. She was named Principal of the Year in 1998–1999 by the Illinois Principals Association, and is active in a number of professional and community organizations. An African American, Gwen grew up in Gary, Indiana. Her educational background includes a bachelor's degree in history and political science from Ball State University (1970), a master's degree in history from Purdue University (1973), a master's degree in administration from Purdue University (1985), and a Ph.D. in education administration and policy studies from Loyola University in 1998.

Gwen describes her career as a "dream come true." She thought others in describing her as a leader would say she was dedicated and very cooperative, maybe a groomer, because "I am always putting someone else in a leadership role, which to me is true leadership." When asked for three words to describe herself as a leader, she chose *proactive, positive,* and *compassionate.* A word that definitely describes Gwen Lee is respect. She embodies respect for herself and others. She maintains her integrity. She is careful to respect the integrity of people she works with because, in her words, "They have a lot to offer." She respects the rules and policies of the bureaucracy in her district while at the same time realizing that she can find ways to make the right decisions for students. Her interviewer characterized Gwen as a "woman of courage." Gwen was honored by IWA with the *Dare to Be Great* award in 2005.

Interviewer: Lynda E. Irvin

Lynda Irvin is a doctoral candidate at Illinois State University and project coordinator for Illinois Technology and Leadership for Change (ITLC), a Bill and Melinda Gates Leadership Challenge Grant. Her bachelor's and master's degrees, as well as her educational specialist certificate, are from Ohio State University. A former principal, she founded *Leadership in Educational Innovations,* a consulting firm working with 26 school districts in Illinois as well as professional organizations and state departments of education in eight states.

DR. ELIZABETH I. LEWIN

Elizabeth Lewin, or Liz as she prefers to be called, is superintendent of Carbondale Elementary District #95, with an enrollment of 2,000 spread out in six different buildings. She began that position in 1995. At the time of the interview, she was the only female superintendent in her regional office of education district that covers two counties in southern Illinois. Her previous administrative positions included an assistant principalship from 1988 to 1992 in Edwardsville Unit District #7, dean of students, and finally a high school principalship in that district from 1992 to 1995. In 1995 she was recruited by the Carbondale Board of Education to come back to her nearby hometown to be the superintendent.

Dr. Lewin was born into a talented African American family in Carbondale. Her parents were first-generation college students and both earned graduate degrees. In fact, her father, who was a gifted teacher and preacher, had five degrees and was a Civil Rights leader in southern Illinois. Dr. Lewin earned her doctorate from the University of South Florida in 1997. Graduate work in educational administration earned her educational specialist credentials from Southern Illinois University–Edwardsville in 1980. Her two previous degrees had been from Southern Illinois University–Carbondale, a bachelor's degree in speech and English in 1970, and a master's degree in communications in 1971. Before becoming an administrator, she taught for 17 years.

Her interviewer wrote about Liz, "Her diligence and drive for detail are to be commended. She is to be recognized for her positive impact upon students, faculty, staff, parents, and community." Liz was honored with the *Dare to Be Great* award in 2004. Asked what three words she thought others would use to describe her as a leader, she chose *consensus builder*, *collaborator*, and *team builder*. In describing herself, Liz said, "I am passionate about my work and have been since I began my career in the classroom." Asked for a word to summarize her career she chose *doer*, saying, "If there's going to be any word that's going to sum up my career, it is that I get things accomplished."

Interviewer: Norma Borgmann

Norma Borgmann retired in 2004 as superintendent of Patoka Community Unit #100 in Patoka, Illinois. She was employed by the same district for

33 years, including the last 14 as an administrator. Her administrative positions have included a year as administrative assistant at the junior high level, and three years as K–12 principal. She has been an IWA member since 1991 and was honored by IWA with the *Dare to Be Great* award in 2000.

DR. HAZEL E. LOUCKS

Hazel Loucks is currently an independent consultant working in the Virgin Islands, Missouri, South Carolina, Arkansas, and Illinois. She most recently worked as an ESEA/NCLB specialist for the National Education Association (NEA), speaking and consulting in all fifty states. She served as deputy governor for education and workforce development in Illinois from January 1999 to 2003. In that position, Dr. Loucks served as spokesperson for the governor on matters regarding education and workforce in Illinois. Hazel earned a Ph.D. in education administration from Saint Louis University in 1987, a master's in personnel in higher education from Ohio State University in 1972, and a bachelor's in education from Southern Illinois University–Carbondale in 1966. She has been an elementary classroom teacher, director of gifted education, high school guidance counselor, director of summer training programs for high school dropouts, elementary/junior high school principal, and professor of education administration at Southern Illinois University–Edwardsville. She served as higher education director for the Illinois Education Association prior to being appointed deputy governor. She was IWA executive director from 1991 to 1994. Hazel has several areas of specialization and has been an education consultant and workshop presenter across the state and nationally. She serves on various national committees and has authored numerous educational materials and coauthored books on integrating students with disabilities in the classroom. She has also written a parent involvement manual for the Illinois state board of education and a book (*Reengaging Families in the Education of Middle School Children*) published by the National Association of Middle Schools in 1971. In 2004 she helped rewrite the training manual for Family, School, and Community Partnerships and trained the trainers for the NEA.

Hazel Loucks is a high-energy person who enjoys a challenge. Her words sum up her philosophy: "Don't worry about the naysayers. Don't agree to the boxes people want to put you in. If it's going to *make a difference* for even one person—go for it!" Her interviewer characterized her as courageous. She elaborated, "Hazel is an incredible woman who inspires without even knowing she's doing it. Her values are solid to the core and they drive her without compromise. She exudes self-confidence, but alongside it a servant heart and a humble spirit." Hazel was honored by IWA with the *Dare to Be Great* award in 1993.

Interviewer: Dr. Linda Searby

Linda Searby is a faculty member at Blackburn College in Carlinville, Illinois, in the department of education. She earned her doctorate in educational administration from Illinois State University in 1999. She has 10 years of experience as an elementary principal in both rural and urban school districts in Illinois. She served several years as an adjunct instructor at Illinois State University before moving into university teaching full time. In addition to her college teaching, Linda has consulted with the Academic Development Institute, helping develop materials for Alliance for Achievement, a national school reform model. Linda began serving as IWA president in 2003.

DR. STEPHANIE PACE MARSHALL

Born in the Bronx in New York City, Stephanie Pace Marshall began her career in education as a fifth-grade teacher in an elementary school outside of Chicago. She has been founding president of the Illinois Mathematics and Science Academy (IMSA) since 1986. Dr. Marshall first became involved with the development of IMSA in 1982 and helped write the proposal and legislation that established the academy. IMSA is an educational laboratory where learning is "competency driven, inquiry based, problem centered, and integrative." IMSA's residential educational program serves Illinois students (grades 10–12) talented in mathematics and science. The school was established by the Illinois General Assembly in 1985, opened its doors in 1986, and graduated its first senior class in 1989. Interestingly, the bill to establish the school was defeated the first time it was proposed.

Stephanie was superintendent for Batavia Public Schools District #101 for two years before accepting the IMSA position. She had also been

Batavia's assistant superintendent for curriculum and instruction. She was director of curriculum for Naperville #203 from 1974 to 1976, and has served as director of gifted programs and chair of a social science department, to name just a few of the leadership roles she has filled. In all those positions, she established her reputation as a designer of innovative learning environments. Dr. Marshall served as president of the Association for Supervision and Curriculum Development (ASCD) from 1991 to 1993. ASCD is the largest international association of professional educators in the world. She earned her bachelor's from Queens City College, New York, in 1967. She received a master's in curriculum philosophy from University of Chicago in 1971, and a Ph.D. in 1983 in industrial relations/educational administration from Loyola University Chicago. As a leader, Stephanie operates from a definition of vision shaped for her in part by Ben Zander, conductor of the Boston Philharmonic. He defined vision as "a possibility to live into, as opposed to a mission which is a purpose to be achieved." Although her cabinet consists of a total of six people, there are about 35 on the IMSA management team. This group meets five times a year for the purpose of sharing information, building relationships, and looking for connections around the strategic issues—the direction in which they're headed, the business plan, and the goals of the institution. She believes in making decisions based on principles. She shared with her interviewer, "To me it goes back to name. Integrity." Reflecting on Stephanie's commitment and ability to integrate *doing* and *being*, her interviewer wrote, "Stephanie Pace Marshall was putting into practice in this school all of the ideas/beliefs/values that have been closest to my heart. And they are working." Stephanie was honored with the *Dare to Be Great* award from IWA in 1988, the first year the award was given.

Interviewer: Dr. Madeline Hafner

Madeline Hafner, author of chapter 8, began her university teaching career at Loyola University Chicago. She is now an assistant professor at the University of Utah in the department of educational leadership and policy. Her prior school district teaching and leadership experiences were in the area of special education. Dr. Hafner's teaching focuses on leadership for social justice, instructional leadership, and qualitative research methods. Her research interests include leadership for students receiving special education services, feminist and postmodern notions of leadership, teaching for social justice in leadership preparation programs, and spirituality and leadership.

DR. VITA P. MEYER

During the 35 years of her professional career, Vita Meyer was a teacher, coach, activity advisor, assistant athletic director, assistant principal, and principal. Although 34 years were spent in Bremen District #22, including 12 years as principal of Bremen High School, her positive influence extends to schools throughout the state. Born in Chicago, she earned a bachelor's in physical education and elementary education from Carroll College in Wakesha, Wisconsin, in 1965. She taught at the elementary level for one year, followed by teaching high school physical education for 22 years. Dr. Meyer's master's degree is from Chicago State University in 1980 in educational administration. She earned a doctorate in leadership and policy studies from Loyola University in 1998. Since retiring as principal in 2000, Vita has been elected to the board of education for Bremen District #228 and serves as president. She is an adjunct professor at Governor State University working as supervisor of the Alternative Certification Program. In that position she is mentoring and evaluating first-year teachers who have changed careers and who teach in at-risk schools on the south side of Chicago. She serves as a consultant for the Illinois State Board of Education Induction/Mentoring Program for Administrators. Having served on the design team, she is training trainers throughout the state. She is also a trainer for the Gates Project for "Illinois Technology and Leadership Change" at Illinois State University.

Early in her career, Dr. Meyer gave leadership to achieve gender equity in school programs. She sued her school district for equal pay for an equal job as coach of a girls' sports team. She gained the respect of the administration and board of education for the professional manner in which she pursued this litigation. As a principal she always viewed her administrative staff members as a leadership team and was known for her inclusive leadership style. The alumni committee at Bremen High School at her retirement established the Dr. Vita Pignatiello Meyer Alumni Scholarship with these words: "We would like to name this scholarship in her honor because of the leadership, academic focus, and community involvement Dr. Meyer has inspired." When asked for one word that summarized her career, Vita answered with *exhilarating*. In describing herself as a leader, she chose the words *visionary*, *risk-taker*, and *motivator*. Her interviewer wrote, "I felt that her story was so filled with commitment and dedication to kids—doing what is best for students. In that pursuit, she sometimes made difficult and unpopular decisions. I admire her fortitude." Vita was honored by IWA with the *Dare to Be Great* award in 2002.

Interviewer: Mary Ahillen

Mary Ahillen is principal of Parkside Junior High School in Normal, Illinois, District #5. She has also been an assistant principal at Chiddix Junior High School. She has been with Normal Community Unit District #5 for four years. Before going into administration, she taught junior high and high school English for 20 years. She holds a master's in curriculum and instruction from Illinois State University.

DIANE MORRISON

Diane Morrison became director of support services for the Northern Suburban Special Education District in 1992 and still serves in that role. Her previous professional positions include coordinator for La Grange Area Department of Special Education (LADSE), as well as school psychologist roles in the Wheaton #200 school district and LADSE. She has been a school psychologist since 1983 and was attracted to working with special education cooperatives because of the leadership opportunities. She has 14 years of administrative experience. Diane earned her bachelor's in education from Ohio State University in 1967. She earned a master's in school psychology from Illinois State University in 1982, followed in 1989 by coursework from Northern Illinois University, qualifying her for Type 75 administrative certification.

Diane Morrison was described by her interviewer as "a driving force in the implementation of Flexible Service Delivery System in Illinois." This FLEX model works to unify the services schools provide for students into a needs-based system. Her leadership practices have been influenced by the ideas of Ronald Heifetz about leadership as adaptive work requiring the facilitation of growth. Diane supervises about 40 people and is always looking to provide opportunities and resources to enable them to develop their own leadership potential. When asked to what she was unalterably committed, she replied, "I would like to have every child in our schools have the same advantages to learn as much as they can and be able to learn how to access what they don't know." Diane understands that what really drives her and helps her hold firmly to her beliefs is the hope that schools will be an inviting and challenging place for students. She would like "for the educational system to become equitable," particularly in terms of access to research-based instruction. She would like to be remembered for "helping people think out of the box, and be supported for taking some of the risks." To summarize her career in a word, she chose *accomplishments*. Diane received the *Dare to Be Great* award from IWA in 2005.

Interviewer: Dr. Mary O'Brian

Mary O'Brian is an assistant professor in the special education department at Illinois State University. Previously she worked as a technical assistant/program supervisor at Livingston County Special Services Unit, as a special education teacher, vocational day training instructor, and school psychologist. She holds a bachelor's and doctorate in special education from Illinois State University. Her master's degree was in school psychology, also from Illinois State University.

MARTHA R. O'MALLEY

Martha O'Malley retired in 1995 after a distinguished career as an educator in southern Illinois for more than 40 years. The last 20 years of her career she served as an elected regional superintendent of schools for St. Clair County. She earned a bachelor's degree in English and social science from Arkansas State University in 1943. Born in Arkansas, she began her career as a fourth-grade teacher, and also taught kindergarten. She found she loved teaching and sought more education, earning a master's in elementary education from Southern Illinois University–Edwardsville, with an emphasis in reading in 1968. She earned two specialist degrees from

Southern Illinois University–Edwardsville—the first in 1970 in elementary education with an emphasis in reading and the second in 1972 in educational administration.

Martha served as assistant to the superintendent and then as assistant superintendent for Signal Hill School District #181 in Belleville before becoming regional superintendent. She was coordinator of elementary education and student services at Southern Illinois University–Edwardsville from 1969 to 1970, teaching in the Education Department from 1967 to 1975. She has served on numerous statewide task forces and served on countless community and civic boards, chaired Catholic Social Services in her diocese, and chaired the diocesan educational program for all the schools in southern Illinois. In 1995 she was elected to the state board of trustees for the University of Illinois, with campuses in Champaign, Chicago, and Springfield. She was the first woman regional superintendent ever elected chairman of the statewide organization and the first woman regional superintendent in the county.

When asked to describe herself as a leader, Martha picked these words: *caring*, *tenacious*, and *creative*. When asked to what she was unalterably committed, she responded, "Advancement of the children. Opportunities. I am still volunteering in the schools, teaching reading to some students. I'm working up to getting more involved in our library." When asked for a word to summarize her career, she chose *luck*. Elaborating, she explained that she "never planned to get out and teach and have a career when I had my eight children and baked my bread and kept my house. So many opportunities came and I dared to accept them." Her interviewer said she was struck by Martha's willingness to stick to her goals when she believed that was in the best interest of children, and the skill with which she would bring opponents into her camp and turn them into loyal supporters. Her interviewer wrote, "It was a privilege to sit before Martha and glean the knowledge she held for me. I am proud to call her mentor and friend." Martha O'Malley was honored with the IWA *Dare to Be Great* award in 1994.

Interviewer: Dr. Shari Marshall

Shari Marshall has been superintendent of Central Community School District #4 in Clifton, Illinois, since 2001. She has been superintendent of two other districts. Her previous professional positions have included being state of Illinois monitor of gifted programs for Region 5, a principal in Collinsville CUSD #10, and a teacher in Madison CUSD #12 and Greenfield CUSD #10. Both her bachelor's and master's degrees, as well as a doctorate in the instructional process, were earned at Southern Illinois University–Edwardsville.

DR. SALLY BULKLEY PANCRAZIO

Sally Pancrazio served as dean of the College of Education at Illinois State University from 1993 until 2001. She continues to be involved with special partnership projects involving the university and Illinois schools. Born in Endwell, New York, she earned a bachelor's in business education and psychology from Illinois State University in 1960, a master's in business education and educational psychology from Indiana State University in 1967, and a doctorate in secondary education and educational psychology from the University of Illinois in 1971. In 1973–1974 she completed postdoctoral work in school finance, organization and development, and educational policy and served as a fellow in educational policy studies at the Institute for Educational Leadership, Washington, D.C.

Dr. Pancrazio was employed with the Illinois State Board of Education (ISBE) for 18 years prior to coming to Illinois State University. Having served as an administrator since 1972, her positions at ISBE included six years as chief of research, planning, and evaluation for the Illinois state board of education, and one year as acting executive deputy superintendent. She was involved in initiatives to bring greater gender equity to the operations of ISBE, was one of the founders of IWA, and published articles and reports on gender equity. When she came to Illinois State University, Sally was hired as chair of the department of educational administration and foundations, a position she held for three years before becoming dean of the College of Education. Prior to taking a position at Illinois State University, she had served as a part-time faculty member for 10 years for the department of educational administration and foundations. Her initiatives as dean included upgrading of DeGarmo Hall, updating of technology, forming partnerships with and establishing professional development schools, development of a college mission statement, developing an Illinois State University presence in Chicago, and involvement in research and policy studies, to name only a few.

Her interviewer characterized Sally as "solidly forthright" and "certain about the immense difference her leadership at ISU has made." Additionally, her interviewer said "It was invigorating to dialogue with someone that is not afraid to say it like it is!" When her interviewer said she sounded like someone who is passionate and visionary, Sally replied, "I would be embarrassed to say I'm a visionary because it smacks of self-importance. I really believe in chaos theory and the notion that you don't know what's going to cause the big things to happen, so a leader must encourage as many little things to happen, some of which will take root and move the programs toward the important goals." When asked, she chose the words *passionate* and *certain* to describe herself as a leader. Sally received the *Dare to Be Great* award from IWA in 1992.

Interviewer: Dr. Donna S. McCaw

Donna McCaw is an associate professor in the educational leadership department at Western Illinois University in Macomb. In addition to an Ed.D. in curriculum and instruction from Illinois State University, she has a master's in speech pathology and in counseling. An Asian American whose mother was a Japanese war bride (WWII), Donna describes herself as a lifelong learner.

AURTHUR MAE PERKINS

Aurthur Perkins has been principal of Harrison Primary School in Peoria since 1993, having taught kindergarten at the school since 1983. Under Perkins' leadership, the teachers and the school, situated on the grounds of a public housing project, have experienced considerable success educating children from extremely low-income families. The school serves a population that is 99.9% low income with a 50% mobility rate, yet the school has not been on the state's academic watch list. Research-based initiatives under her leadership led to development of a phonemic awareness program designed and delivered by classroom teachers. The Harrison

Initiative for Language Learning was developed and implemented in the 1990s. As a result, the scores of children at the end of kindergarten on the Test of Language Segments (TALS) improved in just two years from only 29% being ready for instruction in a basal reader at the end of kindergarten to 79% being ready for reading. Perkins brings her intelligence, life experience, dynamic personality, and personal sense of mission to being the principal of Harrison.

Born in Richmond, Indiana, into a large, extended African American family, Aurthur dropped out of school at age 13 when she had a baby. She attributes part of her success as Harrison's principal to having walked in the same shoes as many of the parents, whom she relentlessly urges to go back to school. Her own return to formal education came in her mid-thirties when, as a volunteer in her children's school, she became outraged that so many African American children could not read and no one seemed to care. She received her GED, then a bachelor's in elementary education from Bradley University in 1982, and finally a master's in educational administration, also from Bradley University, in 1990. Her leadership abilities have received widespread recognition throughout the state and nation. She provides both support and pressure to the excellent staff she has assembled and to whom she gives all the credit for the school's success. Aurthur Perkins was one of two principals featured in *Best Leadership Practices for High-Poverty Schools* by Linda L. Lyman and Christine J. Villani, published by ScarecrowEducation in 2004. When asked to what she was unalterably committed, Aurthur responded, "The success of my children." When asked what one word would summarize her career, she responded with *committed*. Aurthur was honored with the *Dare to Be Great* award from IWA in 2001.

Interviewer: Dr. Ramona Lomeli

Ramona Lomeli is administrator of human resources for the Tolleson Elementary School District #17 in Arizona. She is responsible for personnel, public relations, and technology. At the time of the interview, she was an assistant professor in the department of educational administration and foundations at Illinois State University. Ramona has been principal of an alternative charter school in Arizona and has a doctorate in educational administration from Arizona State University.

DR. MARY M. POLITE

At the time of the interview, Mary Polite was serving as dean of the College of Education at Southern Illinois University–Edwardsville (SIUE). Formerly a professor in the department of educational administration at SIUE, she is now retired from education and working as the general manager of a nature retreat center in South Carolina. Mary began her work in higher education in 1989 and held a variety of administrative and faculty positions at SIUE before retiring. In addition to her university academic and leadership roles, Dr. Polite was actively involved in research and consultation for higher education, and elementary and secondary education. She was actively involved in a variety of research and professional organizations. Prior to moving into higher education, she was an elementary and middle school building principal for three years, and had been an elementary and middle school teacher for eight years. Mary is the author of several book chapters and published articles and reports covering a wide variety of topics. She has been a popular speaker and is an accomplished grant writer.

Dr. Polite earned her master's and doctorate in educational administration from Illinois State University and her bachelor's in elementary education and psychology from Augustana College. Mary wanted to be a teacher from an early age. Moving from playing school to teaching school, she became convinced that schools needed changing to become caring communities of partnership and hope for every child. She began her teaching career in the public schools in Decatur. When asked to describe herself as a leader, Mary responded with the word *passionate*. Her interviewer noted, "I was impressed with how much her passion and values drive her leadership experience. Unlike many higher education professionals, Mary ties the educational experiences at the collegiate level with the instructional leadership at the elementary and secondary level. She radiates an aura of strength and confidence that must be contagious." When Mary was asked how she would like to be remembered, she answered, "I would like to be remembered as a person who made a difference for kids in a way that was fair and had integrity to all the people with whom I work." Asked for one word that describes her career, she answered with *difficult*, because it has been so challenging to maintain balance in her life. Mary was honored with an ISBE *Those Who Excel* award in 2000 for work with the Bridge Program, an integrated teacher–administrator preparation program in a professional development school. She was honored with the *Dare to Be Great* award from IWA in 2003.

Interviewer: Dr. Margaret Noe

Margaret Noe is associate chancellor at the University of Illinois at Springfield. She began her university career at UIS in 2000 as an assistant professor in the department of educational leadership. She received her master's and doctorate in educational administration from Illinois State University and her juris doctorate degree from Southern Illinois University School of Law. She has served in building- and district-level positions, including two superintendencies. Maggie was honored by IWA with the *Dare to Be Great* award in 2004.

DR. CAROL L. STRUCK

A veteran educational leader, the name Carol Struck is synonymous with competence in Illinois. Taking her first administrative position after 5 years of teaching in special education, Dr. Struck has served as an administrator for several districts in central Illinois. Her leadership positions have included principal, assistant superintendent for personnel, acting superintendent for two different districts, and superintendent of Olympia Community Unit School District #16 from 1990 to 1997. Dr. Struck had been an administrator for 24 years when she decided to retire in search of new challenges. These retirement challenges have included being an adjunct instructor at Illinois State University, filling several challenging interim superintendent positions, and establishing two businesses: an educational consulting business and a used-book store.

Dr. Struck earned a bachelor's in education from Culver–Stockton College in 1970, followed by a master's in special education from Illinois State University in 1973. She earned a doctorate in educational administration, also from Illinois State University, in 1988. Her interviewer characterized Carol as a woman whose "professional accomplishments have opened the door for other women." When asked how others would describe her, Carol replied with the words *determined, focused, fair, people-*

oriented, a good listener, and "willing to stand for my beliefs." She finished with the words "and true, true in the sense of being true to friends and relationships." She has always believed in respecting and valuing other people, whether she agrees with them or not. She has gained respect by treating others fairly and with dignity. Protecting herself from political risk was a level at which her competence as always served her well. Dr. Struck's years in administration were marked with several significant and challenging episodes that required all her competence. She received the *Dare to Be Great* award from IWA in 1993.

Interviewer: Dr. Jobie L. Skaggs

Jobie Skaggs is an assistant professor in the department of educational leadership and human development at Bradley University, Peoria. Dr. Skaggs is a nationally certified counselor. She received her Ph.D. (1999) in counseling and counselor education, a master's (1993) in counseling, and a B.S. (1991) in psychology from Idaho State University.

DR. REBECCA VAN DER BOGERT

Rebecca van der Bogert has been superintendent of Winnetka District #36 since 1994. Born in Pennsylvania, she received a bachelor's in psychology in 1967, followed by a master's in special education in 1968, both from Syracuse University. She earned a doctorate in teaching, curriculum, and learning environments from Harvard University in 1991, and is one of the founders of the International Network of Principals' Centers at Harvard. While at Harvard she served on the editorial board of the *Harvard Educational Review*. "A superintendent," said Becky, as she prefers to be called, "is not what I started out to be." Throughout her career she has never gone after a position; she has gone where she believed she could make things happen. For example, she started an innovative program for emotionally disturbed children. When she was a coordinator for gifted and talented, she moved in the direction of how to infuse teaching for critical thinking rather than a pull-out program. She was disillusioned with how schools were run and teachers treated. She became a curriculum director to implement an environment for thinking, working within a district with others to make the appropriate changes. One focus of change was the evaluation system. When asked to be a principal, she implemented democratic leadership practices; when a superintendency followed, she instituted shared leadership.

When Dr. Van der Bogert speaks about her career, she tells of growing up in a rural town in a complex family. During her childhood she developed resilience, learned how to weave behind the scenes, developed clear beliefs, and became achievement oriented. In fact, Becky said during the 2003 acceptance of her *Dare to Be Great* award from IWA, "I was raised by my Sunday school teachers and my teachers in a very real way." Her interviewer said, "Modesty about her achievements was reflected in her comments. Research, reflection, and dialogue about issues and ideas were mentioned frequently." She is the author, coauthor, or editor of numerous publications, including *Making Sense as a School Leader* in 1996, with Richard Ackerman and Gordon Donaldson. Ackerman and van der Bogert serve as codirectors of the International Network of Principals' Centers at Harvard.

Her interviewer characterized her as "a systematic problem solver." When asked to what she was unalterably committed, Becky responded, "Living an honest and ethical life and behaving according to my beliefs." Asked how she would like to be remembered, she said, "Wherever I've worked, I've left a healthy environment behind where everybody can be everything they can be, and continue to be so; that it is not dependent on me, my presence is not a necessary piece." For the word that best summarized her career, she chose the word *fulfilling*. Becky was honored by IWA with the *Dare to Be Great* award in 2003.

Interviewer: Dr. Nancy Gibson

Nancy Gibson is superintendent of O'Fallon CC School District #90 in O'Fallon, Illinois. She is a professional educator with more than 30 years of experience, most of that as a special education teacher in the classroom. Prior to becoming a superintendent, Dr. Gibson had served as a principal and also as an assistant superintendent for curriculum. She earned her doctorate in educational administration in 1996 at Illinois State University. Nancy served as president of IWA from 2001 to 2003. She is currently president-elect of the Illinois Association for Supervision and Curriculum Development.

DR. DOROTHY WEBER

Dorothy Weber, or Dot as she prefers to be called, retired as superintendent of Glenview District #34 in 2004, at the end of her 34th year as an educator and her fifth year with the district. She served previously as superintendent in Arlington Heights Elementary District #25 for 8 years. Her career spanned several districts and included, in addition to the two superintendencies, a central office position as director of curriculum and instruction, principal, gifted coordinator, and 8 years as a teacher. She was chosen Illinois Superintendent of the Year in 1997 by the Illinois Association of School Administrators (IASA). In 2000 she received a distinguished alumni award from the University of Illinois Education Alumni Association. Dot received her bachelor's in elementary education and French from Marian College, Indianapolis, in 1969, and a master's in elementary education from Olivet Nazarene University in 1974. Her doctorate in educational administration was from the University of Illinois in 1981.

Dr. Weber earned her doctorate degree at the end of her first year as an elementary school principal and believes that this degree helped to propel her through the system and rapidly to the top. When she entered the profession as a teacher in 1970, "administration was absolutely a male-dominated field," she explained. She pursued a doctorate while teaching because she knew it would open up opportunities and choices. As a principal she found herself conducting building faculty meetings the way she wished they had been run when she was a teacher. She explained that what she did "was a forerunner to collaborative decision making and teacher empowerment, but at that time there wasn't language or research to describe my leadership style." She was drawn to Glenview because the Glenview constitution matched her leadership style very well. The district "has a constitution that is the contract with our certified staff. Fifteen years ago it actually received national prominence in that it puts into words and practice a common understanding for the board, the staff, and the administration about how decisions are made, and they are made with consensus."

Asked about her unalterable commitments, what she would like to be remembered for, Dr. Weber said, "I am unalterably committed to learning and growth. My goal as superintendent is not to lose the mind, heart, body, or soul of any one student or staff member, and I'd like to be remembered for continually exploring ways to carry out this goal. I hope that people will recall the questions, the discussion, the ideas, the research, the study and review of the different ways of teaching and learning that we've explored." Dot serves as president of a leadership consulting business and has created and conducted numerous workshops and training sessions for both the public and private sector. She has been a keynote speaker for conferences, facilitated strategic plans, and designed training programs for the Administrators' Academy of the Illinois state board of education and the Illinois Association of School Administrators. Dot was honored with the IWA *Dare to Be Great* award in 2004.

Interviewer: Dr. Gwendolyn Lee

Gwen Lee is associate superintendent of Thornton Township High School District #205, in charge of curriculum and instruction. She served previously as principal of Thornridge High School for six years and Hillcrest High School for two years. In 1998 she was Illinois Principal Association (IPA) Principal of the Year. In addition to being an interviewer, Dr. Lee is one of the leaders interviewed for this book.

DR. MAXINE A. WORTHAM

Although now retired, at the time of the interview Maxine Wortham was executive director of early childhood education in Peoria Public School District #150, an urban school district serving 15,000 students. This position included responsibility for an early childhood education center, as well as early childhood programs in all Title I primary schools, two high schools, a middle school, and two community agencies. An African American woman born in Tennessee, Dr. Wortham came to Peoria after graduating from college in 1968. She served the district until retirement, having taken one year off to get her master's in special education from Illinois State University. Her bachelor's in biology was earned at Lane College in 1968. She earned her doctorate in educational administration from Illinois State University in 1985 and continued to take courses that interested her.

Having taught for 10 years before becoming an administrator, Dr. Wortham describes herself as "a lifelong learner and a collaborative decision maker committed to team building." Her administrative positions included being an elementary principal, 8 years as a high school dean, and numerous years in the central office, including 3 years as director of personnel. For much of her time in central administration she was the only woman on the superintendent's cabinet. Whether getting things accomplished for programs, teachers, or students, Maxine is both savvy and fearless. In terms of getting things done she considers herself an insider, but *socially* an outsider. She is regarded as a woman of integrity and was supported as she got things done one way or another because of her reputation as a woman who makes ethical decisions that serve the needs of students. She is an example of a leader whose courage made a difference in countering the oppressions that exist in how things are done in schools. Her interviewer characterized Dr. Wortham's office as "a comfortable living room." She described her style during the interview as "unhurried and thoughtful." "Several times," the interviewer reported, "Dr. Wortham commented that, being a person close to retirement with many years of experience to draw from, she thinks and behaves differently now than she might have in the past." When asked, Maxine said she thought others would describe her as patient, firm, and friendly, as well as a good listener. In describing herself, she chose the words *growing, lifelong learner*, and *predictable*. In summarizing her unalterable commitment, she said, "I do think that most people would say that I believe all children can learn. I believe we all can learn something and learn it well. We just have to learn how to teach them. Everybody can be a productive person. I think everybody has a gift, and we have to find it." Maxine received IWA's *Dare to Be Great* award twice, in 1991 and again in 2000.

Interviewer: Jana Hunzicker

Jana Hunzicker taught eighth-grade language arts in Pekin for 7 years and served as dean of students at Illinois State University's Thomas Metcalf School for three years before becoming an elementary principal in the East Peoria school district. She has taught courses at Illinois Central College in East Peoria in teacher education. She is a doctoral candidate in curriculum and instruction at Illinois State University. Jana is a member of the IWA board.

References

Ackerman, R. H., Donaldson, G. A., & van der Bogert, R. (1996). *Making sense as a school leader*. San Francisco: Jossey-Bass.

AhNee-Benham, M. K. P. (2003). In our mother's voice: A native woman's knowing of leadership. In M. D. Young & L. Skrla (Eds.), *Reconsidering feminist research in educational leadership* (pp. 223–245). Albany: State University of New York Press.

AhNee-Benham, M. K. P., & Cooper, J. E. (1998). *Let my spirit soar! Narratives of diverse women in school leadership*. Thousand Oaks, CA: Corwin Press.

Alston, J. A. (1999). Climbing hills and mountains: Black females making it to the superintendency. In C. C. Brunner (Ed.), *Sacred dreams: Women and the superintendency* (pp. 79–90). Albany: State University of New York Press.

Antrobus, P. (2000). Transformational leadership: Advancing the agenda for gender justice. In C. Sweetman (Ed.), *Women and leadership* (pp. 50–56). Oxford: Oxfam GB.

Arnot, M. (2002). *Reproducing gender? Essays on educational theory and feminist politics*. London: Routledge.

Astin, H. S., & Leland, C. (1991). *Women of influence, women of vision*. San Francisco: Jossey-Bass.

Atlas, B. L. H., & Capper, C. A. (2003, April). *The spirituality of African-American women principals in urban schools: Toward a reconceptualization of Afrocentric feminist epistemology*. Paper presented at the American Educational Research Association annual meeting, Chicago, IL.

Begley, P. (1999). Value preferences, ethics and conflicts in school administration. In P. Begley (Ed.), *Values and educational leadership* (pp. 237–254). Albany: State University of New York Press.

Bennis, W., & Nanus, B. (1985). *Leaders: The strategies for taking charge*. New York: Harper & Row.

Björk, L. (2000). Introduction: Women in the superintendency—Advances in research and theory. *Educational Administration Quarterly, 36*(1), 5–17.

Blackmore, J. (1999). *Troubling women: Feminism, leadership, and educational change.* Buckingham, UK: Open University Press.

Blackmore, J. (2002). Troubling women: The upsides and downsides of leadership and the new managerialism. In C. Reynolds (Ed.), *Women and school leadership: International perspectives* (pp. 49–70). Albany: State University of New York Press.

Bloom, C. M., & Erlandson, D. A. (2003). African American principals in urban schools: Realities, (re)constructions, and resolutions. *Educational Administration Quarterly, 39*(3), 339–369.

Blount, J. M. (1998). *Destined to rule the schools.* Albany: State University of New York Press.

Bolman, L. G., & Deal, T. E. (1995). *Leading with soul: An uncommon journey of spirit.* San Francisco: Jossey-Bass.

Bolman, L. G., & Deal, T. E. (1997). *Reframing organizations: Artistry, choice, and leadership* (2nd ed.). San Francisco: Jossey-Bass.

Bolman, L. G., & Deal, T. E. (2003). *Reframing organizations: Artistry, choice, and leadership* (3rd ed.). San Francisco: Jossey-Bass.

Briskin, A. (1998). *The stirring of soul in the workplace.* San Francisco: Berrett-Koehler.

Brunner, C. C. (1999). *Sacred dreams: Women and the superintendency.* Albany: State University of New York Press.

Brunner, C. C. (2000). *Principles of power: Women superintendents and the riddle of the heart.* Albany: State University of New York Press.

Brunner, C. C. (2002). A proposition for the reconception of the superintendency: Reconsidering traditional and nontraditional discourse. *Educational Administration Quarterly, 38*(3), 402–431.

Brunner, C. C. (2003). Invisible, limited, and emerging discourse: Research practices that restrict and/or increase access for women and persons of color to the superintendency. *Journal of School Leadership, 13*(4), 428–450.

Brunner, C. C., Grogan, M., & Björk, L. (2002). Shifts in the discourse defining the superintendency: Historical and current foundations of the position. In J. Murphy (Ed.), *The educational leadership challenge: Redefining leadership for the 21st century* (pp. 211–238). Chicago: National Society for the Study of Education, University of Chicago Press.

Bunch, C. (1991). Foreword. In H. S. Astin & C. Leland (Eds.), *Women of influence, women of vision* (pp. xi–xiv). San Francisco: Jossey-Bass.

Burns, J. M. (1978). *Leadership.* New York: Harper & Row.

Cantor, D. W., Bernay, T., & Stoess, J. (1992). *Women in power.* New York: Houghton Mifflin.

Carr, C. S. (1994, April). *Verbal and nonverbal micropolitical communication of female school principals.* Paper presented at annual conference of the American Educational Research Association, New Orleans, LA. ERIC Document, ED 373 431.

Chapman, J. D., Sackney, L. E., & Aspin, D. N. (1999). Internationalization in educational administration: Policy and practice, theory and research. In J. Murphy & K. S. Louis (Eds.), *Handbook of research on educational administration* (2nd ed.) (pp. 73–98). San Francisco: Jossey-Bass.

Chase, S. E. (1995). *Ambiguous empowerment: The work narratives of women school superintendents.* Amherst: University of Massachusetts Press.

Collins, J. (2001). *Good to great.* New York: HarperCollins.

Collins, P. H. (1991). *Black feminist thought: Knowledge, consciousness, and the politics of empowerment.* New York: Routledge.

Conway, J. K. (2001). Foreword. In S. J. M. Freeman, S. C. Bourque, & C. M. Shelton (Eds.), *Women on power: Leadership redefined* (pp. xi–xxiii). Boston: Northeastern University Press.

Covey, S. R. (1990). *Principle-centered leadership.* New York: Simon & Schuster.

Curry, B. K. (2000). *Women in power: Pathways to leadership in education.* New York: Teachers College Press.

Dillard, C. B. (1995). Leading with her life: An African-American feminist (re)interpretation of leadership for an urban high school principal. *Educational Administration Quarterly, 31*(4), 539–563.

Dillard, C. B. (2003). The substance of things hoped for, the evidence of things not seen: Examining an endarkened feminist epistemology in educational research and leadership. In M. D. Young & L. Skrla (Eds.), *Reconsidering feminist research in educational leadership* (pp. 131–160). Albany: State University of New York Press.

Drath, W. H. (1996). Changing our minds about leadership. *Issues and Observations, 16*(1), 1–4.

Drath, W. H., & Palus, C. J. (1994). *Making common sense: Leadership as meaning-making in a community of practice.* Greensboro, NC: Center for Creative Leadership.

Dunlap, D. M., & Schmuck, P. A. (Eds.). (1995). *Women leading in education.* Albany: State University of New York Press.

Ericksen, A. M. (1991, Winter). From your executive director. *IWA Newsline, 2*(2), 1.

Freeman, S. J. M., & Bourque, S. C. (2001). Leadership and power: New conceptions. In S. J. M. Freeman, S. C. Bourque, & C. M. Shelton (Eds.), *Women on power: Leadership redefined* (pp. 3–26). Boston: Northeastern University Press.

Freeman, S. J. M., Bourque, S. C., & Shelton, C. M. (Eds.). (2001). *Women on power: Leadership redefined.* Boston: Northeastern University Press.

Fullan, M. (2003). *The moral imperative of school leadership*. Thousand Oaks, CA: Corwin Press.

Furman, G. (2002). Postmodernism and community in schools: Unraveling the paradox. In G. Furman (Ed.), *School as community: From promise to practice* (pp. 51–75). Albany: State University of New York Press.

Furman, G. (2003). The 2002 UCEA presidential address. *UCEA Review, 45*(1), 1–6.

Furman, G. C., & Starratt, R. J. (2002). Leadership for democratic community in schools. In J. Murphy (Ed.), *The educational leadership challenge: Redefining leadership for the 21st century*, pp. 105–133. Chicago: National Society for the Study of Education, University of Chicago Press.

Gardiner, M. E., Enomoto, E., & Grogan, M. (2000). *Coloring outside the lines: Mentoring women into school leadership*. Albany: State University of New York Press.

Gilligan, C. (1982). *In a different voice*. Cambridge, MA: Harvard University Press.

Giroux, H. (1992). *Border crossings: Cultural workers and the politics of education*. New York: Routledge.

Giroux, H. (1994). Slacking off: Border youth and postmodern education. *Journal of Advanced Composition, 14*, 347–366.

Glaser, B. G., & Strauss, A. L. (1967). *The discovery of grounded theory*. Chicago: Aldine.

Goldring, E., & Greenfield, W. (2002). Understanding the evolving concept of leadership in education: Roles, expectations, and dilemmas. In J. Murphy (Ed.), *The educational leadership challenge: Redefining leadership for the 21st century* (pp. 1–19). Chicago: National Society for the Study of Education, University of Chicago Press.

Goleman, D., Boyatzis, R., and McKee, A. (2002). *Primal leadership: Realizing the power of emotional intelligence*. Boston: Harvard Business School Press.

Granoff, J. (2004, July). "World commission on global consciousness and spirituality" roundtable. Roundtable conducted at the meeting of the Parliament of the World's Religions, Barcelona, Spain.

Grogan, M. (1996). *Voices of women aspiring to the superintendency*. Albany: State University of New York Press.

Grogan, M. (1999). A feminist poststructuralist account of collaboration. In C. C. Brunner (Ed.), *Sacred dreams: Women in the superintendency* (pp. 199–216). Albany: State University of New York Press.

Grogan, M. (2003). Laying the groundwork for a reconception of the superintendency from feminist postmodern perspectives. In M. D. Young & L. Skrla (Eds.), *Reconsidering feminist research in educational leadership* (pp. 9–34). Albany: State University of New York Press.

Gupton, S. L., & Slick, G. A. (1996). *Highly successful women administrators and how they got there*. Thousand Oaks, CA: Corwin Press.

Harragan, B. L. (1977). *Games mother never taught you: Corporate gamesmanship for women*. New York: Rawson Associates.

Harris, S., Ballenger, J., Hicks-Townes, F., Carr, C. S., & Alford, B. J. (2004). *Winning women: Stories of award-winning educators*. Lanham, MD: ScarecrowEducation.

Haynes, E. A., & Licata, J. W. (1995). Creative insubordination of school principals and the legitimacy of the justifiable. *Journal of Educational Administration, 33*(4), 21–35.

Heifetz, R. A. (1994). *Leadership without easy answers*. Cambridge, MA: Harvard University Press.

Heilbrun, C. G. (1989). *Writing a woman's life*. New York: Ballantine Books.

Helgesen, S. (1990). *The female advantage*. New York: Doubleday.

Issacs, W. (1999). *Dialogue and the art of thinking together*. New York: Doubleday Currency.

Jackson, B. L. (1999). Getting inside history—against all odds: African-American women school superintendents. In C. C. Brunner (Ed.), *Sacred dreams: Women and the superintendency* (pp. 141–160). Albany: State University of New York Press.

Jamieson, K. H. (1995). *Beyond the double bind: Women and leadership*. New York: Oxford University Press.

Kellerman, B. (2003). You've come a long way, baby—and you've got miles to go. In D. L. Rhode (Ed.), *The difference "difference" makes* (pp. 53–58). Stanford, CA: Stanford University Press.

Keyes, M. W., Hanley-Maxwell, C., & Capper, C. A. (1999). Spirituality? It's the core of my leadership: Empowering leadership in an inclusive elementary school. *Educational Administration Quarterly, 35*(2), 203–237.

Kouzes, J. M., & Posner, B. Z. (1997). *The leadership challenge*. San Francisco: Jossey-Bass.

Lambert, L. (1998). *Building leadership capacity in schools*. Alexandria, VA: Association for Supervision and Curriculum Development.

Larson, C. L., & Murtadha, K. (2002). Leadership for social justice. In J. Murphy (Ed.), *The educational leadership challenge: Redefining leadership for the 21st century* (pp. 134–161). Chicago: National Society for the Study of Education.

Lashway, L. (1996). *Ethical leadership*. Eugene, OR: Author. ERIC Digest, Number 107, ED397463.

Leithwood, K., & Duke, D. L. (1999). A century's quest to understand school leadership. In J. Murphy & K. S. Louis (Eds.), *Handbook of research on educational administration* (2nd ed.) (pp. 45–72). San Francisco: Jossey-Bass.

Leithwood, K., & Prestine, N. (2002). Unpacking the challenges of leadership at the school and district level. In J. Murphy (Ed.), *The educational leadership challenge: Redefining leadership for the 21st century* (pp. 42–64). Chicago: National Society for the Study of Education, University of Chicago Press.

Leithwood, K., & Steinbach, R. (1995). *Expert problem solving: Evidence from school and district leaders*. Albany: State University of New York Press.

Lyman, L. L. (2000). *How do they know you care?* New York: Teachers College Press.

MacBeath, J. (2002). Leadership, learning, and the challenge to democracy. In A. Walker & C. Dimmock (Eds.), *School leadership and administration: Adopting a cultural perspective* (pp. 103–122). New York: Routledge Falmer.

Machievelli, N. (1992). Winning the shell game. *Executive Educator, 14*(11), 35–36.

McPherson, R. B., & Crowson, R. L. (1994). The principal as mini-superintendent under Chicago school reform. In J. Murphy & K. S. Louis (Eds.), *Reshaping the principalship* (pp. 57–76). Thousand Oaks, CA: Corwin Press.

McPherson, R. B., Crowson, R. L., & Brieschke, P. A. (1986). Marjorie Stallings: A walk through a mine field. *Urban Education, 21*(1), 62–85.

Mendez-Morse, S. E. (1999). Redefinition of self: Mexican-American women becoming superintendents. In C. C. Brunner (Ed.), *Sacred dreams: Women and the superintendency* (pp. 125–140). Albany: State University of New York Press.

Mendez-Morse, S. E. (2003). Chicana feminism and educational leadership. In M. D. Young & L. Skrla (Eds.), *Reconsidering feminist research in educational leadership* (pp. 161–178). Albany: State University of New York Press.

Merriam, S. B. (2001). *Qualitative research and case study applications in education*. San Francisco: Jossey-Bass.

Morris, V. C., Crowson, R. L., Porter-Gehrie, C., & Hurwitz, E. (1984). *Principals in action: The reality of managing schools*. Columbus, OH: Charles E. Merrill.

Muller, R., Lazlo, E., & Singh, K. (2004). *Awakening global consciousness and spirituality as key to planetary cultures in the 21st century*. (Available from Global Dialogue Institute, Haverford College, 370 Lancaster Avenue, Haverford, PA 19041-1392.)

Murphy, J. (2002). Reculturing the profession of educational leadership: New blueprints. In J. Murphy (Ed.), *The educational leadership challenge: Redefining leadership for the 21st century* (pp. 65–82). Chicago: National Society for the Study of Education, University of Chicago Press.

Murtadha-Watts, K. (1999). Spirited sisters: Spirituality and the activism of African American women in educational leadership. In L. Fenwick (Ed.),

School leadership: Expanding horizons of the mind and spirit (pp. 155–167). Proceedings of the National Council for Professors of Educational Administration. Lancaster, PA: Technomic.

Noddings, N. (1992). *The challenge to care in schools*. New York: Teachers College Press.

Noddings, N. (1999). Care, justice, and equity. In M. F. Katz, N. Noddings, & K. A. Strike (Eds.), *Justice and caring: The search for common ground in education* (pp. 7–20). New York: Teachers College Press.

Olesen, V. L. (2000). Feminism and qualitative research at and into the millennium. In N. K. Denzin and Y. S. Lincoln (Eds.), *Handbook of Qualitative Research*. Thousand Oaks, CA: Sage.

Ortiz, F. I. (1999). Seeking and selecting Hispanic female superintendents. In C. C. Brunner (Ed.), *Sacred dreams: Women and the superintendency* (pp. 91–102). Albany: State University of New York Press.

Palmer, P. J. (2000). *Let your life speak*. San Francisco: Jossey-Bass.

Patton, M. Q. (1990). *Qualitative evaluation methods*. Thousand Oaks, CA: Sage.

Piazza, A. G. (1996). Principals' perceptions of decision-making related to tenure status. Unpublished doctoral dissertation, University of Alabama at Birmingham.

Polkinghorne, D. E. (1988). *Narrative knowing and the human sciences*. Albany: State University of New York Press.

Reitzug, U. (1994). Diversity, power and influence: Multiple perspectives on the ethics of school leadership. *Journal of School Leadership, 4*, 197–222.

Reynolds, C. (Ed.). (2002). *Women and school leadership: International perspectives*. Albany: State University of New York Press.

Rhode, D. L. (Ed.). (2003). *The difference "difference" makes*. Stanford, CA: Stanford University Press.

Riessman, C. K. (1993). *Narrative analysis*. Newbury Park, CA: Sage.

Rimm, S., with Rimm-Kaufman, S. (2001). *How Jane won: 55 successful women share how they grew from ordinary girls to extraordinary women*. New York: Three Rivers Press.

Rimm, S., with Rimm-Kaufman, S., and Rimm, I. J. (2001). *See Jane win: The Rimm report on how 1,000 girls became successful women*. New York: Running Press Book.

Rosener, J. B. (1990). Ways women lead. *Harvard Business Review, 68*(6), 119–125.

Seidman, I. E. (1991). *Interviewing as qualitative research*. New York: Teachers College Press.

Senge, P. M. (1990). *The fifth discipline*. New York: Currency Doubleday.

Sergiovanni, T. J. (1992). *Moral leadership: Getting to the heart of school improvement*. San Francisco: Jossey-Bass.

Sergiovanni, T. J. (1994). *Building community in schools*. San Francisco: Jossey Bass.

Sergiovanni, T. J. (1999). *Rethinking leadership: A collection of articles*. Arlington Heights, IL: Skylight Training.

Shakeshaft, C. (1987). *Women in educational administration*. Newbury Park: Sage.

Shakeshaft, C. (1999). The struggle to create a more gender inclusive profession. In J. Murphy & K. S. Louis (Eds.), *Handbook of research on educational administration* (pp. 99–118). San Francisco: Jossey-Bass.

Shields, C. M. (2003). *Good intentions are not enough: Transformative leadership for communities of difference*. Lanham, MD: ScarecrowEducation.

Shores, P. (1989, Fall). Charter IWA member maintains IWA connection. *IWA Newsline, 2*(1), 2.

Skrla, L. (1998, April). *Women superintendents in politically problematic work situations: The role of gender in structuring conflict*. Paper presented at annual meeting of the American Educational Research Association, San Diego, CA.

Skrla, L., & Young, M. D. (2003). Introduction: Reconsidering feminist research in educational leadership. In M. D. Young & L. Skrla (Eds.), *Reconsidering feminist research in educational leadership* (pp. 1–8). Albany: State University of New York Press.

Slattery, P. (1995). *Curriculum development in the postmodern era*. New York: Garland.

Smith, M. K. (2002). Mary Parker Follett and informal education. *The encyclopedia of informal education*. Retrieved August 4, 2004, from http://www.infed.org/thinkers/et-foll.htm

Smulyan, L. (2000). *Balancing acts: Women principals at work*. Albany: State University of New York Press.

Starratt, R. J. (1991). Building an ethical school: A theory for practice in educational leadership. *Educational Administration Quarterly, 27*(2), 185–202.

Starratt, R. J. (1994). *Building an ethical school: A practitioner's response to the moral crisis in schools*. Washington, DC: Falmer Press.

Strachan, J. (2002). Feminist educational leadership: Not for the fainthearted. In C. Reynolds (Ed.), *Women and school leadership: International perspectives* (pp. 111–126). Albany: State University of New York Press.

Tannen, D. (1990). *You just don't understand: Women and men in conversation*. New York: Morrow.

Terry, R. W. (1993). *Authentic leadership: Courage in action*. San Francisco: Jossey-Bass.

van der Bogert, R. (2002). The Winnetka public schools: Traditions, transitions, transformation. [Electronic version]. Early Childhood. Retrieved November 3, 2004, from http://winnetkaalliance.org/PAST_ARTICLES/wpstraditions.htm

Wheatley, M. J. (1992). *Leadership and the new science: Learning about organization from an orderly universe*. San Francisco: Berrett-Koehler.

Wheatley, M. J. (1999). *Leadership and the new science: Discovering order in a chaotic world*. San Francisco: Berrett-Koehler.

White, K. (1995). *Why good girls don't get ahead but gutsy girls do: 9 secrets every working woman must know*. New York: Warner Books.

Willower, D. J., & Forsyth, P. B. (1999). A brief history of scholarship on educational administration. In J. Murphy & K. S. Louis (Eds.), *Handbook of research on educational administration* (2nd ed.) (pp. 1–24). San Francisco: Jossey-Bass.

Wilson, M. C. (2004). *Closing the leadership gap: Why women can and must help run the world*. New York: Viking Press.

Young, M. D., & Skrla, L. (Eds.). (2003). *Reconsidering feminist research in educational leadership*. Albany: State University of New York Press.

Index

About the Authors

Linda L. Lyman is a professor in the Department of Educational Administration and Foundations at Illinois State University. She has a B.A. in English from Northwestern University, an M.A.T. from Harvard University, and a Ph.D. in administration, curriculum, and instruction from the University of Nebraska–Lincoln. Dr. Lyman's career has included positions as secondary English teacher, regional consultant for staff development and gifted education in Nebraska, and administrative assistant at the Nebraska Department of Education. Her scholarship focuses on leadership with an emphasis on issues of gender, caring, and poverty. She teaches courses in the master's and doctoral programs. During the spring semester of 2005 she was a Fulbright Scholar in Greece, teaching about women's leadership and conducting research.

Dianne E. Ashby currently serves as professor and 10th Dean of the College of Education at Illinois State University. Dr. Ashby earned her bachelor's degree in speech and theater arts from MacMurray College, her master's degree in educational administration from the University of Illinois–Springfield, and her doctorate in educational administration from Southern Illinois University–Carbondale. She began her career as a middle school teacher of English and speech. Other career highlights include serving as a school administrator for the Illinois Department of Corrections, staff to the Illinois State Board of Education, and as a faculty member and administrator for Illinois State University. Her scholarship focuses on school reform with an emphasis on leadership.

Jenny S. Tripses is an assistant professor in the Department of Educational Leadership and Human Development at Bradley University in Peoria, Illinois. She has a B.A. in education from Bradley University and an M.A. in reading and a Ph.D. in educational administration from Illinois State University. She taught at the elementary school level and later served as an elementary school principal in rural and suburban schools. Dr. Tripses teaches graduate courses at the master's level in the principal preparation program at Bradley. Her scholarship focuses on leadership with an emphasis on gender, social justice, and poverty.